# HAUNTED CATSKILLS

LISA LAMONICA

Haunted America

Published by Haunted America
A Division of The History Press
Charleston, SC 29403
www.historypress.net

First published 2013

Manufactured in the United States

ISBN 978.1.62619.011.5

Library of Congress CIP data applied for.

# CONTENTS

# ACKNOWLEDGEMENTS

This book would not have been possible without help and collaboration from many great people:

Roy Davis of the Windham Historical Society; Karrie Allen of the *Chatham Courier*; Douglas Stalker, Judith Rundell and Steve Pec of the Vedder Library; the *New York Times*; Bruce Bergman, Rick Allen and Ed Klingle at the Van Hoesen House; Emily Benson and Ms. Terwilliger at the Hudson Area Library; Enid Futterman and Rachel Waldholz of *Our Town* magazine; Tim Duerden of the Delaware County Historical Society; archivist Ray LaFever; Margaret Kenyon, Nancy J. Haynes, Ellen McHale and Libby Tucker of the New York Folklore Society; Roderic H. Blackburn, PhD, at the Albany Institute of History and Art; John Craig at the Hudson Area Library History Room; Nina Shengold at *Chronogram* magazine; Ron Toelke Associates; Peter Pehrson at the Stoddard Corner Bookshop; Stephen Kent Comer and Barbara Allen of the Stockbridge Library Museum and Archives; Andrea Lain of the New York State Museum in Albany; Donald Shriver and Jennifer Palmentiero of the Southeastern New York Library Resources Council; Jason Korbus; Andrew Amelinckx; Amy Levine; Mason Winfield; Christopher J. Hack; Skip Hommel; and Gail Hommel.

I'd also like to thank my neighbors Ed and Antoinette Bratton for their assistance and Marcy Groll for her hospitality. Gratitude to Mary Bartolotta for bringing me to a great house to write a book in, and also to my son, Patrick Robert Mason.

# ACKNOWLEDGEMENTS

Many thanks also to Whitney Landis, my editor at The History Press, for her guidance. I am grateful to her and The History Press for making this project a reality.

# INTRODUCTION

The Catskills and upstate New York are what Washington Irving called "this spellbound region." The Catskill Mountains are two hours north of New York City and forty miles south of Albany. The mountains saw erosion from glaciers during the last two Ice Ages, as evidenced by exposed rocks around the region. The valleys of the Catskills and its rounded mountains are a result of the once-great sheets of ice that traveled through them.

Discovered in 1609 by Henry Hudson, this region offers four hundred years of history and lore. Settled by seventeenth-century Dutch and written about in Washington Irving's *Rip Van Winkle*, the area was then known as "Kaatskill," meaning "Cat Creek." Catamounts, as they were then known, were the mountain lions that inhabited the region. As the story by Washington Irving goes, Rip Van Winkle fell asleep in the Catskill Mountains for twenty years after an encounter with the ghost of Henry Hudson and his men. This is one of America's most well-known and beloved folktales.

Rip Van Winkle awoke from his twenty-year sleep next to Kaaterskill Falls, a two-tiered waterfall whose dual cascades total 260 feet, making it the highest waterfall in New York State. It's been more than one hundred years since Washington Irving wrote his tale, and the falls are still a breathtaking sight. You can reach the base of the falls via the Kaaterskill Falls Trail, a lovely state-maintained path that begins where Route 23A crosses Kaaterskill Creek between the hamlets of Haines Falls and Palenville. From the trailhead, the path runs uphill, alongside the creek, for about a half a mile until the falls come into view.

Kaaterskill Falls. *Library of Congress.*

Each fall for the last two years, when foliage season shows us the rich colors of the trees and the brisk fireplace smoke scent is in the air, I have wanted to put together the stories of our region. Many of these stories have been nearly lost over the last thirty years or gathered sporadically in many publications. It also gave me joy to combine the stories with some of the old photographs, which hasn't been done with many of these older tales.

# INTRODUCTION

In writing this book, I had the pleasure of reading many classic books for research purposes. My reading helped me gain even more knowledge about some of the tales and mythology of the Catskills. *Body, Boots and Britches* is still considered to be the best collection of New York State folklore there is. *Things That Go Bump in the Night* and *Spooks of the Valley*, both published in the 1950s by Louis C. Jones, are classics and must-reads. But my absolute favorite was the 1970s book by James McMurry, *The Catskill Witch and other Tales of the Hudson Valley*. This now-out-of-print book allowed me to correspond with the author via email, and I have since made a new friendship with a fellow author who wrote tales about my Columbia County when I was a child wishing to grow up and write books of my own. I came across this book rather late in my research process, and I'm so glad I found it.

When Halloween approaches, people of Celtic descent focus a bit on Samhain (pronounced SAH-win), a harvest festival marking the end of summer and the beginning of the Celtic New Year. The Celts believed that during Samhain, the veil between the living and the dead was at its thinnest, making communication with the spirit world possible. According to *Our Town* writer Rachel Waldholz, "The result, it seems, is that ghosts are woven into the fabric of life in the country, along with the chickens and woodstoves and gravel mines."

Considered by many to be America's first great writer, Washington Irving gathered material and then fame for his characters in *The Legend of Sleepy Hollow* and *Rip Van Winkle* in this Hudson Valley/Catskills region. Now, over one hundred years later, we all know the story of Ichabod Crane and the Headless Horseman of Sleepy Hollow, who some believe were based on people residing in Kinderhook. The Jesse Merwin farmhouse in Kinderhook has long held stories of being haunted. Merwin was a friend of Washington Irving's and is believed to have been the model for the Ichabod Crane character.

Some of the first streets and houses of America are located in the Hudson Valley, well trodden, and many with residual energy from the past. New York State built the first concrete road in Ulster County: the New Paltz Turnpike to Highland.

I also can't stress enough our region's pre-history—the history of the Mohicans and other Indians who first inhabited our Hudson Valley and the Catskills area—and it is important to me to acknowledge their stories as well. On the journey of writing this book, I had the profound pleasure to meet the last lineal descendant of the Mohican tribe of my county, a member of the Stockbridge-Munsee Band of Mohicans, the only descendant community of

The Catskills. *Courtesy of Hudson Valley Weather.*

the Original People of Columbia County. I have formed a new friendship there also.

Some stories in this book are perhaps just folklore, resonating from or with social and class differences, immigrant mythology or historical upheaval of the time. Patrick Frazier, author of *The Mohicans of Stockbridge*, wrote, "In times of upheaval, stress, or significant social changes, people often turn to religion or change religions, seeking a supernatural solution to their plight." And similar to how a rumor gets started, these stories took on lives of their own.

But others don't fit any of these categories. They seem to require research on another level—a scientific or spiritual level—especially when the person experiencing a sighting doesn't want to or has for many years been unwilling to speak about it. These events then take on new meanings. Some stories do not appear to be merely the retelling of a long-ago folktale but rather, in this generation, a place or house having some kind of disturbance from former occupants. In this case, I appreciate those who came forward to share their experiences.

For the introduction to the 1986 book *Ghosts in Residence*, Roderic Blackburn wrote, "The special quality of Hans von Behr's accounts is that they are first-person witness to events inexplicable and supernatural. We are present at the creation of stories which will become folk legends in the twenty-first century."

# THEORIES

A spirit or ghost is believed to be the soul and consciousness of a person who has passed away—his personality left imprinted on the environment. For many reasons, such as tragedy, unfinished business or attachment to someone or someplace, a spirit is condensed energy that is left behind.

Thermodynamics holds that energy cannot be destroyed; rather, it simply takes another form and instead of dissolving goes back into the atmosphere or becomes part of something else. One theory states that if conditions are right, events of the past or even a once-living person's mind can be copied or imprinted on the environment by way of electromagnetic resonance. An example of this would be the way in which a tape recorder works. Some theorists suggest that a specific brainwave or state is needed to experience this, such as the Alpha State.

Conversely, another theory proposed by Professor Max Bruin, PhD, must also be considered:

> An impression upon the subatomic weave of the universe, created via strong emotion of a sentient observer. Ghosts are created when the observer's emotions create a semi-permanent "indentation" into the quantum tapestry of the universe. Like the scent of burned toast that remains long after the offending bread is discarded, ghosts are impressions of emotions that remain long after the cause has been resolved.

Time and space, always thought to be linear, are now considered to possibly fold over onto one another, so that past events may be experienced today.

A "residual haunt" is believed to be displaced energy that plays itself over and over again, like a recording—for example, a ghost following the old layout of a house.

"Messenger haunts" are believed to visit shortly after a person's death, interacting with the living to deliver a final farewell. They seem to appear briefly and sometimes only once, but their purpose is to bring comfort to those left behind and to halt or shorten their grieving. Sometimes, one who is dying appears elsewhere than his place of death, such as a story from the 1940s of a woman seen praying in a New York City church at the exact time her body was being removed from the East River.

In a 2008 interview with Jeff Belanger, Hans Holzer explained the difference between a ghost and a spirit:

> *A ghost is a residual entity, like a psychic imprint left in an area that some people can pick up, whereas a spirit is intelligent and interactive. Holzer also mentioned a third category I hadn't heard about before: the "stay behinds." "Stay behinds are relatively common," he said. "Somebody dies, and then they're really surprised that all of a sudden, they're not dead. They're alive like they were. They don't understand it because they weren't prepared for it. So they go back to what they knew most—their chair, their room, and they just sit there. Next, they want to let people know that they're still 'alive,' so they'll do little things like moving things, appear to relatives, pushing objects, poltergeist phenomena and so on."*

Many primitive societies incorporated banishing rituals at the time of burial to prevent a spirit from lingering. The ancient Celts and Native Americans both burned sage and used salt as protection and banishing herbs. It's interesting that these two cultures, so far removed from one another, shared the same belief in the correspondences of these herbs and the spirit world.

## CHAPTER 1

# THE *REGISTER-STAR* BUILDING

The *Register-Star* building in Hudson, New York, was originally the town's jail. The first woman to be executed in New York was hanged here, and her ghost is known to haunt the location.

On October 17, 1817, Margaret "Maggie" Houghtaling (aka Houghthling) was hanged in Hudson, Columbia County's county seat, for murder.

One website states that Houghtaling was convicted of killing her baby but that after the execution, a neighbor confessed to the crime. Women were often executed for the murder of their illegitimate children; it was a great stigma to have a baby outside of marriage, and this was why some of them decided to risk killing these unwanted children. Concealing the birth of a child was also a capital crime at one time, and five women in U.S. history were hanged for the crime. It did not need to be proven that the baby was murdered; the woman could be convicted even if the baby had actually been stillborn or had died of natural causes in the first hours of its life. The website does not explain the basis for that assertion, but the information may have come from an 1887 pamphlet mentioned on two other sites. The publication's title reads, in part, "MAGGIE HOUGHTALING. AN INNOCENT WOMAN HANGED. THE TRUTH REVEALED AT LAST. A STARTLING CONFESSION."

And then there's this story, taken from the UFO-Free Paranormal website (www.ufofreeparanormal.com), about the same building:

> Hudson is a small city about 30 miles south of Albany on the Hudson
> River. It began as a whaling and trading town and as such developed a

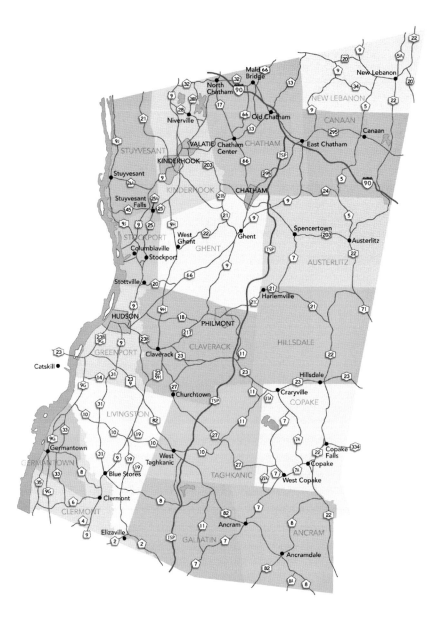

Map of Columbia County. *Courtesy of Ron Toelke.*

certain element. For a time, it was, in fact, the red light district for upstate New York.

It was in this context that a young "lady of negotiable affection" was arrested for the murder of one of her clients. She was tried and convicted

The *Register-Star* building. *Courtesy of Hudson Area Library.*

*and spent the last few months of her life in the town jail awaiting execution. After the sentence was carried out, it was discovered that her boyfriend had actually committed the deed. Ever since, the ghost of the woman has haunted the building.*

*The jail has long since been moved, and the site was occupied by the offices of the local paper, the* Register-Star *for quite some time. The ghost, however, remains. It takes the form of a small woman with long black hair. She can even be mistaken for a living woman but disappears if approached for a closer look.*

Employees at the *Register-Star* can sometimes hear someone walking around at night in parts of the building after their co-workers have gone home, and over the years, townspeople have claimed to see images of hanging people from inside the windows at night while walking down Warren Street.

## CHAPTER 2

# THE HALLENBECK HOUSE

Peter Hallenbeck was murdered by his nephews on Christmas Eve 1901. Now uninhabitable, the Hallenbeck home has been the site of unexplained disturbances over the years. In those days, the home was located in what was a hamlet of Greendale within Greenport. Following are excerpts from local newspapers at the time of the murder:

*HUDSON, Dec. 27—The coroner's inquest in the case of Peter A. Hellenbeck [sic] of Greenport, who was murdered at his home last Tuesday, was continued today by Coroner Lisk. The four young men under arrest on suspicion of being implicated in the murder are Willis, Burton and Frederick Van Wormer and Harvey Bruce. Hellenbeck [sic] was shot down in the doorway of his house, about eighteen miles from Kinderhook, where the prisoners reside.*

*At the inquest this afternoon, Mrs. Van Wormer, stepmother of the Van Wormers; Pearl Louise Van Buren, sweetheart of Willis Van Wormer; George H. Brown, a liveryman; and Mrs. Maria Conner and two daughters testified on behalf of the prisoners, swearing to their being in Kinderhook, eighteen miles from the scene of the murder, between one and two hours after the crime was committed. They were positive in their statements, which were not taken under examination.*

*Demond Vernon, a notion dealer in Kinderhook, swore that on Monday, two of the prisoners purchased two masks in his store. The masks represented devils' faces. They wore their coats turned inside out. On Tuesday evening, he testified, the other prisoners bought two more. The murderers wore masks when Hellenbeck [sic] was killed.*

—Columbia County at the End of the Century

*Tell-Tale Wagon Wheel Tracks*

*The wheels of a wagon which the prisoners hired on the day of the murder are said to correspond exactly with the tracks leading from the scene of the crime. The horse driven to the wagon had a peculiar shoe and an impression identical with this peculiarity was also, it is stated, found in the soft earth in the vicinity of the Hallenbeck home. The shoes worn by the prisoners on the day of their capture are said to correspond with the shoe prints left in the snow. Interest in the case is intense. The prosecuting officers declare they are confident the right men have been arrested. So far, however, the evidence is entirely circumstantial, and the defense declare they can establish an alibi.*

—Post Standard, *Syracuse, New York, December 28, 1901*

*HUDSON, N.Y., Dec. 30.*—*The confession of Harvey Bruce, one of the four young men under arrest for the murder of Peter Hallenbeck at Greenport on Christmas Eve, caused an enormous crowd to assemble when the coroner's inquest was resumed to-day. The courtroom became densely packed, and the coroner announced that owing to the illness of the widow and advanced age of the mother of the murdered man, court would adjourn to the private office of the District Attorney for their testimony. The confession of Bruce has not been made public, being kept secret by the officials.*

*The testimony of Mrs. Margaret L. Hallenbeck, wife of the murdered man, to-day showed that four men took a hand in the killing, offsetting the previous belief that one held a horse near the barn while three others went to the house. Mrs. Hallenbeck declared she and her mother-in-law were the only persons present in the house with her husband at the time of the murder. Her husband had called her attention to a wagon passing on the highway and two men walking behind. A short time afterward, four men came walking back wearing coats inside out. They passed down the road toward the church. The murdered man, herself and mother-in-law all saw them from the window. Her husband said they must be chicken thieves and watched them 'til out of sight. Shortly afterward, there was a knock at the kitchen door. Her husband went to open it, and she went to the door with him.*

*Four Pistols Thrust in His Face*

*As he opened the door, four pistols were thrust in his face and fired. Her husband jumped back and gave his wife a push out of the way. The four men jumped into the room after him, and all fired again. Mrs. Hallenbeck said her husband turned toward the stairway for his gun, when his assailants fired again. The men were masked and had coats turned inside out. One was tall, two medium size and one short. "I begged them not to kill my husband," she continued. "Seeing I could not do anything, I ran to the next room and upstairs. The men kept shooting. I met my mother-in-law on the stairs and pushed her back. I could not recognize any of the men. They ran through the house and departed."*

*The evidence of Mrs. Aletnina Hallenbeck, mother of the murdered man who is 80 years old, bore out the testimony of her daughter-in-law concerning the happenings of the evening of the tragedy. She confirmed the statement that four men entered the room and that all of them fired.*

*Sheriff Harry J. Best testified to having visited the Hallenbeck house on the night of the tragedy. He examined the various footprints and wagon tracks in the snow, their location and the directions of the footsteps to and from the house. He told how he and his assistants went to Kinderhook on Christmas Day and arrested the three Van Wormer brothers and Harvey Bruce. The officers searched the house, finding three revolvers, a fourth one being found next day. Three of the weapons were of 32-caliber and one of 36. The prisoners all wore shoes when arrested. These shoes Sheriff Best took down to Hallenbeck's house on Christmas Day and in the presence of other witnesses fitted them in the prints in the snow near the Hallenbeck house. The four pair of shoes fitted all perfectly, the tracks leading about the kitchen door and from there toward the highway and in the vicinity of the barn. One of the footprints had a peculiar impression as though the shoe had a heel-plate, while the other prints indicated shoes of "bulldog."*
—*The Associated Press, 1902*

A family feud had existed between the Hallenbecks and Van Wormers for years. Peter Hallenbeck had prospered, but John Van Wormer, his brother-in-law, eked out a precarious living as a river boatman. Before his death, however, Van Wormer managed to buy a cottage across the road from the handsome home of his brother-in-law. It was mortgaged, however, to Hallenbeck. Although the latter frequently aided the Van Wormers, he finally, after John Van Wormer's death, gradually withdrew all assistance *and pressed the family for the interest and principal. The mortgage was finally foreclosed in September last, and the Van Wormers were turned out. They removed to Kinderhook, 16 miles away. This increased the hatred of the brothers for the uncle, and this was the alleged motive for the crime. It is expected that the defense will try to prove an alibi, and the trial promises to prove one of great interest.*

—Trenton Times, *Trenton, New Jersey, March 31, 1902*

*BURIAL OF VAN WORMER BOYS*
*Funeral Will Be Private—Interment in Kinderhook Cemetery*

*Hudson, N.Y., Oct. 3.—The bodies of Frederick, Willis and Burton Van Wormer, who were electrocuted on Thursday at Dannemora Prison, arrived at their old home in Kinderhook. Undertaker Birchmyer removed the bodies to the rooms of Estella Van Wormer, their step-mother.*

*The funeral will be held this afternoon and will be private. The coffins will not be opened. The burial will be in the Kinderhook cemetery, where the body of Martin Van Buren rests. The feeling in Kinderhook is strong against the cemetery commission in selling Mrs. Van Wormer a lot for interment there.*

—Altoona Mirror, *Altoona, Pennsylvania, October 3, 1903*

At least one thousand people from around the county viewed the bodies in the Kinderhook home's parlor. Apparently, after the brothers had been executed and laid out in the autopsy room, a guard saw one of them, Frederick Van Wormer, move a hand and then an eye. The prison doctor was called for. A stethoscope held to the presumed dead man's heart discovered that it was still beating. Frederick's heart was bigger than that of anyone executed up to that date, so two full charges of current had failed to kill him. The convict was carried back to the chair and kept there until he was dead beyond the shadow of a doubt. The *New York Times*, in an October 2, 1902 article, stated that the brothers decided who would be executed first, with all taking fifteen minutes and being carried out in a most humane way. Peter Hallenbeck's wife and mother passed away shortly after him, and a brother was left "broken in health and nerve by the awful tragedy."

To see some old photos of Peter Hallenbeck and newspaper articles, visit the Facebook page of Ghost Walk Hudson.

## CHAPTER 3

# 608 COLUMBIA STREET AND THE SANFORD GIFFORD HOUSE

What is now the DMV parking lot on Columbia Street in Hudson was once a majestic family home. Across the street were the "three sisters"—three adjoining houses built for three daughters. In one of these houses, I lived for a period of time and experienced some interesting phenomena.

A few years after a boyfriend had passed away, I sold my house and began staying at one of my brother's houses on Columbia Street. I lived in the house for three years, and I loved the staircase in the entryway, the downstairs kitchen and scullery area and the overall Victorian feel of the place. But I had experiences there that I know to be otherworldly.

On Halloween day in 2007, some workmen refinishing a house next door were leaving the job. The contractor called and asked if I would move my car, as a dumpster would soon be arriving. On the sidewalk in front of the house, while we were standing next to each other, I felt like I had to keep looking over my shoulder. I felt this sort of breeze—it felt strange, like nothing I had ever experienced before or since. It was like something swirling around, almost watching me. After the roofer left, I went inside to take a nap, but out of the corner of my eye, I saw something amiss. A pumpkin, which had previously been sitting on a wide windowsill, was now on the floor several feet away in front of the fireplace. Next to it was my ChapStick, which had been on the table in the adjoining room. There was just no way these two items could have gotten there. I lived alone, and I was outside for only about ten minutes. It felt like a very long time of me standing there, looking at these items and trying to make sense of everything. The significance of the pumpkin was obvious to me, as Halloween had been my first date with Rob. But the ChapStick didn't make sense until much later in the day, when I recalled the details of that first date, in that dark movie theater in Hudson. I remembered that after our first kiss, he leaned back, licked his lips and asked me if I was wearing ChapStick—the same kind that was now on the floor near the pumpkin. The experience gave me chills, but it also made me smile.

I never told the roofer. I still miss Rob, and I know there is a spirit world.

The other experience I had in the Columbia Street house was also surprising. At that time in my life, I was hostessing at a very nice restaurant in Chatham and would come home on cold nights to take bubble baths in the old clawfoot tub. Two nights in a row, right above me as I was in the tub, I heard what sounded like a child running around in circles. My mother was downstairs in the den, and on the second night of hearing this, I mentioned it to her after I had eventually wandered downstairs. I had commented on how the tenant upstairs must have been letting her children stay up late and run around. My mother laughed and told me that the tenant had moved out a few weeks ago but would return at some point in the daytime to retrieve a few boxes that she left behind. Baffled, I said, "That's impossible—there's

The Sanford Gifford house. *Courtesy of Peter Jung and Historic Hudson.*

someone up there. I've been hearing a child running around for the past two nights while I was taking a bath." "You couldn't have," my mother said. "There's no one up there now, and no one has come into the house tonight except you…the tenant moved out a while ago." It gave me chills. I knew what I had heard.

A year later, I had moved on and into my own house but had bumped into my brother's new tenant at a local coffee shop. She had a very unsettled look on her face and asked if I had ever heard noises while living in my brother's house. She went on to say that a male tenant who had lived above her had moved out weeks ago but that she kept hearing someone walk around above her whenever she was home at night. She knew that she was alone in the house, yet she was hearing this often. This surprised me, and I told her about my experiences in the house. It was clear to me that she was not happy about living there by herself.

## CHAPTER 4

# THE WEINTRAUB HOUSE

*I've actually seen a ghost walk through our bedroom. I can't pin down the exact year…sometime between 1990 and 1992. It was on a weekend during the middle of the night. He looked at me and went out a back door (which didn't exist until the 1900s), which leads me to think it was one of Herb Weintraub's family…we bought the building from him in 1990. His family had owned it since 1900, when a back door was added on the second floor. Everyone's take on this "event" that I've talked to is that it was a good thing. Whoever he was, we think he was just making sure the building was being cared for. I'd put his "look" circa 1920–30. He was whitish-translucent, in his sixties and had a moustache…taking all of about five to ten seconds at best to pass by the bed and through the door. Then I hid under the covers!*

Such was the experience of the current owner of the home and gallery now located at the former Adams town house and gardens in Hudson, New York.

Mr. Adams was a Scottish architect, having done most of his work in England about the time of the American Revolution, and this Warren Street home is the only remaining Adams-type house in the Hudson Valley, according to the New York State Historical Society. The house was the first Bank of Hudson in 1809, after which it was converted to a private residence in 1819. The first residents of the house were the Hogeboom family, principals in the bank. After being converted to a residence, the doorway, which was originally located at the center of the building, was moved to the side. So when I heard this experience from the current owner, it made sense to me—it was some sort of entity following the old layout of the house.

In the 1920s and '30s, when Diamond Street was about to be renamed Columbia Street, Hudson had a reputation for vice. A 1994 *New York Times* article written by Harold Faber quotes Bruce Edward Hall from his book *Diamond Street*:

> *Gambling, bootlegging and prostitution flourished in Hudson because generations of local police officers and public officials either averted their eyes or were corrupt. These houses were neatly managed and protected by the mayor and the police department. It was sort of like Andy Hardy visits Sodom and Gomorrah.*

Herb Weintraub, retired at the time and also interviewed for the *Times* article, said he had "fond memories of old Hudson and the red-light district. It was a marvelous cottage industry." The vice era came to an end in 1950, when state troopers made raids and arrests without giving a heads-up to the local police. Mr. Hall's book and the *New York Times* article are great sources of information regarding Hudson's scarlet past.

Wolf Weintraub, father of Herb, was born around 1886 in Austria, and according to a 1940 census, was a businessman with a shop at 554 Warren

St. Winifred's Awe. *Courtesy of Dan Region (www.regionsphotos.com).*

Street. Was there an emotion, event or a weather condition that triggered the sighting, and why did the sighting occur only once?

The current owners stated:

> *We never got to talk to Herb Weintraub, the previous owner, about our experience, but it might have made sense that it was his father. The back addition to the building was added in the 1920s, and the figure I saw had the same build as Herb. There is a store opposite Town Fair, which was the Wolf Weintraub paint/wallpaper store. It was a one-time time event, but I know what I saw. He left and never came back.*

## CHAPTER 5

# SPOOK ROCK ROAD

When leaving the city of Hudson on State Route 23B, if you turn right just past the Old Tollhouse on the right, you'll be on Spook Rock Road. The ghost of a Native American girl has been sighted on the road, where legend holds that when her father forbade her to be with her chosen man, she threw herself into the waters of Claverack Creek.

The rock in the creek is where another story states that an Indian boy and girl from differing tribes, engaged in a forbidden love, died as a result of being punished by their angry gods. Some say the young brave can still be heard calling for his maiden lover. The following tale was told by Miss Bertie Sagendorph of Claverack and printed in Ruth A. Stickles's *Folklore of Columbia County*:

> *This chief had a lovely dark-eyed daughter whose lover was the son of an enemy chieftain of a neighboring tribe. One evening, as the tribe slept and only the glow of the campfire remained of the day's activities, this beautiful Indian girl sped swiftly over the trail to meet her lover on a huge rock overhanging a small creek. Obedience to parents was one of the most sacred Indian beliefs, and this happy pair was rudely violating this ancient Indian tradition. As the Great Spirit looked down upon the lovers, he became exceedingly angry. He was, indeed, so indignant that he sent the crashing thunder rolling over their heads and the forked lightning playing over the rocks. In the midst of this tumult, the lovers clung to each other. Then suddenly, a swift bolt of lightning struck the great boulder, which crashed*

*down to the stream below, carrying the lovers with it. The storm was soon over. One by one, the stars began to twinkle in the dark heavens; the brook flowed placidly on, but the great rock had found a new resting place for all time. The Great Spirit had had his revenge. The boulder rests now in the winding creek, a memorial to the two young Indians who are supposed to be lying beneath it. It has since been added to the story that every time the great rock hears the old Claverack church bell, it is supposed to turn over.*

There are several possible explanations and dynamics to consider when exploring a folktale haunting like this, along with differing points of view. Stephen Kent Comer, a Mohican descendant, explained to me that the above tale is merely a Victorian-era narrative demonstrating how Caucasians thought about the people that they had displaced—a sort of rationalizing of Europeans pushing the native Mohican tribe away from the Columbia County area. He notes, "Our history and culture is like a clay pot that's been broken and scattered, and we're still trying to piece it together."

Comer offers another version and explanation of this common tale:

*A young Indian brave once fell in love with a white girl living in a nearby settlement. He took every opportunity to court her, and she was willing to have him do so, but her parents, with the backing of the whole community, would not allow her to see the young brave anymore, let alone marry him. The young brave was devastated by this turn of events and began wandering through the wilderness, uncaring of food or shelter. Before long, he came to the edge of a high precipice and in his melancholy pitched himself over the edge to fall dead on the rocks below. This typical "Indian" story could be interpreted as a colonialist explanation for the reason why the Original People seemed to "melt away" at the encroachment of Euro American society. In this case, the young brave is symbolic of Native People presumably wanting to integrate into colonial society but unable to do so because they cannot meet the requirements of white civilization. The Native Peoples then destroy themselves because of their regrets and inabilities, rather than from any aggression or repudiation on the part of the invaders.*

The Mohican language, for example, is now extinct. As with any language, you need a certain number of people still speaking it to pass it on. Comer went on to say that his grandfather was one of the last speakers of the language in the tribe. Around 1736, the Mohicans left Claverack,

Distant view of the Van Hoesen House. *Courtesy of Rick Allen (vanhoesenhouse.org).*

The initials of the first occupants of the house were worked into the masonry in black clinker headers. This is the only surviving regional example of this type of monogramming from the 1715–50 period. *Courtesy of Rick Allen (vanhoesenhouse.org).*

Hudson and the area now known as Columbia County and traveled west, eventually settling in what is now Stockbridge, Massachusetts. Although the Massachusetts Court assured the Stockbridge Indians that their land would never be sold, the agreement was not upheld. And despite aiding the colony

The Van Hoesen House, built around 1720, was one of the grandest on the Hudson. It stands on a tract of land purchased from the Mohicans by Jan Fransen Van Hoesen, the grandfather of its builder. *Courtesy of Rick Allen (vanhoesenhouse.org).*

during the Revolutionary War, the Mohicans were forced to relocate—first back to New York State, on to Oneida and then to Wisconsin.

In 1609, Henry Hudson arrived in the area of Catskill to Stockport, riding to shore in an Indian canoe three days after his arrival. Later visitors included Shlectenhorst, who purchased flats along the Claverack Creek (Greenport and Claverack), and Abram Staats, who purchased a tract at the mouth of Stockport Creek (Oosterhoeck). The first actual settlement being around 1660 and we know there are records of a land purchase from the Mohicans by Jan Fransen van Hoesen at Claverack Landing (which is now Hudson). Later, in 1667, land patents were also granted to his widow.

It is also important to know and remember the native Mohican's friendly acceptance of these early visitors; showing them their way of life, their tools made of shells and stone, their food supplies and cooking methods, as well as hunting techniques. Author Shirley Dunn wrote about a symbolic and reassuring gesture in which "the natives broke their arrows and threw them into the fire so Hudson would not be afraid."

According to journals kept at the time, Henry Hudson also entertained some of the Mohicans aboard his ship the *Half Moon*. Fur trading with the Mohicans would begin a year after Hudson left and returned to his homeland

*Right*: A 1909 postcard depicting "Hendrik Hudson" and published by Jerome H. Pemick & Co. Image from the collection of Vivian Yess Wadlin. *Courtesy of the Hudson River Valley Institute (www. hrvh.org).*

*Below*: Edward Moran's circa 1898 painting of Sir Henry Hudson entering New York Bay on September 11, 1609, with an Indian family watching from the shore in the foreground. *Library of Congress.*

in the Netherlands. The Dutch would then come up the Hudson River every summer for furs.

When researching this local Spook Rock tale, I came across more information and variations in the New York State Folklore Society's archived articles, one of which was written by one of its board members, Libby Tucker:

> *Stories about places called Spook Rock—of which there are several in New York State—seem more complex and interesting. They usually tell of an Indian's or settler's murder, with parental disapproval, greed, and human sacrifice as motivating factors. I first heard a Spook Rock story from one of my students at Binghamton University in the spring of 1978. As part of her term project, Regina Hoefner collected a legend from a female friend about a young Dutch woman who habitually met her Indian lover at Spook Rock in Rockland County. Outraged by this mixed-race courtship, Dutch settlers climbed up to the rock by moonlight and murdered the young lovers. The legend says that moonlight still casts the shadows of the murdered lovers and that people can hear their screams in the woods along Spook Rock Road.*

Northbound parkway view near Snydertown Road. *Library of Congress.*

*Right*: An Indian dart used before the invention of the bow and arrow. *Courtesy of the author*.

*Below*: Detail from a 1616 Hendrickson map of the Columbia County area. *Courtesy of Ron Toelke and the Columbia County Historical Society*.

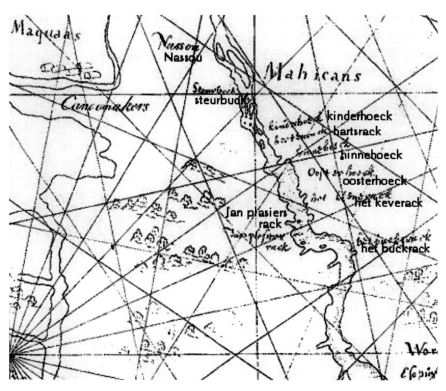

I was interested to learn that this was a common story throughout New York State, and one that had landed in my county as well. The fields still contain a trove of arrowheads and other artifacts; they're out there.

The Mohicans were numerous and strong at the time of Henry Hudson's arrival on the Hudson River in 1609, and for about twenty or so years afterward. The Mohican lands extended from what is now Vermont to Lake Champlain and south nearly to Manhattan Island, including land on both sides of the Mahicannituck (Hudson) River, as well as present-day Windham. It also stretched west to Schoarie Creek and east into Massachusetts and Connecticut. In 1984, historian Kenneth Mynter wrote in a Hillsdale newspaper, "Indians were living here in this county before the building of the pyramids at a time when our own ancestors were living in the new Stone Age in Europe."

Donald Shriver, president emeritus of the Union Theological Seminary in New York, and Stephen Kent Comer, last lineal survivor of the Mohican Nation in the vicinity of Columbia County, added a historical marker alongside the already-existing History of Columbia County marker at the northernmost overlook of the Taconic Parkway. The original marker tells of Henry Hudson's arrival in 1609 with no mention of the Mohicans.

Historical marker at the northbound overlook. *Library of Congress.*

After years of fundraising and work with a variety of state agencies, and also with the help of St. Peters Presbyterian Church in Spencertown, the men decided it was necessary to commemorate the Mohicans who had greeted Hudson and his crew. Comer noted, "I can say that when I came to this area thirty years ago, I was amazed to find virtually nothing about my people in their native land. It was though we were a ghost people."

I think it's important to honor and share some these Native Peoples' folklore as well:

*A Mohican Culture Hero: Snowshoe Man*

*Retold by Steve Comer*

*A culture hero amongst Indigenous peoples is a mythical person who has lived among the people in the indefinite past and is typically the one who has made the world a better, safer place by destroying monsters and teaching the people for the first time those arts that became fundamental elements of their traditional ways. By good fortune, a Congregationalist minister recorded something of the Mohican hero myth. Here the cultural hero is called simply Snowshoe Man, and a version of the story goes like this.*

*Among the people there once lived a man who was seen to come down from heaven with snowshoes on. He was the one who gave the people the knowledge of snowshoes and how to make them. He also gave them much other knowledge and taught them the ways that made them who they are. He was considered to be a seer (prophet) who knew things that were neither present nor obvious. It was he who destroyed the monsters that then inhabited the country.*

*Eventually, he married a woman among the people and had two children by her. He became the Powwow (shaman, or priest) of the people and led their spiritual ceremonies. At times, however, he forgot to offer prayers, and that caused the people to criticize him behind his back. When he learned of their dissatisfaction, he apologized and said that he would be sure to offer prayers the next time.*

*When that time came, he started praying with his two children sitting on his knees. Soon he began to rise into the air with them as he prayed, but as he rose to the top of the wigwam, he was entreated to leave at least one of his children behind for the good of the people. He handed one of the children down and disappeared into the heavens with the other one. The child left behind grew up to be an exceptional human being who led a great life and also accomplished many things for the people.*

## CHAPTER 6

# DRAGGED TO DEATH; CONDEMNED TO THE NOOSE

Ralph Sutherland, who early in the last century occupied a stone house a mile from Leeds, in the Catskills, was a man of morose and violent disposition. His servant, a Scotch girl, was virtually a slave, as she was bound to work for him without pay until she had refunded him for her passage into this country. Becoming weary of bondage and of the tempers of her master, the girl ran away. The man set off in a raging chase, and she had not gone far before Sutherland overtook her, tied her by the wrists to his horse's tail and began the homeward journey. Afterward, he swore that the girl stumbled against the horse's legs, so frightening the animal that it rushed off madly, pitching him out of the saddle and dashing the servant to death on rocks and trees. But knowing how ugly-tempered Sutherland could be, his neighbors were better inclined to believe that he had driven the horse into a gallop, intending to drag the girl for a short distance as a punishment before reining up in lieu of doing any serious damage. On this supposition, he was arrested, tried and sentenced to die on the scaffold.

The weakness of circumstantial evidence, coupled with pleas advanced by influential relatives of the prisoner, induced the court to delay sentencing until the culprit should be ninety-nine years old, but it was ordered that, while released on his own recognizance, in the interim, he should keep a hangman's noose about his neck and show himself before the judges in Catskill once every year to prove that he wore his badge of infamy and kept his crime in mind. This sentence he obeyed, and there were people living recently who claimed to remember him as he went about with a silken cord knotted at his throat. He was always alone, and he seldom spoke—his rough, imperious manner had departed. Only when children asked him about the rope were his lips seen to quiver, and then he would hurry away. After dark, his house was avoided, for gossips said that a shrieking woman passed it nightly, tied at the tail of a giant horse with fiery eyes and smoking nostrils; that a skeleton in a winding sheet had been found there; that a curious thing, somewhat like a woman, had been known to sit on his garden wall, with lights shining from her fingertips, uttering unearthly laughter; and that domestic animals reproached the man by groaning and howling beneath his windows.

These beliefs he knew, yet he neither grieved, nor scorned, nor answered when he was told of them. Every year deepened his reserve and loneliness, and some began to whisper that he would take his own way out of the world—though others answered that men who were born to be hanged would never be drowned. So, on Ralph Sutherland's ninety-ninth birthday, there were none who would accuse him or execute sentence. He lived yet another year, dying in 1801. But was it from habit (or was it self-punishment and remorse) that he never took off the noose? For when he drew his last breath, though it was in his own house, his throat was still encircled by the hangman's rope. This legend has a number of versions, and *The Sutherlands*, a novel published in 1862, is one of them.

William Salisbury was indicted for the murder of his servant, Anna Dorothea Swarts. An eighteenth-century bill of indictment in the Greene County Historical Society in Coxsackie, New York, gives information about William Salisbury, who in 1755 tied Swarts to his horse and dragged her to death. The Vedder Library of the Greene County Historical Society maintains genealogy file folders on both Sutherland and Salisbury.

In 1824, a Colonel William Leete Stone, an editor of the New York City newspaper *Commercial Advertiser*, visited the newly opened Catskill Mountain House resort. He later recounted the following for his newspaper:

> *Sometimes, sighs and lamentations were heard in the air, like the plaintiveness of the soft whistling wind. A white horse of gigantic size, with fiery eyeballs and distended nostrils, was often seen to run past the spot, with the fleetness of wind, dragging a female behind, with tattered garment and streaming hair, screaming for help. At other times, the horse would appear to drag a hideous skeleton, clattering after him, enveloped in a winding sheet.*

This version, taken from the June 1883 issue of *Harper's New Monthly Magazine*, is very lengthy and descriptive indeed:

*In a faded letter lying before me, and which is dated from Greenwich Street, in New York, fifty years ago, the writer says: "I could wish the Hudson were in better condition for my trip to Catskill. I shall be four or five days in going, but I will start well prepared for the journey." I wonder what the anxious gentleman of that day would say were he to sit in his own library on this morning and listen to and observe the changes in this beloved Catskill since that period of green fields and wide-spreading orchards, fine old country estates and farms that stretched down to the very water's edge. Where the Indians grew their corn, and the Duboises and Van Vechtens built their homes, a great arena of summer traffic has developed. Boats and trains are coming and going, the bustle of arrival and departure stirs all the "Point," animating the village in the way peculiar to American towns near a "resort," and the whole community to a new-comer seems to be on the alert for signs of travel.*

*But to the right of this provincial crowd and clatter, one sees, directly on landing, a vista of very fair and quiet country. The river curves about the greenest of banks, the sky shines above a rim of close dark foliage, and the flight of the bird is across a peaceful stretch of land and water. But this is not the Catskill of Indian romance and one's imagination. One longs to leave the concentration of the village life, the bustle of the wharves and station behind one, and be up and away to the hills, whose everlasting beauty is the background for this picture of activity, thrift, and speculative lounging.*

*I recall my first visit twenty years ago to these grand old mountains. It seems only the other day, yet such trips were then matters of much more calculation, as well as duration. We took the night boat, and though it was a rather poor affair, I am afraid, to my childish eyes, it seemed a floating palace, and the ladies' cabin a mingling of the fascination of the theatre with the luxuries of real life. The cabin was presided over by a colored woman, portly and affable, and full of a rather weird sort of anecdote which charmed me greatly. She impressed me as being about as old as people ever were, but I presume she was not over fifty. And she told me stories of slave times in the Northern States, which seemed to me ghastly traditions, I remember, for that peaceful moon-lit country.*

*She had been brought up in the mountains and loved the suggestions of old Rip and of the Indian period with a fervor worthy of a larger intelligence that she owned, and from her I first heard any of the romance of the region about which I am writing.*

*When our boat landed, we took a large lumbering old coach, which stopped at all the public houses and various private ones and deposited and* took up letters, packages, and messages. Our driver was a man of amiable though meager physiognomy, and he idled over his employment in a way that gave the child beside him ample opportunity to fill her eyes and heart—indeed, perhaps, to touch some glimmerings of her soul—with the majesty, the gigantic wonders of the scene before her. High upon every side rose the mountains, their pathways cleft with gorge and ravine, their indomitable silence broken only by the rushing of their many waters or the quiet summer wind moving through the pines. God's grace and bounty spoke through it all, in the green splendor of their height and depth, their width and vastness.

Those old days have passed away. Progress has come sweeping over the country, setting much at defiance, but it can never destroy what nature has reared there. To this hour, the message of the Catskills may be read as reverently and as awfully as when their depths echoed Indian voices or their waters carried the Indian's canoe.

And herein I find the greatest charm of this country. Nothing seems to take away the fearless beauty of the hill. No intrusion seems to disturb the solemnity of the peaks and gorges, the sweetness of the mountain streams, the innumerable brooks and torrents.

The Catskill of to-day is a large, active place, characterized by the usual appearance of the American village. A long main street with shops and hotels and idly speculative loungers, and almost nothing to indicate what the place once was, unless it be in the names which have descended through many generations since Dutch and colonial and provincial times. Around about, in a sort of stately indifference to the activity of the place as a "resort," are the houses of olden time, belonging to families who have authorized Americans in their feeling that pride of race may be consisted with the most simply republican sentiment. And these old places give a dignity to the town. He who runs may read their story, since in few instances have the original forms been altered. They preserve their Dutch symbols, the heavy cross-beams, the generous fire-places, or the English architecture of the last century so perfectly that their tale is assuredly written in stone and woodwork, and I will be pardoned, I am sure, for returning to some mention of these later.

But what would the writer of the letter before me say were he to arrive at the "Point" in Catskill on a summer's morning in 1882? Everything bespeaks not only bustle and enterprise but also the exhilaration of something very new, since a railroad has been established from the Landing up to Laurenceville, just at the mountain's foot. Surely this is something to awaken the Van Vechtens and Van Dusens and Livingstons and Fieros from their slumbers, but, as is sure to be the case in all American enterprises, *it has been received with the most matter-of-course thankfulness and patronage. Is it, we question, possible to overcome the American tourist with any contrivance for his comfort or luxury? I believe he is not to be moved to surprise in any such direction, and certainly the manner in which the travelers leave the boat and step on to the brand-new little train awaiting them is worthy of study.*

*The train rushes down into the placid loveliness of the shore where the boat lands, with little shrieks and starts and various signs of its being new to this existence, and I think it is disappointing to most people to be met with so much bustle and crudity when their destination is such an old and grand region. But once away from the bank, you will find that the trip can include the romance of the hills, for the route is well chosen and leads you away over a country full of richness and peace, of idly growing things, great fields of corn, stretches of buckwheat with the bloom of August on it; into ravines where the water rushes with an ancient melody in its movement, and out and over a plain beyond which the mountains rise, relegating all smaller things to insignificance. I think nothing can be more perfect than the slow evolution of the dusk and change to moonlight over this country; then arises some understanding of the lore which all old Catskillians cling to, and which, let us hope, no strength of enterprise, no congregation of the "summer boarder" can ever take away.*

*The train takes us up around Catskill proper and into Leeds, and Leeds was really old Catskill—in very truth the place which gave this part of the country a name. Whence comes the name, I believe the most faithful chronicler cannot say. It is found in various old records. In a letter dated over one hundred years ago, and which the present owner kindly allowed me to read, "Catskill Village" is mentioned, but the place now known by that name was then referred to as the "Strand" or the "Landing," for, as I have said, the village of Leeds was then Catskill proper.*

*I think it nurtured in men a curious feeling of permanence, proprietorship, of desire to keep Nature unchanged, glorious and true to her first, best impulses, for there at Leeds one finds so few marks of the impress of destroying man, so little which could jar the student of form and color as God has laid it upon His earth. Whether this has come from jealousy, listlessness, or perhaps the appreciation of vastness, one cannot say. All that can be reduced to fact is that Leeds village, the old Catskill, lies simply embosomed by the hills and vales which the Indians and Dutch must have known, and it seemed to me a most perfect relic of the past, which is fast becoming too traditional to seem our own.*

*In 1678, a solemn company of Dutch gentlemen, at the Stadt Huis in Albany, effected the purchase of Catskill. They bought the "plain and land" for four miles around.*

*I think the picture of that morning an intensely significant and American one. There was the old room in that quaint Dutch town, and there were his Majesty's humble though enterprising and shrewd servants, Robert Livingston and Marten Gerritsen Van Bergen and Sylvester Salisbury, Esquires, and with them the magistrates of the jurisdiction and those strongly pathetic figures of the time, Mahak-Neminaw and his six head-men, representatives of an Indian tribe who were, as they had been for years, in possession of the solemnly beautiful Catskills, where their corn grew and their campfires burned.*

*The Dutch and English gentlemen bought the Indian country; the deed was executed with writing and hieroglyphics. If the Indians were stoical, the purchasers cared but little for tradition, since we can find no records of the original occupants of old Catskill valuable enough to give them a place. They disappeared, wandering we know not where, and the only tradition worth preserving is of a handful of the tribe who sometimes came quite peacefully to the new settlement, simply from a desire to visit their forefathers' ground. They never lingered long; finally they disappeared entirely; and then descendants of that 8th of July, 1678, woke up to the fact that the Indians' idea of the hills must have been picturesque and colored strongly enough by romance to bear comparison with the print and canvas of their own more varied, progressive period.*

*I think no one is quite certain what was at first done with the new purchase, yet this last example of enterprise, the mountain railroad, leads past the very houses which were built by the sons and grandsons of the earliest Dutch and English owners. In those days, Albany was a thriving town, and certain smaller settlements had gained reputation as being habitable, sociable, and "worthy of domicile," but this new settlement in the country of the Indians must have had its origin in the merest speculation, since the few who gathered there seem to have made almost no effort to found or encourage a community.*

*Francis Salisbury built in 1705 the fine house still standing. One of the Van Vechtens had a dwelling deeper in the hills, and we are told that here and there houses were built, but there could scarcely have been anything like the feeling of an active community in a region that was all wilderness, silence, and the impenetrable grandeur of mountain, clove, and forest.*

*Gerritsen Van Bergen's house is still upright, and one cannot but wonder what was the story of those early buildings. Tiles and bricks imported from*

*Holland, woodwork put in with slow and patient hands—what a picture one can conjure up as the train goes rushing by, past Leeds, into the dim silence of the real mountain country, where one waits for the stages up the grand old hills!*

*Of all the old landmarks just at this point, the Salisbury house is, I think, most interesting. We drove to it one sunshiny day when the mountains were like great purpling monuments ahead of us, the greener country looking strangely fresh and young for that old country; and as we went past corn fields and buckwheat meadows, we talked to the Indian and Dutch traditions of the land almost as though we had all of us the associations with them to which one of our party could lay hereditary claim, and the story of the Salisbury house was told as I faithfully give it here.*

*Francis Salisbury built it, on his share of the land purchased from Makak-Neminaw, in 1705, when it must have been a very stately dwelling. After his occupancy there lived in it a man whose life included a romance which Hawthorne would have illumined with his weirdest fancies. He was*

The first Salisbury House, built in 1705 by Francis Salisbury. *Courtesy of the Vedder Library, Greene County Historical Society, Coxsackie, New York.*

*a person of strange and arbitrary temper, and so ill-used a slave or bound girl in his service that she fled from the old house, aided, it was supposed, by her lover, a young Dutch settler. Infuriated by her escape, her master rode up the mountains in search of her, discovering the girl at night-fall. He tied her to the tail of his horse and started furiously back to Catskill. As might be expected, the horse dashed the unfortunate girl to pieces on the rocks; and slight as was the law of the land, it found means to arrest the murderer and put him on public trial. His family united political power with great wealth, and when the man was brought to trial and justly condemned to death, they obtained a respite of the sentence. But herein lies the curious part of the story. The decree of the magistrates was that he should be publicly hung in his ninety-ninth year, and meanwhile, he was condemned to wear about his neck a halter, that all might know him to be a murderer doomed to death.*

*From this time forth, the criminal lived in a strange and gloomy seclusion, rarely coming into the village of Catskill, isolating himself from his fellow creatures but doggedly wearing his halter, which on certain occasions had to be shown in public. Until quite recently, there lived in Catskill aged people who could remember having seen this strange recluse wearing his halter, and singular as it seems, he actually lived to complete his hundredth year! But times had changed, King George's rule gone, and the new order of things seems to have swept into oblivion the curious decree of that colonial magistrate, and the unhappy owner of Salisbury house was left to die in his bed; but his singular story affected the neighborhood, as might be expected, with a belief that the house was haunted, and strange tales used to be told of a spectral horse and rider, with the shrieking figure of a girl flung from it. One old lady told me that when a child she used to live in terror of the peaceful spot where the Salisbury house stands, firmly believing that its ghostly occupant, with a halter about his shriveled neck, could at any moment appear.*

*Certainly any such ideas were dispelled by the sunny look of things about it the day we spent at the old house. It is a large two-story building, with walls of sandstone and regular windows, and the date 1705 in iron letters along the upper ledge of stone. There is not much shade about it, yet enough to shut out all glare, and the garden and orchards are a pretty tangle of growing things, which give it an air of homely comfort rather than any ghostly dread. Within, on entering, is a hallway running the length of the house, with a quaint staircase to the left, and on either side doors open into living-rooms which are treasures for the antiquarian.*

*The ceilings are supported by heavy beams, the windows are deep, and the panes of glass small and old, while the fire-places are the deep caverns of the early eighteenth century. At present, these rooms, the scene of much festivity in the early Salisbury days, are furnished quietly but in quaint enough style to suggest the origin of the house; a suggestion of lavender and dried roses lingers in the drawing-room as of summers long gone by; and the low-footed chairs, the old brass, and Chippendale book-cases might have been there when the Salisbury house was very young, and the orchards without mere striplings.*

## CHAPTER 7
# THE SUTHERLAND BURIAL PLOT: THE VISION IN THE VAULT

H er body was found in the crypt with two other coffins—hers was cast-iron with an eight-by-ten window. When the glass was cleaned, people saw a beautiful young woman dressed in a bridal gown, holding a rose in her right hand over her breast. Her features were perfectly preserved, and even the rose seemed fresh. Considering what embalming procedures must have been like in the 1800s, this is extraordinary.

In 1936, a young boy discovered that the door to the crypt had been broken. He also found a baby's bronze coffin and three disintegrated wooden coffins containing skeletal remains. For weeks, there was a steady flow of people coming to see the sight, carrying torches and candles. State trooper Dwyer had been posted there to protect the vaults against further vandalism. The metal coffin contained the remains of Mrs. Caroline Sutherland Layton, placed there on the first anniversary of her marriage. She was born in Chatham Center, the only daughter of John and Maria Wilbur Sutherland. She died in childbirth.

The Sutherland burial plot, on the Thomas Farm, was located three miles from Chatham, New York—between Chatham and Chatham Center. The

*Next page, top*: The Sutherland crypt was violated three times by curiosity seekers trying to remove the coffin of the young woman whose perfect features could be seen through a transparent pane. *Courtesy of Doug Stalker, Chatham Courier.*

*Next page, bottom*: The Sutherland crypt. *Courtesy of Doug Stalker, Chatham Courier.*

*Right*: Caroline Sutherland. *Courtesy of Doug Stalker,* Chatham Courier.

*Below*: Sutherland Pond. Taken from the Spring 2006 issue of *Columbia County History & Heritage Magazine. Courtesy of Ron Toelke and the Columbia County Historical Society.*

farm was originally owned by the Sutherlands, who lived there until 1867, when it passed to the Harris family.

The burial plot became inaccessible, being in a grove of trees about one hundred yards west of the farmhouse. A vault in this burial plot contained a coffin in which the wife of one of the John and James Sutherland doctors was buried. The lady was one of unusual beauty, and when buried, her coffin was made with a glass top. She was holding a white rose.

Hans von Behr, author of the 1986 book *Ghosts in Residence*, retells this story and also states that his neighbors, having seen it for themselves, would not have believed otherwise. Von Behr's neighbors, Dr. and Mrs. Estabrook, told him what they saw when he came back from a trip abroad, and Dr. Estabrook commented at the time that it would be hard to explain her preservation.

Someone, in an act of vandalism, broke the glass, and the corpse crumbled to dust. The tomb was later moved and closed up. It was on the anniversary of her wedding day that Caroline received last rites, the year being 1855. Eleven days after her death, the child she had just given birth to also passed away.

Officer Dwyer engaged help of the local undertaker to move the bodies to the Chatham Center Cemetery. Residents in Chatham Center say that sometimes, they've seen a young lady in a white bridal gown walking through local fields on June 13. It may be a coincidence, but that was also the date of her marriage to John Layton in 1854.

## CHAPTER 8

# HISTORIC HUGUENOT STREET AND NEW PALTZ

In the 1600s, French Huguenots purchased forty thousand acres from the Lenape (also known as Esopus) Indians and were soon after joined by Dutch families, settling in New Paltz. Although now a quaint college town, in the past, New Paltz was the site of several grisly murders and suicides. Since olden times, many stories have endured about various locations of New Paltz being haunted. The New Paltz Cinema is reported to be haunted by a little girl, heard by employees to be laughing and playing. On its surveillance cameras, the Elting Memorial Library picked up a shadow that seems to belong to a person moving around during the time the library was closed and locked up. The identity of the ghostly shadow was never determined, but prior to 1920, two deaths had occurred there.

A short distance from New Paltz's hip main street is Historic Huguenot Street, a National Historic Landmark District and home to the oldest inhabited street in America. The district offers yearly tours in the fall. Its original seven stone houses, some of which acquired the reputation of being haunted, are shown on its website. The site holds a wealth of knowledge, photographs and collections pertaining to New Paltz's history. The tour takes you back to days before electricity, as candlelit nights mark the end of summer and the beginning of the dark season, and includes three murder stories. The first story involves a 1970s New Paltz student who killed a resident for undetermined reasons and was then sent to an insane asylum across the river. There's also the story of Abraham Hasbrouck, one of the twelve original purchasers of the New Paltz land, who has been seen in

Spooky night. *Courtesy of Dan Region (bluemesaproductions.com).*

Colonial garb carrying an axe near one of the houses—sometimes with a large, black dog following him.

Ashley Hurlburt, manager of collections and archives at Historic Huguenot Street, wrote the following to me in an email:

> *It is here around this house that the most frequent apparition on Huguenot Street has been seen. In the dark of night, many people have seen a tall man wearing a long, dark coat and carrying an axe. With him on his lonely vigil is a large, black dog. The man approaches and enters the house, although footprints are never seen—even in the snow. Inside, he haunts the upper windows, at times staring down at those who pass by and at other times yelling and swinging his axe violently, perhaps over a sleeping occupant. No sound is ever heard, and the identity of this lurking man and his dog remains a mystery.*

Alf Evers (February 2, 1905–December 29, 2004) was an American historian who lived in Ulster County, New York, where he wrote histories of the Catskills and later served as historian of Woodstock. Evers and his

The Abraham Hasbrouck house. *Library of Congress.*

wife, illustrator Helen Baker, eventually settled in Connecticut, where they wrote and illustrated fifty children's books. But for a time, Evers lived in the Hasbrouck house with his mother, a clairvoyant who insisted that a child was buried in the basement. And just as she said, a child's remains were later found buried in the basement. This cellar or basement, as with several of the houses on Historic Huguenot Street, was the home of slaves and the place where most of the heavier domestic chores and cooking occurred.

At the bottom of a well (which is still standing) on Huguenot Street, near the Bevier-Elting House, Annie DuBois was found after an apparent suicide upon losing her romantic interest, Hugo Freer, who died of appendicitis. A ghost with long, dark hair, believed to be that of DuBois, has been seen wearing a white nightgown. The apparition holds her hands close to her while looking out toward the driveway and making a sobbing noise.

Jemima Wilkinson, born in 1752 in Rhode Island to Quaker parents, settled near New Paltz during the American Revolution to escape religious persecution and the rigidity of Christianity. After her death, Wilkinson allegedly sat up in her coffin and said, "I have passed through the gates of a better world, and I have seen the light. But they asked me to come back to you." Her promise to her followers before she died was to become visible a few hours before someone was to die in order to comfort them. Some of her followers had come from Connecticut, landed in Ulster County, bought land and called their settlement Penn Yan, named for the numerous Pennsylvania Yankees living there. It was later to be known as the Pang Yang Settlement.

Apparently, two portraits of Jemima still exist, and there are numerous stories of her having been seen on roads and near windows of homes of people who shortly thereafter experienced losing a loved one. After her resurrection, Jemima wanted to be known as the Publick Universal Friend to her followers. Some of her followers reached the area near the Finger Lakes and built a house dedicated to her, still standing. Her followers were the first white people that the Native Americans in this region ever saw and traded with. In 1785, scouts under her younger brother Jeptha were sent to the new Genesee Territory of western New York to determine habitability there in what was Iroquois land. The friendly experience led to the sending of a small exploring party of three of her followers in 1787 up the Susquehanna River to the new Genesee Country. She had brought 260 believers to Yates County, creating a utopian community and the largest settlement in western New York State. A powerful preacher and forceful personality, Wilkinson espoused plain dress, pacifism and the emancipation of slaves. The sect declined after her death in 1819.

Today, the Yates County Genealogy and Historical Society (YCGHS) owns the largest known collection of artifacts and manuscript materials relating to Wilkinson and her community, the Society of Universal Friends. These collections include her portrait; a hat worn by her; her bible; gifts given by visitors to the community, including Seneca baskets and a pocketbook from a French aristocrat; and items of daily use, including pewter, china, chairs and a saddle. Manuscript materials include her last will and testament, the Society's Death Book and a large body of correspondence and other written materials.

Jemima was a person ahead of her time. She favored an equality of the sexes at a time when women had no legal rights in the United States. Enemies put her on trial for blasphemy in 1800, but the court ruled that it could not try blasphemy cases due to the separation of church and state in the U.S. constitution. Jemima became a pioneer in establishing freedom of speech and freedom of religion in American law.

When Jemima Wilkinson "left time," as her followers put it, her body was buried. To this day, her burial location is known only to the two who buried her and their descendants. She was the first American-born woman to found a religious movement.

## CHAPTER 9
# THE GHOST OF DELAWARE COUNTY AND OTHER TALES

*The following tale is reprinted with permission from Tim Duerden, director of the Delaware County Historical Association (DCHA). It originally appeared in a 1968 DCHA newsletter written by Roy Gallinger.*

The ghost of Delaware County was laid many years ago, and the once haunted house past which the children ran in terrified excitement is now gone and the scene overgrown with brush and wild berries. Even the cemetery where ghostly horses vanished is now a dark and impenetrable forest, silent and fearsome, dotted with the gravestones of those who lived and witnessed the scene that was even then the beginning of a legend.

The story goes back to the year 1811, when William McCrea, a highly respected man and a relative of the famous Jane McCrea, whose fate awakened a thrill of horror and indignation throughout the colonies in 1777, when she was killed by Indians on Sunday July 27th near Fort Edward during Burgoyne's invasion, from Saratoga, settled near what is now Masonville. In the 1939 Harold W. Thompson book, *Body, Boots and Britches,* Jane McCrea's death is described more in detail:

> *Of all the incidents connected with the Saratoga victory, the most romantic is the death of Jane McCrea, whose body lies near Duncan Campbell's. Jane McCrea was the daughter of a Scotch-Irish minister in New Jersey, descended from an old Highland clan. As the British army approached, Jane had the cruel choice of escaping South with*

*her Patriot brother or waiting to see her loyalist lover. She made the romantic choice.*

American General Gates to Burgoyne:

*Miss McCrea, a young lady, lovely to the sight, of virtuous character and amiable disposition, engaged to an officer of your army was with other women and children taken out of a house near Fort Edward, carried into the woods, and there scalped and mangled in a most shocking manner. The miserable fate of Miss McCrea was particularly aggravated by her being dressed to receive her promised husband, but met by her murderers employed by you...Upward of one hundred men, women, and children have perished by the hands of the ruffians, to whom it is asserted you have paid the price of blood.*

William McCrea built a mansion-like house on his land and became a leader in the community. In 1829, he was elected a member of the state legislature. Soon after that, he died, leaving his widow to live in the big house and operate the farm.

The widow McCrea hired one Pangborn, an odd sort of character, and his wife to assist her on the farm. Mrs. Pangborn was a beautiful woman and when addressed by another man was sure to bring a flare of jealous rage from her husband. Apparently, there was no cause for these outbreaks, for Mrs. Pangborn's character was above reproach, and she had the respect of her mistress and the entire community.

One day, Mr. and Mrs. Pangborn were putting a load of oat sheaves into the barn when suddenly, the horses bolted and went galloping toward the house, the remains of the farm wagon clattering behind them. The maddened animals did not stop but tore across the road to the cemetery and, according to the legend, were never seen again. In a few minutes, Pangborn came to the house, washed his hands and told Mrs. McCrea that his wife was dead on the barn floor, killed by the team of horses. Mrs. McCrea ran to the barn and found the attractive Mrs. Pangborn bleeding from the wounds around her head—dead.

An informal inquest was held, and Mrs. Pangborn was buried in the little cemetery across the road. A few days later, an ironwood flail, an implement used in that day to thresh out grain, was found in the weeds, with some of Mrs. Pangborn's hair and much dried blood still clinging to it. The body was exhumed and examined, and it was found that she had been struck three times on the head with the flail. It was also established that she was not near the horses when she was struck and killed and that the team was probably struck by the flying flail, which startled them.

Pangborn was arrested and tried. On May 23, 1836, the Court of Oyer and Terminer convened in Delhi, with Circuit Judge Charles H. Ruggles presiding. After four days, Peter Pangborn, somewhat surprisingly, was acquitted. He immediately left the community and went west, where he remarried.

Soon after the death of Mrs. McCrea, the owner of the farm, things began to happen around the old homestead. Eerie lights began to flicker in the vacant house, and on the anniversary of the murder, a pair of fiery, dashing horses would race up to the door at midnight and disappear into the cemetery across the road. The old house, avoided by everyone in the neighborhood, finally crumbled into ruins. Old-timers said that ghostly screams continued to come from the barn at intervals but finally ceased. Not long after, Pangborn's second wife was found dead. He was accused of killing her, tried summarily before "Judge Lynch," condemned and righteously hung by the people, in accordance with frontier law.

Another old ghost tale of Delaware County concerns the Octagon House, one of only eight octagon houses built in the United States during the 1850s. Legend has it that long ago, a newlywed bride still wearing her gown and riding her horse was thrown when the horse became spooked. She died after hitting her head on a rock, and her ghost has been seen over the years, still riding atop that horse late at night. It was to be her bridal home.

Judith Richardson's must-have 2003 book *Possessions: The History and Uses of Hauntings in the Hudson Valley* documents numerous examples of a "link between regional hauntings and transience; hauntings that seem to take place at sites of transition, such as roads, bridges and taverns." Richardson referenced the frequency of stories about ghosts of transients such as hitchhikers, gypsies, peddlers and drifters. Keep this in mind as you read here and further into this book about transitional locations of the region.

In his 1939 book *Body, Boots and Britches*, Harold W. Thompson recounts the following story about Delaware County's Spook Woods:

*A Mr. Williams had been hired to work on Cornelius Mayham's farm. He had heard tales of Spook Woods which he hardly believed; yet when he entered the woods on his way home one moonlit night, he felt some trepidation. All went well until he was in the middle, when he saw something moving over the snow beside the road ahead. On reaching the*

Octagon House, Delaware County. *Courtesy of Delaware County Historical Association.*

*object, he found two cats dragging between them a third which was dead. Although he hurried along, the cats kept up with him, and to his horror, one called his name. Mr. Williams had not the slightest desire to enter into conversation and hurried on. Just before he left the woods, one of the cats called out again, "Mr. Williams, tell Molly Meyers she can come home now; old Hawkins is dead."*

*Mr. Williams was soon home. He was hesitant about revealing his experience, but finally, when the family was seated about the fireplace, he told what had happened. As he came to the passage "tell Molly Meyers she can come home," the old family cat jumped from Mrs. Mayham's lap, ran to the open fireplace, leaped up the chimney, and was never seen again.*

In the 1970s, Nancy J. Haynes gathered much research and wrote a paper on her interviews with both young and old county inhabitants concerning the legend of Spook Woods in the town of Kortright, Delaware County, and the murdered peddler believed to be haunting those woods. Her friend Peg Kenyon, a member of the Route 10 Historians, gave me a copy of the paper, which had been included in a spring program the historians held entitled "Mysteries Along the Route 10 Corridor."

At the time of her interviews, locals were recalling a very old tale from 150 years prior. The tale was that of a peddler who passed through monthly with his wares and would stay at an inn on the old Catskill Turnpike owned by the Blakeleys. The legend holds that the peddler was either disappeared or was murdered and then set about haunting the woods and the inn.

The farm/inn was originally composed of 1,000 acres but was later split into parcels of 333.3 acres given to each of Blakeleys' sons. After the Blakeleys owned the inn, the structure changed hands over the years. Subsequent owners told of a window that would never stay shut or retain glass when fixed, as well as a bloodstain on the floor of the ballroom—where the peddler's murder is believed to have taken place—that could never be removed by cleaning or even sanding of the floor.

On his last visit to the inn, the peddler disappeared after checking in. It was said that he always carried with him a large sum of money, and the people who owned the tavern seemed to become rich after his disappearance. The inn always had lots of young people stopping by, and they often held parties. One night, some of the guests at one such party heard strange noises coming from the cellar, broke up the party and at 4:00 a.m. heard running water. One person, deciding to investigate, saw Mrs. Blakeley (the innkeeper's wife) doing some washing. There was blood in the water in which she had washed the clothes, and from then on, everyone assumed that the Blakeleys had murdered the peddler.

Locals told tales of the peddler running through the woods near the inn with his head in his hands, and some believed he was killed in either the woods or ballroom and then possibly walled up in the cellar.

There was also the story of a man from Bloomville who went to the inn to talk to Mr. Blakeley and, finding him at the well, remarked at how large a stone Mr. Blakeley had atop of the well and how heavy it was. The man allegedly saw blood around the rim of the well as Mr. Blakeley lifted the stone.

Apparently, whoever killed the peddler also decided that his horses and wagon must be done away with. Legend has it that the horses were taken into Spook Woods and shot and the wagon burned. Since the two horses were standing side by side and hitched to the wagon when shot, neither fell to the ground but rather fell against each other. This apparently scared the shooter, who ran off and left a lantern burning on the wagon. People later traveling through the woods claimed to see a lantern light following them. From that time up until the 1970s, when the stories were collected, people still "wouldn't ever go through the woods for love nor money," and horses would not go near the place where the peddler's horses were shot. Once near the location, they would rear up and run.

Blakely Inn. *Courtesy of Carolyn McPherson.*

The following excerpt is taken from the *1797 Illustrated History of Delaware County, New York*, published in 1880 by W.W. Munsell and Co. of New York:

*John Blakeley came to Kortright about 1798 from Schenectady. Mr. Blakeley built a cabin with his ax, and with his ax and auger made furniture for it. He took from a huge tree timber sufficient to make a table and left the tree still growing. He hewed the material and finished the table; it had "fall leaves." This table was used by the family until they were able to have a better one. Mr. Blakeley soon became noted as a businessman. "The turnpike," running from Catskill, on the Hudson, to the Susquehanna, afforded good facilities for keeping a hotel. He erected suitable buildings, and for forty years was the jolly host of the home-seeking traveler. He was one of the most prosperous businessmen of his day. He died in 1855, aged 78 years, leaving an inheritance which will be enjoyed for generations by his descendants. Two of his sons, James G. and G. Banyar, live on parts of the old homestead. His other son, John D., moved to Tully, NY and is still living. The other brothers and their descendants are unknown to the writers.*

Locals still believe that some of the inheritance was the peddler's money.

## CHAPTER 10

# THE VAN SCHAACK HOUSE AND KINDERHOOK

B uilt in 1774 with brick baked in Holland and imported to this country by David Van Schaack, the Van Schaack mansion was fortified against intruding Canadian Indians but known for its hospitality. The Van Schaacks were among the first Kinderhook inhabitants coming from the fur trade in Albany of their ancestors. David and his brother Peter, whose house was next door, both practiced law, as did their father. For a time, both David and Peter were exiled in England during the Revolutionary War but were then allowed back to Kinderhook and their homes.

The Van Schaacks were involved with groups opposed to British rule, events and actions precipitating the war. Their grand house entertained Chief Justice John Jay, Alexander Hamilton, General Philip Schuyler and, later, *Legend of Sleepy Hollow* author Washington Irving. History happened there.

In October 1777, uniformed American Revolutionary soldiers, under the command of General Phillip, approached the house to journey Major General John Burgoyne as a prisoner of war and his army to Massachusetts after a defeat at Saratoga. Burgoyne's troops were in a wooded area nearby as he prepared to dine at the Van Schaack mansion. From a ballad of the time:

> *For the bold Burgoyne was marching,*
> *With his thousands marching down,*
> *To do battle with the people,*

*To do battle for the crown.*
*But Stark he lay at Bennington,*
*By the Hoosic's water's bright,*
*And Arnold and his forces,*
*Gathered thick on Bemis height.*

Several of Burgoyne's German soldiers were won over by the attractiveness of Kinderhook women and deserted the army and made their permanent homes there. To the rear of the estate is a small cemetery that was used to bury one resident's slaves. This cemetery is located at the present village playground on Rothermel Avenue.

Dinner guests were gathered again at the house in winter 1942, when the house was to be sold. Contemplating current events and sitting near a fireplace after the meal, feeling a slight breeze, the diners saw a figure on the wall carrying a musket and marching away, causing alarm and bringing fear to all present. It has long been said, "American patriots do not sleep in their graves when the nation is in peril." Could there be something to the conditions and energy of both fireplace-lit evening dinners during wartimes?

*Legend of Sleepy Hollow* author Washington Irving spent time at many locations in Kinderhook, including Lindewald, the home of his friend William Van Ness, whose children he was tutoring. (Lindenwald later became the home of Martin Van Buren and is now a National Historic site.) In the legend, Yankee schoolmaster Ichabod Crane (based on Kinderhook resident Jesse Merwin) courts Katrina Van Tassel (based on one of the Van Alen girls), the only

Dishes used at the time of Burgoyne's visit to Kinderhook. Photo by William Wait. *Courtesy of Rick Roberts, Global Genealogy.*

*Above*: The Van Schaak House. Photo by Mimi Forer. *Courtesy of Columbia County Historical Society.*

*Right*: Monument to Peter Van Ness, builder of Lindenwald, 1013 Old Post Road, Kinderhook. *Library of Congress.*

daughter of the town's wealthiest landowner, arousing the wrath of fellow suitor Brom Bones (based on Abraham Van Alstyne).

Leaving after a harvest party at the Van Tassel house during which Crane had hoped to propose to Katrina and failed, Ichabod wanders home in the dark but is afraid of the local legend of the Headless Horseman, believed to be a Hessian soldier who lost his head to a fired cannonball. Upon encountering the terrifying specter, both race to the bridge adjacent to the Old Dutch Burying Ground, where the Hessian is said to "vanish, according to rule, in a flash of fire and brimstone" upon crossing it. Ichabod rides for his life but is never seen again.

In 1941, model and actress Esther Tuttle and her husband bought the Merwin residence. When interviewed in her nineties, Mrs. Tuttle said she had never experienced anything herself but that her family had encounters with an apparition on the porch. She also said that the door to the bedroom where her mother-in-law typically stayed would unlock and open repeatedly. The mother-in-law described hearing the thumb latch on her door lift on many successive nights and said that she was wide awake at the time of hearing this. Mrs. Tuttle's grandson described a "white mommy" on the porch that he was afraid of. Much later, Mrs. Tuttle had visitors to the house, elderly descendants of the Merwins, who explained that their sister would often sleep on the porch to ease her ailments and that she had died there in 1917.

In her memoir, Mrs. Tuttle described a signed letter she had, written by President Martin Van Buren, that stated that Merwin was the prototype for Ichabod Crane. The two marble slabs in front of the Merwin House front door are believed to be the tombstones of Merwin and his wife, and Mrs. Tuttle was cautioned upon buying the house that if she ever moved the stones, the Headless Horseman would return.

## CHAPTER 11

# THE UNDERGROUND RAILROAD, UPSTATE NEW YORK AND GHOST STORIES

It is hard to believe that slavery ever occurred in our country. The Compromise of 1850 replaced the Fugitive Slave Law of 1793, which put the onus on the states from which the slaves had escaped to capture them. It was expensive business, as there were few police to apprehend runaway slaves.

The "compromise" mandated that officials of free states must assist slave catchers if there were runaway slaves in the area and granted slave catchers national immunity to do their job when in free states. So just because escaped slaves were in non-slave territory, it did not mean that they were automatically free and safe from being recaptured. It was also possible for black Americans who lived in the North to be captured and sent into slavery by judges, who were paid a ten-dollar fee if they allowed freed slaves to be sent back to the South. As a consequence, the Underground Railroad operated deep into Northern territory, often taking escaped slaves into Canada. New York was one of the biggest states in the abolitionist movement, as Harriet Tubman and Frederick Douglass were both active in upstate New York. The Underground Railroad shielded escaped slaves as they fled toward freedom. Tubman, in her role as a conductor along the Underground Railroad, helped some three thousand slaves escape from slavery. Tunnels connecting houses afforded secrecy to these runs. Often, there would be a church's cemetery along the house routes, and sometimes, tombstones in the cemetery were shaped like a very small coffin—this was the way to get into the tunnel from the outside or to get out if there was trouble. Often times, though, the tunnels would collapse, tragically leaving panicking slaves trapped with no way out, perishing in a horrible fashion. And many times, the bodies were just left there. This is also where and when the African American slander "spooks" came from. The following is taken from *Skaneateles Journal* and is reprinted with permission from David Wilcox:

> *A few years after settling into her home, Regina awoke to the growls of her Irish setter, Lady. Startled, Regina looked for the disturbance provoking her dog. Her eyes landed on the bedroom closet. There, Regina saw something that would ultimately lead to a visit from Syfy's show* Ghost Hunters. *"It looked like an actual person crouching in the closet—like a slave—with a kerchief on her head, looking down, with her arms around her knees," she said. "It looked like a person; you couldn't see through it."*
>
> *Regina's sighting of a ghost slave made sense—or at least as much sense as any paranormal experience can make. Regina's village home since 1998, the historical James and Lydia Canning Fuller House, was once part of the Underground Railroad. James was active in the Anti-Slavery Society, and abolitionist Frederick Douglass called him "a fast, faithful, and noble friend of the slave" in the April 13, 1849 edition of Douglass' newspaper,* The North Star.
>
> *A representative of the Preservation Association of Central New York's Freedom Trail project confirmed to Regina that the house hosted slaves venturing north on the Underground Railroad and had since been the subject of ghost sightings. Regina would add more evidence to the list in the years following the closet experience. The sound of footsteps, the image of a face in the window, the feeling of a presence in her midst—all added up to a supernatural suspicion on Regina's part.*

Regina was the only one who had that suspicion, though. Then, late one night in 2003, Regina's daughter Amanda was on the porch with a friend. They witnessed "a guy going through a wall." "It was tall…it was over six feet, but you could definitely make out a figure. I got this really uneasy feeling, and I actually left," she told the *Ghost Hunters* crew.

Concerned about her mother living alone among whatever paranormal phenomena the house hosted, Amanda contacted The Atlantic Paranormal Society (TAPS) of *Ghost Hunters* about coming and checking out the Fuller house. TAPS wouldn't pay its visit until late June, when they were in the upstate New York area working on another case.

The team spent about a week there, providing the family a room at the Holiday Inn while they combed the house. Led by investigators Jason

Hawes and Steve Gonsalves, they set up cameras in two bedrooms and the parlor (also called the "ghost room") and spent a night in the darkened house exploring, asking questions and being receptive to unusual phenomena. "I remember being in a basement with Jason, and all of a sudden, a marble or some sort of sphere rolled at our feet," Gonsalves said. "It definitely wasn't explained."

Ultimately, though, TAPS didn't have much in the way of hard data to present Regina, aside from an odd orb of light that, they told her, video didn't do justice. But they did corroborate feeling many of the same sensations that spooked Regina: unusual noises, opening doors and the presence of people behind them when there were none. Off camera, TAPS suggested to Regina that the Fuller House may actually host two kinds of spirits: an interactive one that could respond to human activity and a residential one that goes through the motions of the time when it was alive. The latter spirit might be that of James Canning Fuller, she said. Regina hopes to dig into its paranormal possibilities even more—starting with the tunnels that brought slaves there more than 150 years ago.

# CHAPTER 12
# POINT LOOKOUT, WINDHAM MOUNTAIN

The first travelers to this area were the Mohican Indians, who stayed here during the winter months, leaving their homes along the Hudson River to hunt. The Windham Mountain, which is two thousand feet high in the Catskills, offers an unprecedented five-state view into Vermont, New Hampshire, Massachusetts, Connecticut and New York.

The Point Lookout Inn, located on the mountain, went through a transformation and rebuilding after a long-ago fire. The following was submitted by David Dorpfeld, Greene County Historian:

> *Much of what I know about East Windham comes from a small booklet written by Margaret Radcliff Olsen. Mrs. Olsen says that her great-great grandfather, Barney Butts, began to settle the hamlet when he built the Summit House in 1848. It was operated as a boardinghouse for many years and was finally destroyed by a heavy snowstorm in March of 1959. Olsen says that Mr. Butts was quite the hunter and trapper, having captured over 100 black bears over the years and in 1882 had three bears in captivity at the Summit House.*
>
> *Mrs. Olsen dates the 90-guestroom Grand View Mt. House erected by Mrs. E. Dickerman at 1872. Barney Butts' son Isaac built the Butts Hotel in 1875, and this was followed by another named the Barrymore in about 1880. Other summer resorts and homes were built, and a general store/post office was built in 1900. By the beginning of the 20th Century, East Windham, with its panoramic view of portions of 5 states—New*

*York, New Hampshire, Vermont, Massachusetts and Connecticut—was a very popular summer vacation spot.*

*Mrs. Olsen says, " Summer guests of the earlier 1900s, in addition to enjoying the relaxed vacation and abundant food, enjoyed picnics and hikes on the nearby hills. Swimming in [nearby] Silver Lake and square dances in the evening were most popular." "Sherman's Hall" was a long, barn-shaped building on the ledge on the northwest side of Route 23. Mrs. Olsen says: "People came from miles around to dance to Mr. Sherman's fiddle. The inside of the hall boasted a small stage for the musicians, and the area was lighted by kerosene lamps. Long wooden benches provided the seating for the customers. In the '20s and '30s, Aunt Nellie [Mrs. Sherman] and her mother, Grandma Kearns, provided hot dogs and soda at the stand beside the road for the Saturday night festivities." A small remnant of the old hall can still be seen on the right embankment just past the few homes that still remain in East Windham.*

*Much more can be said about the "good old days" and the hostelries in East Windham, but it would be incomplete without a discussion of Point Lookout, which continues today as the Point Lookout Mountain Inn. According to Mrs. Olsen, Point Lookout started out as Gates Tea Room about 1920, but the name was quickly changed. It became widely known as a restaurant and gift shop where visitors could climb a 75-foot observation tower for a better view. Fire destroyed the original building in 1965. A new building was constructed, but the business was not successful, experiencing six owners in 12 years. According to the Point Lookout Mountain Inn website, by 2001, the building, in great need of repair and refurbishment, was bought by Ron and Laurie Landstrom, who now run it as an inn and restaurant.*

*In the end, East Windham is not what it once was, but visitors can still visit there, spend the night or enjoy a meal while experiencing the five-state view that attracted so many earlier vacationers. There is much more in Mrs. Olsen's 20-page booklet, and for the interested, the Vedder Research Library in Coxsackie still has a few for sale. A genealogy researcher recently sent me the following excerpt from the Catskill Messenger of March 30, 1833:*

*"On Monday last, Mr. Alexander Stewart committed suicide by hanging himself. Mr. Stewart is a Scotchman by birth and formerly lived in the town of Andes, Delaware County, from whence he moved to Troy, and during the cholera in that city last summer, he came with his family to this village. His occupation was that of a silversmith, at which business he worked*

*up to Friday of last week in the employment of Mr. Willard. We are told that for some time past, his mind has been greatly exercised upon the subject of religion, and that his doubts and fears had driven him to a state bordering upon if not of actual despair. The aberration of his mind were so apparent on Sunday that it was not deemed prudent to leave him alone, and he was accordingly watched during Sunday night, notwithstanding which, he eluded the vigilance of his keepers, escaped from the house, and subsequently found upon the [Catskill] creek in search of a hole in the ice where he might drown himself. The next day, he again effected his escape, wandered across the river, and was found upon the premises of Dr. Benham, suspended from a tree by a silk handkerchief around his neck. He has left a wife and two young children."*

*Three things interested me. One is how differently we report an event like this today. Unless the person who committed suicide is someone of note, it is usually hushed by the paper, and the death is usually reported as "died suddenly." The second thing is that the river was still frozen enough that it could be walked on at almost the end of March. As many of us have observed recently, some years, the river does not even freeze over. This event happened during the period that is often referred to as the "little ice age." Author Brian Fagan, in* The Little Ice Age, *gives the dates as about 1300 to 1850. So, this event would have occurred within that period.*

Current owners Ron and Laurie had long been interested in the hospitality industry and started looking to purchase property to start their own business. Not familiar with the area, they soon began hearing stories from locals about the inn they had just purchased. They dismissed it all, having their hands full with opening and running a new business.

The first thing they noticed was the odd behavior on the part of their cat, which they also dismissed, not having time nor interest in reading too much into. It has long been believed that animals and small children are the most attuned, sensitive and aware of paranormal activity; they are able to sense spirits that can't be seen or heard by many humans.

Not long afterward, Laurie noticed a bad smell in Room 12 but thought it must be a dead rodent in a wall or attic and promptly had all checked out. Nothing to this end was found, and the smell was always present—some days worse than others. Ron and Laurie tried everything to rid the smell, but nothing worked. Now they were both starting to get concerned, as it was beginning to hurt their business.

The only solution seemed to be to gut the entire room and totally renovate it—which they did. Floors, walls, ceiling—everything was redone. And for a short time, it seemed to have worked. But the odor came back. Ron was especially disappointed after all of that work. "I just couldn't believe it," he said.

Housekeepers soon began noticing lights on in the room when it had been vacant, and they were not interested in working in that room.

Laurie, working alone in the office one night, said she heard voices but couldn't make out who was talking or what was being said. Upon leaving the office to investigate, she found that no one else was on that floor. She and Ron again dismissed it, thinking that there must be some sort of natural explanation. One of their waitresses, who was living in one of the guest rooms at the time, was also skeptical of anything she heard. But one week into living at the inn, at closing time, she started experiencing a feeling of uneasiness and dread in her room. She heard and felt something and, looking down a hallway, saw a figure near Room 12. She described the figure as a petite female with long hair who was just hovering there. She ran downstairs to find and tell the owners and then quickly moved out.

Worried about negative affects of this on their business and still wanting to dismiss it all, neither Ron nor Laurie wanted it talked about. For a few months, it remained quiet and seemingly uneventful.

Then, one night, a guest checked in, and having only Room 12 available, he was given to staying there. He was fine—but only for a short time. A housekeeper told the owners that the man was screaming in his room, and they decided to investigate. What they found was a totally different person from the man who had checked in an hour earlier; he seemed possessed. The owners called 911 wishing to have him removed.

Tom, a now-retired sheriff, recalls hearing the man screaming in the background when he received the call from the owners of the inn. Upon his arrival, the guest was screaming about the smell in the room but refusing to leave. He was removed by police and, upon leaving, said he didn't understand his own behavior.

It became clear to Ron and Laurie that the time had come to get some much-needed answers. Three years ago, at the request of the inn's owners, the Pennsylvania Paranormal Association (PPA) performed an investigation. The group described a sense of "heaviness" in the room and immediately noticed a "smell of decay," an odor never before experienced by him or his team. Their EMF (electro magnetic frequency) meter spiked and reacted to questions asked regarding whether or not a female entity was present.

Upon attempting communication with the entity, the odor became even more pungent. The group attributed this to the possibility that the entity was uncomfortable with anyone being in this particular room.

A psychic, Virginia, was also present to do a reading. She believes that a hanging on the property occurred around the mid- to late 1700s. The PPA noted:

> *When Virginia walked into Room 12, she was immediately approached by a female energy in great distress. She was moving quickly and was very confused and frightened. Virginia picked up the name Ann Marie or Anna Marie with this energy. Virginia felt she was in her twenties, with blond or dirty blond hair. Virginia was receiving that this female came down from Albany, had a drug problem and had died an accidental death of a drug overdose by another person using a needle to administer the drug and fell to the floor in the back left corner of the room. Virginia felt the girl also lost some blood from her arm where the needle went into the wrong spot. There was also something to do with prostitution connected to this female. The girl kept asking Virginia where Chuck and Larry were. Virginia felt that this female's body was discarded somewhere after her death due to fear of the law and that her body was never recovered. Virginia also picked up on a male energy in Room 12 with a J name, possibly John. This male was very large in size, and Virginia felt that the female was very threatened by him and that both would move between Rooms 12 and 14.*

The psychic had no knowledge of the local area and stated that the corner of the room seemed to be where the energy was at its worst. Laurie, as the inn's owner, was mortified upon being told the findings. She simply did not want to believe that any of this could be true. Upon being asked to look further into the matter, local police said that there was no evidence of a murder or death at the inn. It seemed like the owners had come to a dead end.

Then, one night, an unknown woman came into the inn and decided that she should tell the owners what she had heard about the inn as a child. She recalled hearing that a couple had checked in one night and that the man told staff at the inn not to disturb his companion, who was ill. He put a Do Not Disturb sign on the door and then simply vanished. He was never heard from or seen again. It was a week before any of the staff went to check on the room and its occupant, and when they did, they discovered a deceased woman wearing a white gown. Apparently, this was never documented anywhere. The original town hall building having burned down, many wondered if this could be the explanation of the murder not being recorded.

The inn's owners decided to again contact the Pennsylvania Paranormal Association again with this new information. This time, two cadaver dogs were brought in. Separately, both dogs went straight to the corner of the room previously mentioned, and both reacted as trained to show the indication of death. Some of PPA's findings are as follows:

> *The clients have owned and operated this inn for the past nine years. Since they moved in, they have witnessed sporadic activity, mostly at night, in different areas of the building, but most pronounced in Room 12. The clients, employees and a few guests have reported strange odors, items moving, changes in temperature, and seeing shadows and other figures. They have also reported hearing strange sounds and seeing changes in someone's disposition. The clients report that the TV and light would often turn on by themselves in Room 12 with the door locked and no one present in the room. The clients have heard of a local legend that a woman was killed in Room 12, possibly over a lover's quarrel. The clients want to find answers and get some final closure as to whether a woman could possibly have been murdered in the room and may now be haunting the inn.*

One investigator, sitting in the small dining area on the main floor facing a door that leads into the kitchen, noticed a small, illuminated digital clock coming though the window of the door. In a split second, she observed someone walk right in front of the clock very fast from left to right and then right to left, completely blocking out the illuminated clock. Another investigator immediately went into the kitchen and verified that no one was there. The cause could not be found. The PPA reported:

> *Virginia felt that the male energy was very threatened by our presence, especially when he saw the cadaver dogs and their handlers in uniform. Virginia related that it felt like he didn't want something to be found out. Investigators did have numerous personal experiences throughout the investigation, including hearing voices, feeling multiple anomalous cold spots, seeing shadows with no known cause and having the feeling like someone was walking or standing with them. And our K-9, Ben, reacted in a very unusual manner in the great room, which is inconsistent with his normal behavior. The amount of personal experiences by investigators was above the normal and validates many of the claims by guests and*

*employees. The Rescue International cadaver-dog team was brought in on this case to rule out the possibility that the smell coming from Room 12 was caused by a cadaver or somehow connected to a dead body or that body's spirit in some way. Being that it was more probable that the cadaver dogs would not alert on anything and that a non-cadaver control dog would show interest in what would probably be a dead rodent, the hopes were to dismiss the idea that the smell was connected to a human cadaver and rule out the chance of anything paranormal. In this particular case, what occurred was that the control dog did not show any interest in the smell, while the two cadaver dogs independently alerted on the same back left corner of the room, as if a cadaver was there. This is the same spot where Virginia psychically picked up on the overdose death of a girl who may have had some blood loss in this area and died. The PPA was not able to rule out a potential paranormal cause using the cadaver dogs, but the dogs seemingly reinforced the clients' belief that someone may have died in that room, which could be connected to the activity.*

The psychic and the PPA finally did a blessing ritual to cleanse the space and assist with the crossing over of any lingering spirits. Since the blessing, Laurie states that the odor, as well as whoever might have been lingering there, seems to have disappeared. "I wanted her to be free," she said.

## CHAPTER 13

# HANK, THE ONE-ARMED
# BRAKEMAN OF TANNERSVILLE

For nearly one hundred years, some say Hank is still running around the Tannersville woods, looking for his arm. The following was told to me by a local Tannersville resident:

> *While they were repairing a switch track near Cortina, there was a train waiting at the switch to head west into Tannersville. The guy was right in front of the train, and the stupid engineer thought the work was done and it was clear, and he started up…he severed the guys arm off somewhere around the elbow, and the guy bled out because he was basically alone. The arm went with the train along the current bike path and finally fell off somewhere before Tannersville Park* [the boathouse was originally a train station]. *So now this pissed-off dead guy wanders up and down the bike path with a lantern. He hasn't really sought vengeance on anyone—the poor man just wants his arm back. All my husband knows is that his name is Hank and that he walked with a lantern on the train tracks up there for the switch…and something about a white dog.*

Skip Hommel's version was told to him by his grandfather and later published in a 1995 issue of *Hemlock*, the Mountain Top Historical Society's quarterly publication:

> *My grandfather told me the story when I was twelve, no doubt to scare me, since I was trapping mink and muskrats in the swamps and ponds alongside*

Rip Van Winkle Railroad. *Courtesy of John Curran, Mountain Top Historical Society.*

Tannersville. *Courtesy of John Curran, Mountain Top Historical Society.*

the train track beds. In the 1920s and '30s, there were two railroads that went from Tannersville through Haines Falls and up to North Lake—just north of what was the Catskill and Tannersville Railroad, which was also known as the Huckleberry.

The incident happened on the Kaaterskill branch of the Ulster and Delaware. The trains back then had a man that they called the brakeman. The job of the brakeman was to switch the track from one track to the other. To do this, there was a long lever to switch the tracks back and forth. The brakeman would carry an axe because often the levers would get rusty, and it would be hard to switch the tracks back and forth. At nightfall, the brakeman would carry a lantern so he could see where he was going. There was a spot where the train track separated just to the east of Tremper Lake.

One night, the train stopped, and the brakeman went ahead to switch the track. He had his lantern and his axe with him, and as usual, the track got stuck. He tried to use his axe to get the track unstuck. As he was trying to get the track unstuck, his arm got caught between the tracks. He grabbed his lantern to get a better look at his arm so that he could figure out how to get his arm unstuck. The engineer on the train thought that the brakeman was waving his lantern to motion the train on through. The train came barreling through and tore the brakeman's arm right off. The brakeman went running through the woods with his axe and lantern, screaming in pain. He left his arm lying next to the side of the track. People searched for the brakeman for days but couldn't find him.

At about the same time, there was a Civilian Conservation Corp. camp down by Tannersville just to the south of the lake. Back in the Depression, during the 1930s, the Conservation camp used to give teenagers and young men work, working on park trails, roads and things like that. There were about 150 kids all camped out in the Conservation camp lot just above Tannersville Lake.

One night, some maniac got into the camp amongst the kids and chopped off the left arm of eleven kids, killed them, gashed them across their heads with an axe and then took off. It was the one-armed brakeman getting revenge for having his arm torn off by the train. Police and bloodhounds were out looking for the one-armed brakeman. They were never able to find him. Legend has it that the one-armed brakeman still patrols up and down the track looking for kids to chop their arms off.

I was told by my grandfather that you could only see him at nightfall. He said that you had to look for the lantern. You could see the lantern coming down the track. The lantern had a candle in it, with a square opening and a little door to keep the candle from going out.

*After I heard about this, I went down to the old railroad tracks at about 10:30 at night down by Tremper Lake. The first time was in winter. I waited and waited and just about froze. All of a sudden, at about eleven o'clock at night, I saw a light way down at the other end of the tracks. The light was coming closer and closer, and as I was watching it, I was getting more and more afraid. It looked like the light was swinging from side to side. I quickly jumped into the woods, and I was really afraid. I thought what I would do was sneak through the woods and try and get behind the light. I looked back the other way, and there was the light, the exact same distance away as when I first went into the woods. Needless to say, by this time, I was scared stiff.*

*Another time I had a girlfriend—her name was Theresa. I took her down to see the one-armed brakeman during the summer. Theresa was from Park Ave down in Manhattan. She didn't believe a single thing I had told her about this legend. I took her down to Tremper Lake on the back of a big old black Indian motorcycle. We went to the other end of Tremper Lake, shut off the motorcycle and sat there. We sat there for an hour and a half,*

Train station at Tannersville. *Courtesy John Curran, Mountain Top Historical Society.*

View of railroad in Catskill Mountains at the turn of the century. *Courtesy of New York State Archives, A3045-78.*

A panorama of Tannersville. *Library of Congress.*

*and Theresa said, "There's no one-armed brakeman—you're just making this all up to scare me." All of a sudden, there was this light shining on her face. I said, "Now what do you think that is?" She turned, and she just screamed when she saw the light just coming down the track toward us. It actually got me a little nervous, so we jumped on the motorcycle, and I said to her that when the light got close, I was going to start the motorcycle and run right over it. As soon as I kicked the motorcycle over, it started right up, and I drove right over the light just as fast as I could. With the motorcycle's light on, we couldn't see a thing ahead of us as we went barreling right down the track.*

I've probably seen the one-armed brakeman ten or twelve times, and believe me, if you go down to Tremper Lake in the middle of the night and wait long enough, and you have enough nerve, you will see…THE ONE-ARMED BRAKEMAN.

## CHAPTER 14
# THE DIETZ HOUSE

Hudson is a town with a scarlet past, but I like Hudson. The town was named after explorer Henry Hudson, who in 1609 encountered the native Mohicans in this area as he came upriver in his ship, the *Half Moon*. In 1783, a group of men from Massachusetts and Rhode Island arrived in search of safe harbor for their vessels against British naval attacks. In the spring of 1783, they purchased the land that was then called Claverack Landing but is now Hudson and Greenport. By fall of that year, two families arrived, followed by more families the next spring, also bringing with them prefabricated houses from Nantucket. These settlers called themselves the Proprietors, many of them being Quakers. In 1785, the city of Hudson was chartered. It was the third city in the state of New York.

Mabel Parker lived all her life in a stately house on South Sixth Street in Hudson. John Craig of the Hudson Area Library History Room was instrumental in filling in more details to me of the Parker family. Mabel was the granddaughter of Byron Parker, a businessman who ran a plumbing business along with his family, which is still fondly thought of today. Five Parker sons were also to become plumbers in the family business, which in the 1940s, was sold to the Hover family.

In the 1870s, Mr. Parker lived above his business on Warren Street. Mabel Parker eventually took over running the family business after her father George. The following is taken from *Illustrated Hudson, N.Y.*, published in 1905:

Statue of the St. Winifred ordered by General DePeyster and created by scuptor George E. Bissel in Paris, 1896. *Courtesy of Chad Weckler.*

*MR. BYRON PARKER—Plumber, Gas and Steam Fitter. No. 436 Warren Street. In a general review of Hudson and its progressive institutions, it is quite necessary to make honorable mention of that "old reliable" plumber and gas fitter, Mr. Byron Parker. This house is the oldest of its kind in the city, having been established for thirty-five years. Mr. Parker, by personal attention to his business and energetic methods, has steadily increased his trade, until now it necessitates the help of eight skilled and careful workmen. These men are all able to take a plumbing job and do it in a neat and satisfactory manner. Some good samples of his work may be seen in the plumbing and heating system of the Court House and also of the Fireman's Home. A profitable specialty is made of job work of all sorts; the firm is also the agent for the famous Welshbach [sic] light. Mr. Parker carries a large stock of goods in his line and makes every effort to please his customers. The proprietor himself, and indeed the business, has always been closely identified with all the makes for progress and business energy in Hudson.*

The 1893 book *Decennial Souvenir*, written by Mrs. J. Rider Cady of the Home for the Aged in Hudson, shows an advertisement for Byron Parker services on page 30. The Parker ancestry is further documented in *Columbia County at the End of the Century, Volume II:*

*PARKER, Byron, of Hudson, N.Y., was born in Coxsackie, N.Y., on August 28, 1830. His father was Jonas Parker, a native of Vermont; he was married to Hannah, daughter of Allen Breed, whose ancestor came to America from England in 1630. Byron Parker secured his education in the public schools, and after leaving school, he devoted his attention to river navigation in various capacities until 1865, when he settled in Hudson and established a plumbing, gas and steam-fitting business, which he has since continued. He has been successful in his efforts and sustains the reputation of an honest, industrious, and in every way valuable citizen. He was a charter member of the Hudson Building and Loan Association. In 1854, he was married to Mary L. Hollenbeck, who has borne him five sons and four daughters, all worthy children of worthy parents.*

Professor Hans Holzer, PhD, a well-known author of more than one hundred books on the paranormal and teacher of parapsychology for eight years at the New York Institute of Technology, at one time visited Hudson. He was interested in interviewing the Dietzes, who bought the house after Mabel Parker passed on. He wrote about his interview in his 1997 book *Ghosts: True Encounters with the World Beyond.*

The Parker house was built between 1829 and 1849, with a variety of owners up to our present time. The Parkers acquired the house around 1904, and Mabel, while living there, was described as "a happy person with a zest for life." But in her sixties, she contracted a serious illness, apparently suffered enormously and then passed away at a nearby hospital. It was said that she was a house-proud person, not wanting to leave her house to deal with the cold and the hospital environment. It was after her passing that the house then came into the hands of Mr. and Mrs. Jay Dietz. Mrs. Dietz found employment at one time with Mabel Parker's father. To the Dietzes, the house was simply "peaceful."

Some tenants prior to the Dietzes living there would not sleep in one of the upstairs bedrooms, a room later to be used by Mrs. Dietz's mother. They described something uncanny about that particular room. But the Dietzes were not interested in the stories—until they themselves started experiencing the unexplained. Sometimes they would hear footsteps going up and down the stairs and into the hallway, where the sound would stop. This was heard by Mr. and Mrs. Dietz, as well as her mother, on many occasions. One of those occasions happened just before Christmas of that year while Mrs. Dietz was in the hallway "attending to some sewing" while her husband was in the bathroom. When she thought he was coming down the hall, she realized that

Creaky stairs. *Courtesy of the author.*

she hadn't heard him leave the bathroom or a toilet being flushed. Some nights later, after going upstairs, she had a strong feeling that someone was with her in the room. Another night shortly thereafter, she was awakened by someone pulling at her blanket from the foot of the bed. When she sat up, it stopped. But it happened again a few nights later, and this time, as she slept with the blanket covering her ear, she felt the covers being pulled off. Many times after having turned out the lights, she was aware of someone standing beside the bed looking down at her.

In February of the year that Professor Holzer met with the Dietzevs at their house, they recounted how both women in their respective rooms were awakened at 5:00 a.m. by the sound of slow, heavy footsteps coming up the stairs, going down the hall and stopping. But the women stated that these footsteps sounded different than what had been heard in previous times. Mrs. Dietz noted, "It sounded as if a very sick person was dragging herself up the stairs, trying not to fall but determined to get there nevertheless. It sounded as if someone very tired was coming home." Was Mabel Parker returning to her home to be in her resting place?

Hans Holzer passed away a few years ago, and it would have been interesting had he returned to the Dietz house to investigate further.

*They are kept in place, both in time and space, by their emotional ties to the spot. Nothing can pry them loose from it so long as they are reliving over and over again in their minds the events leading to their unhappy deaths.*
*— Hans Holzer*

## CHAPTER 15

# THE CATSKILL WITCH

This story is being added to my book with permission from the author, James McMurry, who wrote me a lovely letter at the request of his publisher. The only place I could find this legend was in his book, *The Catskill Witch and Other Tales of The Hudson Valley*, published by Syracuse University Press in 1974. A story known to Washington Irving, this was once a very old Indian legend. The Dutch updated the Old Squaw of the Mountains and called her the Catskill Witch.

### The Catskill Witch

*Solomon Brink was known to be the boon companion of Rip Van Winkle. He was an agile man, long of limb and light on his feet, much accustomed to climbing about the Catskill cliffs. He often accompanied Rip Van Winkle when Rip would sneak off with his dog and musket to go hunting in the mountain forests. But while Rip was a lazy soul who could spend an entire hunting trip sitting on a hemlock stump puffing at his pipe, Solomon was a curious man and would never be satisfied until he had tracked down the haunt of the last bobcat or fox in the Catskill range. We all know what Rip Van Winkle's laziness brought him to, but the curiosity of Solomon Brink proved even more calamitous when it at last brought him face to face with the Catskill Witch.*

*It all began one September day in 1769, about a week before Rip Van Winkle began his long sleep of twenty years. Solomon Brink and Rip had gotten their muskets and powder and set out early in the morning before the town—and more specifically, their wives—had begun to stir. They roamed through the woods together with Wolf, Rip's faithful dog and companion in idleness, nine miles westward until they came to the mountains, where the real game was to be found: bobcats. They wended their way up along a mountain trail beneath lofty spears of pines and cedars, far from the villages of men, where the only sounds were the din and roar of waterfalls and the cry of birds. At last, the two companions stopped beneath the highest of the waterfalls.*

*"We'll climb to the top of this falls, and there we'll catch us a cat when he comes to drink," said Solomon.*

*"Well," said Rip, "mightn't the cat come to drink at the bottom of the falls just as well? Then we'd save ourselves a climb and have time for a pipe besides."*

*"It's plain to see," said Solomon, "there's no cat here; but how do we know there's not one standing at the top of the falls this very minute?"*

*So up the boulders of the falls clambered the two men, one swiftly, as though pulled up by the strings of his curiosity; the other rather more laboriously. Their climb was well rewarded, for there at the edge of a pool where the falls began to form stood the largest bobcat either of them had ever seen. Old Wolf bristled up his back, and giving a low growl, skulked to his master's side, looking fearfully at the wild beast.*

*"This one's mine," said Solomon, "the next one's yours." And he raised his gun and fired. The burst of white smoke from the old musket's barrel clouded their vision for a moment, but when the smoked cleared away, they both got the surprise of their lives. Instead of the dead or wounded bobcat they expected to see, there stood before them a magnificent buck. The animal turned its antlered head toward them and seemed to grin; then off it went, leaping and braying, and disappeared among the trees. The two hunters stood dumb with amazement, while Wolf curled his tail between his legs.*

*"Now I've seen such things as this before," Solomon managed to say at last, "after a seventh, eighth, or ninth pint of ale on a Saturday night at George III's. But we've had not a drop to drink this day, either of us."*

*"True enough," said Rip. "Strange things are happening here, and that's good reason to rest our bones awhile before going anywhere else to hunt."*

*"Why nonsense!" said Solomon, "Witch or goblin, fairy or angel, I'm going to get myself that game. A buck is not a bobcat, but it's a fine trophy all the same." And he went bounding off through the woods with Rip following reluctantly behind.*

*After awhile, they came to the grove of smaller trees with finely carved branches and scant foliage. "There's no buck here," said Rip, "only trees, that's plain to see."*

*"Perhaps," said Solomon, "but if those branches I see are not the antlers of a buck, then a tree grows from the body of a doe yonder there." He raised his gun and fired. There was a crashing sound among the bushes which they took to be a buck falling dead. But lo and behold! Out from behind the bushes came a great black bear, baring its teeth and seeming to grin, and off it lumbered through the woods.*

*"There's no more doubt a spell of magic is being cast for us," said Rip in despair, "and as good and fearless Christian men, we're duty bound to get our souls out of here."*

*"Why, if it's the devil," said Solomon, "we'll catch him and make him tell all his secrets; and if it's an angel, we've nothing to fear."*

*"And if it's the Catskill Witch who plays these pranks on us," retorted Solomon, "we'll be the last men she tricks or know why!" And off he sprang on his long legs, leaping logs, boulders, and stumps or whatever else fell in his path, while Rip, pipe in hand, stumbled along behind with Wolf casting many a sidelong glance into the shadowy woods.*

*At length, they came back to an outcropping of rocks and huge boulders black with moss.*

*"It seems your bear's given us the slip," said Mr. Van Winkle, "if that's what it is we're chasing."*

*"Perhaps," said Solomon, "yet if I'm not mistaken, that one boulder down yonder has small ears like to any bear's I've ever seen." He lifted his gun and fired again, but when the smoke from the old musket cleared away, there stood in place of the black bear a small red fox grinning from ear to ear. The fox turned, wagged its bushy tail, and went leaping off through the woods. But the greater his perplexity, the greater the tenacity with which Solomon Brink tracked down his prey. So off he went, this time in pursuit of a fox. He darted through a pine grove, waded through a swamp thick with mosquitoes, climbed a rocky pass and at last came out into a small batch of barberry bush all brightly spotted with berries.*

*"Well, he lost us this time," said Rip, when he finally straggled up beside Solomon, who stood intently eyeing the clearing.*

*"Perhaps," said Solomon, "but that one barberry bush yonder has a long snout and gleaming eyes I thought peculiar to the fox." He lifted his gun and fired again, and this time out of the burst of white gunsmoke came the old Witch in her true form at last—for it had been she they had been chasing*

*all the while. Off she went flying across the gorge into the distant woods, her scream of mocking laughter echoing through the mountain range.*

*When Rip Van Winkle saw that, he came so near to fainting he had to sit down on a log and light up his pipe. But Solomon Brink only grew the more determined. "Cursed Witch!" he swore, "for a bobcat she gave me a buck, for a buck a bear, for a bear, a fox, and now—nothing!"*

*"Well, nothing is better than being boiled alive in a witch's caldron," said Rip, who had pulled his hat down over his eyes and sat there puffing furiously on his pipe.*

*But Solomon was too angry for such good advice. "I'll skin her alive like any prey and mount her head on the tavern wall as though it were a ten-point buck!"*

*"Now, Solomon Brink, listen to some good advice," said Rip. "You know as well as I that curiosity and determination can be a fine fellow's virtues, but in this instance of the Catskill Witch, they would be vices of the worse sort. Follow my example for once, and let laziness and indolence adorn your Christian soul."*

*And in other such words did Rip try to dissuade his friend from so ill-advised an adventure, but all to no avail.*

*"You sit here and rest yourself and have a pipe or two," said Solomon, "while I hunt down the Catskill Witch. And I'll be back before you've filled your pipe a third time."*

*And so Solomon Brink settled to his fate. With a run and a jump, he made a leap across the gorge—a feat an agile deer would scarcely attempt—and landing on the other side, he went running off through the forest.*

*For several hours, he continued on the trail of the Witch. He has a sharp eye, and her path was not hard to follow. Little signs told him which way she had passed: here the leaves of a tree were strangely withered, a little further, a small bird lay dead on the ground; a hundred paces of a patch of tall grass was blanched and parted as though in terror. At length, Solomon found himself approaching the top of Rundy Cup Mountain. As he climbed higher up the mountainside, the sky grew darker. Thunder rumbled in the distance, and lightning flashed over his head. At last, near the mountaintop, he spied a cave opening into the mountain, and at the mouth of the cave sat the Catskill Witch, spinning black clouds and flinging them to the winds. By her side was a pile of magic gourds. She cast them one by one against the rocks, and torrents of water burst forth down the mountainside and fell as thundershowers from the skies round about. As she spun the dark clouds and broke the gourds, the Witch sang to herself:*

The Catskill Witch. *Courtesy of the author.*

*Blow, blow, winds of ice,*
*Down the mountain pass;*
*Thunder and lightning*
*Rumble and roar,*
*And darkness fill the air*
*Til gone is all weather fair.*

*Never had Solomon Brink seen so ill-omened a sight in all his life, and the fear in his heart bade him turn back from his foolhardy adventure. But his determination to avenge himself on the Witch for her deceitful tricks and his curiosity to see more closely how she spun the clouds and made the rain fall goaded him on. So he climbed higher yet up the mountain. But at just that moment, the Witch turned and saw him. She looked him full in the face and said with a terrible gleam in her eye, "You are too curious a man, Solomon Brink! Have you come for your trophy? Then you shall have it!"*

*And picking up the largest of the magic gourds, she dashed it on the rocks where he stood. The last thing poor Solomon heard was the Witch's scream of laughter, for the gourd burst before him, and a spring welled up in such volume the unhappy man was engulfed in its waters. He was swept to the edge of Kaaterskill Clove and dashed on the rocks two*

The Rip Van Winkle House, the oldest house in the Catskills, 1787. *Library of Congress.*

*hundred and sixty feet below. Nor did the water from the magic gourd ever cease to run, and in these times, the stream born of the Witch's revenge is known as Catskill Creek.*

*When his friend failed to return, Rip and Wolf made their way back home, alone and sorrowful. He was not one to meddle with the Catskill Witch and risk the loss of his soul; and yet some say it was to search for Solomon Brink that Rip Van Winkle went into the mountains a week later.*

*But that time, Rip met with other adventures, as we all know well.*

## CHAPTER 16
# HARPER

Under the roof of the former H.W. Rogers Hose Company, a long-ago tale originated. The home of the second-oldest volunteer fire company in New York State, originally chartered in 1794, has been respectfully renovated to showcase the original brick walls, wood floors and grand staircase and is now home to a restaurant.

The Honorable Gerald Solomon, when speaking in the House of Representatives in 1994, mentioned the H.W. Rogers Hose Co. with plenty of praise:

> *We could only imagine how many buildings have been saved and how many lives and livestock rescued by the prompt action of these dedicated volunteers. And the H.W. Rogers Hose Co. No 2 has been doing it for 200 years. But above all, they are marked by a spirit of civic pride and desire to help their neighbors, especially when trouble arises.*

Long ago, a fireman from the H.W. Rogers Fire Company had a dog that followed him to fires and once climbed a ladder to the top of a burning building to join his master. But this is not Harper. Harper is believed to be Harper W. Rogers, and most of the activity experienced over the years has occurred on the second floor of the building.

Long ago, people with money would build firehouses as a way of protecting their interests, especially if they owned multiple properties. Harper Rogers was one such individual. Harper was born in Warren County in 1819, lived on a farm until the age of ten and then moved to Stockport with his family. His ancestors were the early settlers of Rhode Island. As an adult businessman, Harper purchased an interest in the paper mill at Claverack, was one of the managers of the House of Refuge For Women in Hudson, was elected mayor in 1864 and was one of the trustees for the Hudson City Savings Institution in 1894. He was described in Ellis's *History of Columbia County, New York* as a "man of commanding presence, and readily wins the confidence and respect of his associates."

As noted in the *History of Secret Orders in Columbia County,* Harper Rogers was also a member of the Order of Free and Accepted Masons. The Masonic Club of Hudson was originally organized on January 14, 1899, but the first meeting was held at the John McKinstry house on December 18, 1786. McKinstry had been captured during the Battle of Cedars in 1776 but was saved by Captain Brant, a Mohawk chief, and was spared from being burned at the stake.

In the past, firefighters cooking and eating in the basement had heard footsteps upstairs and went to investigate only to find that no one was there. The current owner and staff have arrived many a morning to find that things have been moved around and in disarray. Amusingly, mannequins bearing restaurant logo T-shirts have been "tampered with."

In January 1914, Hudson's newspaper at the time, the *Hudson Register,* ran a story about the H.W. Rogers banquet dinner celebrating one hundred years of firefighting:

> *The main floor was completely filled up with dining tables, ferns and carnations being the table decorations, while about the room were hung bunting and flags most artistically arranged. Thomsen's orchestra was present and played during the hour given to social intercourse before the banquet and also during the dining. The menu was as follows: Gherkins, celery, mustard, pickles, olives, fricassee of chicken, biscuits, fresh ham, dressing, cranberry sauce, boiled onions, mashed potatoes, salmon salad en mayonnaise, American cheese, saltines, coffee and cigars.*

County Clerk Milton Van Hoesen gave a speech after the dinner:

> *Hudson had its first fire in 1793, when the office of the* Hudson Gazette *and the bookstore of Asafoel Stoddard were burned. There was no fire extinguishing apparatus, no firemen's organization, and no adequate water supply. This fire proved a warning, and at the next session of the*

*Legislature, a petition was presented asking for authority to organize fire companies. The desired act was passed March 19, 1794 ordaining that the Common Council appoint Fire Wardens in this city, whose duty it was immediately upon cry of fire to repair the place. Then it was further directed that in case of fire, the inhabitants of the city should place lighted candles in the windows of their homes so that inhabitants could pass through the streets in greater safety. In the same year that the first fire occurred, a number of public-spirited citizens circulated a subscription paper to raise funds for the purchase of a fire engine. We learn from the records that the membership of the company from time to time contained the very best citizens and businessmen of Hudson.*

My neighbor Ed, a longtime firefighter himself, put me in touch with a colleague of his. George, a fifty-five-year veteran of the fire company, shared some of his father's stories with me. George's father, a sixty-five-year member of H.W. Rogers, passed down his experiences, which George talked fondly about. The "old-timers," as George referred to them, had their first television set at the fire station in an upstairs room. Many people felt weird sitting in this room, even though they were very interested in the new technology. Many had heard chains rattling throughout the upstairs, but mostly in the higher hose tower. The hose tower was a small room in which the hoses were hung to dry before being put back on the firetrucks. Despite the room being checked for wind leaks, no one could attribute the sound of chains to anything in particular. Many of the men wandered throughout both the upstairs and downstairs in search of the source of the noises but never found anything.

To some, it was too unsettling. They felt that maybe it was the ghost of Harper Rogers himself and that, perhaps, Harper didn't want newcomers or old-timers in his space without him. To others, it was Harper letting fellow firefighters know that he was still around and that he approved of them being there with him. If theories about ghosts and spirits are to be believed, maybe Harper simply wanted to make his presence known and to participate with his fellow firefighters in any festivities going on in his building.

At the fifty-first State Fireman's Convention, held here in Hudson in 1923, it was decided that a building would be constructed to serve as a firefighting museum. The museum would celebrate the history of firefighting in New York and would house many relics, including the oldest fire engine in New York State. The museum was built on the grounds of the Fireman's Home on Harry Howard Avenue, and in November 1925, relics were donated to the new space, which was to become the Firemen's Association of the State of New York (FASNY) Museum of Firefighting. The new museum space was dedicated on Memorial Day in 1926. Here you can see the artifacts, as well as old photographs of Harper and his fellow firefighters. Today, the FASNY Museum of Firefighting houses the best collections of firefighting relics in the world. And this, we know, would make Harper very happy.

# CHAPTER 17
# THE VANDERBILT

P eople love this old place, and so do I," says Bob Mansfield, the third Mansfield to own and operate the Vanderbilt House Hotel & Restaurant. Built in 1860 by the Vanderbilts to serve their railroad employees and upstate travelers, Bob's great-grandfather Leverett bought the property in 1890. The train station that was across the street no longer exists, but at one time, guests could step off the train and onto the hotel porch thanks to the spur the Vanderbilts added to the main line. The nearby railroad was a big boost to business at the hotel. In time, Bob's grandfather Douglas became the innkeeper, and Bob's father Leverett and his aunt Madalyn were both born in Room 12.

The hotel still proudly displays the original staircase and banister, as well as the original hardwood floors. Many who have trodden there still remain. "I grew up hearing great stories about life in the hotel from my grandma, my dad and especially my aunt," Bob recalls. "Even after my grandfather died in 1937 and the hotel was sold, everyone in my family always thought of the Vanderbilt House as ours."

Whenever a Mansfield visited Columbia County, it was a ritual to check on the hotel. On a trip back east in 2009, Bob made the pilgrimage to the Vanderbilt House, then a restaurant owned and operated by Marcy Groll. In the tavern, Bob saw a picture of the hotel, circa 1900, that included his great grandfather. When he tried to buy the photograph, Marcy told him, "Sure, but you have to buy the hotel first!"

By November 2009, the Vanderbilt House, with its eight rooms and two bathrooms, was back in the Mansfield family. Bob renovated the first floor,

*Above*: Old Vanderbilt. *Courtesy of Bob Mansfield.*

*Left*: Bob Mansfield's parents. *Courtesy of Bob Mansfield.*

including the tavern, dining room, Victorian parlor and restrooms. The restaurant opened in April 2011. He also added a two-level outdoor deck overlooking Summit Lake, which once served as Philmont's reservoir. Since then, he's renovated and restored the guest rooms upstairs, adding private baths to each. Their numbers run from 1 to 7, but there's still Room 12, where Bob's father was born. Visitors to the hotel's website can view a 1901 register of guests and where they traveled from, along with nostalgic old photos of the area and hotel, right on up to the renovation photographs.

Louise lives across the street from the Vanderbilt and, along with her now-deceased husband, Bud, was also a prior owner. Louise never experienced anything herself, but now the current owners and staff members claim that they can smell Bud's ever-present cigarette smoke and the smell of the popcorn he always made while they're working in the office and bar area. Many visitors and staff members, both past and present, have had similar experiences, none of which they considered negative.

Last October, a customer having been there many times finally decided to tell Marcy that the place was haunted. He would never go upstairs and had asked about the downstairs "ladies' sitting room." He also claimed that while in a restroom, an older woman had yelled at him to get out, startling him a bit—but she was from another time. Often times, a headless girl in white has been seen by both customers and staff hovering downstairs. Over the years, four different mediums (none of whom know one another) from four different states have also asked Marcy about this girl in white. All that seems to be known about her is that she may have been a local schoolteacher from long ago. She has also been seen dancing in one of the upstairs rooms.

One overnight guest commented on how he saw a woman upstairs in the hallway with her hand on her hip. He mentioned it only because the next day, he saw her portrait in the downstairs lobby. He swore it was the woman he saw the night prior. The portrait is of Bob's grandmother, who has long been deceased.

One earlier group of guests staying upstairs had opened the door to the attic and was very frightened to have seen "three black people that were hiding for the Underground Railroad." They were dressed as if they were from another era. Similar sightings were reported later on by other guests, as well as those who tried venturing into the same area.

The manager's niece, Lindsay, once stayed overnight at the Vanderbilt and had an unsettling experience. Lindsay had occasion to be there early one morning, around 10:00 a.m., because even though there was a snowstorm going on, guests had booked a huge party for the dining room that night.

*As to why only some people can see, hear, feel or smell the unexplained, some theories have been suggested:*

*A clairvoyant is someone who seems to have intuitive knowledge of both people and things—a sixth sense that not all are capable of. A clairvoyant sees images in her mind and reports what she sees, even though it often does not makes sense initially. She can often go into a place and report on possible past or even upcoming events, sometimes in great detail.*

*A clairsentient is an empathic person who feels or senses what may have occurred in spaces of the past. This type of overwhelming feeling can also come with very physical symptoms, including feelings of sickness, impending doom and profound sadness. A clairsentient can even experience wounds on her own body that sometimes correspond with those of a person from the past.*

*Clairessence is the ability to actually experience certain smells from the past. These smells are often unexplainable at first but become clear after more details emerge.*

*A clairaudient person has the ability to hear beyond the normal hearing range. These sounds are known as electronic voice phenomena (EVP) and are often captured on tape.*

Lindsay, who works doing prep in the kitchen, decided to get there early and stay as needed.

After the party ended and the restaurant had been cleaned up, Lindsay decided to stay overnight in one of the rooms. She was the only person staying there that night. During the late evening, while she was in her room, she heard laughter upstairs, but she knew that everyone had left the building some time ago. Needless to say, it took her a while to fall asleep.

The next morning, she awoke to the sound of all of the upstairs doors opening and closing several times—and she also heard footsteps. This was confusing to her; she knew that there would be absolutely no one in the building in the morning and that there were no guests upstairs either. When she looked out her door, there was no one around, and all the upstairs doors were closed.

Staff members at the restaurant have reported not wanting to walk through the empty dining room at night because they feel like they are being watched. In one upstairs room, the strong smell of a man's cologne is always present, despite the room being thoroughly cleaned and all linens laundered after guests depart. Windows have been left open to air it out, sometimes with the room being vacant for up to two weeks, but the cologne smell always returns.

James, a former Vanderbilt employee, explained to me how he had once asked other staff members about the little boy watching him in the kitchen. James had seen the boy twice in his first few days of working there. Both times he saw a small boy, with his fingers pressed against the glass pane of the kitchen door, looking back at him. He wondered who this little boy was and why he was in the kitchen unattended. No one knew who he was.

James had also inquired about a "guy in a cowboy hat" smoking a cigarette on the front porch. No one seemed to know why he was there, and when the man didn't come into the restaurant, James looked outside for him but couldn't find him. Since he looked like a person from long ago, someone remarked that maybe he was someone from olden times waiting for the train.

As the manager, Marcy frequently works in the office with her dog. Sometimes, the dog's eyes seem to follow something, and then the dog will flinch or jump, as if being startled or poked with something.

The kitchen seems to be an area where pranks happen, and it was always brushed off until psychics later started visiting the hotel. A cook working alone in the kitchen would have the ranges set on low flame, leave the kitchen for a short time and come back to find a high, raging flame and his cooking burning. Upset with the constant hijinks, the cooks started looking for explanations. Things on shelves in the kitchen would sometimes fly off and fall to the floor. More than once, patrons at the bar saw a glass leave the bar, suspend itself in midair and then crash to the floor.

On one occasion, Marcy stayed overnight in one of the upstairs rooms and had an experience of her own, although not scary or unpleasant. She heard what sounded like someone giggling and playing with jacks—the sound of a little ball bouncing and the jacks being scooped up.

Over a period of time, about five psychics and four mediums started to visit the inn by chance, each giving their observations to the owners and staff. They all stated that the hotel had many otherworldly presences and more than one or two entities. Their observations are interesting because they mirrored what guests had been telling the owners for some time.

While outside the hotel, several guests have reported seeing a man looking out an upstairs window when no guests are staying upstairs. Apparently he's waiting to see Lincoln go by on the train.

A white-haired man sitting in the back of the dining room smoking a cigar is seen by guests and psychics alike. He fits the description of and is thought to be Cornelius Vanderbilt. Vanderbilt's railway ran from Manhattan up to nearby Chatham Four Corners in the 1800s, and it's possible that he could have been a visitor to the hotel that his family built during those days.

One of the psychics informed Marcy that the hotel was home to a little boy named Michael. A friend, a little girl named Tabitha, is frequently with him as well. Prior to this psychic visiting, hotel owners were baffled at guests telling them that a little girl was jumping on the bed in one of the upstairs rooms. Each time this was reported, the owners explained that there were no children currently staying in the hotel. The psychic went on to say that Michael was currently upstairs and crying because he can't find his jacks. This gave Marcy chills, and she said, "Not to worry. Tell Michael I think his jacks are upstairs, around the corner from where my room was."

While managing the hotel, Marcy experienced the loss of her father, who on his deathbed complained to her of all the people in his room. Marcy explained that these might be people helping him to cross over. Before he passed, Marcy asked her father to let her know of his presence by leaving her two specific coins known only to her. On several occasions, guests have found these coins—a penny and a dime—in the oddest places and brought them to Marcy. Before he passed away, author David Pitkin dined at the Vanderbilt. David wrote many books while studying the folklore of this country and in the Caribbean, having collected over eight hundred stories. One of his two accompanying male guests used dowsing rods, which are typically used to search for electromagnetic energy, mines, tunnels, corpses or substances that may explain sightings by picking up vibrations, at the Vanderbilt. Dowsers used in finding a missing person may first hold their instrument over a personal item belonging to that person. One of David's guests said that he felt there was a little boy still present who had mischievous energy. Dr. Hans Holzer said of Pitkin's efforts:

> *Ghosts of the Northeast by David J. Pitkin is a painstakingly accurate collection of true ghost stories in which Mr. Pitkin, a teacher by profession and a resident of the area he writes about so knowingly, reports the true experiences people have had with the denizens of the Other Side who somehow have not yet found their way to that world. The book is genuinely fascinating and lovely.*

It has been a multi-generational assumption that the Vanderbilt has many past and present visitors, all perhaps interacting with one another in the same space and time. If some of the theories are correct, perhaps time and space do fold over onto one another, two dimensions sort of superimposed upon one another.

# BIBLIOGRAPHY

Brodhead, John Romeyn. *Documents Relating to the Colonial History of the State of New York*. Albany, NY: Weed, Parsons and Co., 1856.

Callan, Albert. "The Vision in the Vault." *Chatham Courier*, December 30, 1976.

Donaldson, Harold, and Cortlandt Van Dyke Hubbard. *Historic Houses of the Hudson Valley*. New York: Bonanza Books, 1942.

Ellis, Captain Frank. *History of Columbia County, New York*. Philadelphia: Everts & Ensign, 1878.

Foderaro, Lisa. "The Librarians Call It an Anomaly (It Wasn't Rattling Chains.)" *New York Times*, April 20, 2008.

Gallinger, Roy. "The Ghost of Delaware County." Dehli, NY: Delaware County Historical Association, 1968.

Holzer, Hans. *Ghosts: True Encounters with the World Beyond*. New York: Black Dog and Leventhal, 1997.

Hudson, David. *History of Jemima Wilkinson, a Preacheress of the Eighteenth Century*. N.p.: S.P. Hull, 1821.

*Hudson Gazette*, ed. "History of Kinderhook, NY (Part 1)" from *Columbia County at the End of the Century*. Hudson, NY: The Record Printing and Publishing Co., 1900.

*Hudson Register*. "110th Anniversary of Rogers Hose Company No. 2, This City Observed With A Banquet." January 29, 1914.

Matthews, Kathryn. "This Old House Has Ghosts." *New York Times*, October 13, 2006.

# BIBLIOGRAPHY

New York Correction History Society. "An NYCHS Timeline on Executions by Hanging in New York State." http://www.correctionhistory.org/hangings/hangdates8.html.

Richardson, Judith. *Possessions: The History and Uses of Hauntings in the Hudson Valley*. Cambridge, MA: Harvard University Press, 2003.

Riservato, Rochelle. "Hudson Valley's Most Haunted." VisitVortex.com http://www.visitvortex.com/magazine/Hudson-Valleys-Most-Haunted.

Rockwell, Reverend Charles. *The Catskill Mountains and the Region Around*. New York: Taintor Brothers & Co., 1873.

Skinner, Charles M. *Myths and Legends of Our Own Land*. Philadelphia: J.B. Lippincott & Co., 1896.

Stickles, Ruth. *Folklore of Columbia County*. Albany, NY: State College for Teachers, 1938.

Stockbridge-Munsee Band of Mohicans. "Origin & Early Mohican History." http://www.mohican-nsn.gov/Departments/Library-Museum/Mohican_History/origin-and-early.htm.

Tucker, Libby. "Voices." New York State Folklore Society Newsletter 32, Spring/Summer, 2006.

Waldholz, Rachel. "Ghost Town." *Our Town* (Winter 2009): 42.

Wikipedia. "Hudson Valley." http://en.wikipedia.org/wiki/Hudson_Valley.

Wilcox, David. "Syfy's Ghost Hunters Pays Visit to Underground Railroad House." *Skaneateles Journal*, November 6, 2012.

# WEBSITES

www.catskillarchive.com
www.cityofhudson.org
www.historicaldigression.com
www.hudsonarealibrary.org

# ABOUT THE AUTHOR

L isa LaMonica is an author and award-winning illustrator living in upstate New York. She was nominated for the Columbia County Council on the Arts Artist of the Year award in 2001. She is currently working on *Folktales of the Caribbean*, a favorite travel place of hers, and *Halloween Stories of the Hudson Valley*. LaMonica gives private art lessons and also teaches at her community college and the Hudson Youth Department. With her books and portfolio in tow, she has attended the Hudson Children's Book Festival, the largest such festival in the Northeast, every year since its inception.

Visit us at
www.historypress.net

This title is also available as an e-book

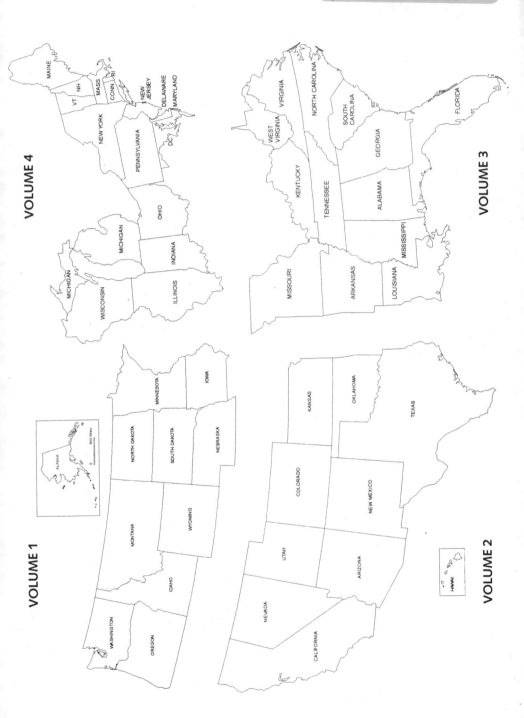

VOLUME 4

VOLUME 3

VOLUME 1

VOLUME 2

S0-BTD-980

## Who Should Read This Book?

We've all heard the scenario: the family on vacation stops at a road-side "dig your own" gem mine. Junior finds a sapphire the size of a peach and ends up on national television telling the world how he will spend his fortune.

*T* This book is for those who have read these stories and want their chance to find their own fortune. It is also a book for those who would enjoy the adventure of finding a few gems, getting them cut or polished, and making their own jewelry. It is a book for those people who want to plan a gem hunting vacation with their family. It is a book for those who study the metaphysical properties of gems and minerals and would like to add to their personal collections.

*T* This book is for those who would like to keep the art of rock-hounding alive and pass it on to their children. It is a book on where to find your own gems and minerals and on how to begin what for many is a lifelong hobby.

*T* This is a book for those who aren't interested in the "hidden treasure map through mosquito-infested no-man's-land" approach to treasure hunting but do want to find gems and minerals. It is for those who want to get out the pick and shovel and get a little dirty. (Although at some mines they bring the buckets of pre-dug dirt to you at an environmentally temperature controlled sluicing area.)

Many an unsuspecting tourist has stopped at a mine to try his or her luck and become a rockhound for life. Watch out! Your collection may end up taking the place of your car in your garage.

Good hunting!

# This volume is one in a four-volume series.

VOLUME 1: **Northwest States**
Alaska
Idaho
Iowa
Minnesota
Montana
Nebraska
North Dakota
Oregon
South Dakota
Washington
Wyoming

VOLUME 2: **Southwest States**
Arizona
California
Colorado
Hawaii
Kansas
Nevada
New Mexico
Oklahoma
Texas
Utah

VOLUME 3: **Southeast States**
Alabama
Arkansas
Florida
Georgia
Kentucky
Louisiana
Mississippi
Missouri
North Carolina
South Carolina
Tennessee
Virginia
West Virginia

VOLUME 4: **Northeast States**
Connecticut
Delaware
District of Columbia
Illinois
Indiana
Maine
Maryland
Massachusetts
Michigan
New Hampshire
New Jersey
New York
Ohio
Pennsylvania
Rhode Island
Vermont
Wisconsin

*The Treasure Hunter's*

# GEM & MINERAL GUIDES TO THE U.S.A.

### 4TH EDITION

## Where & How to Dig, Pan, and Mine Your Own Gems & Minerals

### VOLUME 3: SOUTHEAST STATES

by KATHY J. RYGLE AND STEPHEN F. PEDERSEN
Preface by Antoinette Matlins, PG,
author of *Gem Identification Made Easy*

### GEMSTONE PRESS
Woodstock, Vermont

*The Treasure Hunter's Gem & Mineral Guides to the U.S.A.* 4th Edition:
*Where & How to Dig, Pan and Mine Your Own Gems & Minerals*
Volume 3: Southeast States

2008 Fourth Edition, First Printing
© 2008 by Kathy J. Rygle and Stephen F. Pedersen
Preface © 2008 by Antoinette Matlins
2006 Third Edition
2003 Second Edition
1999 First Edition

30405 1384
S

For information regarding permission to reprint material from this book, please mail or fax your request in writing to GemStone Press, Permissions Department, at the address / fax number listed below, or e-mail your request to permissions@gemstonepress.com.

**The Library of Congress has cataloged the third edition as follows:**

Rygle, Kathy J., 1955–
Southwest treasure hunter's gem & mineral guide : where & how to dig, pan, and mine your own gems & minerals / Kathy J. Rygle and Stephen F. Pedersen—2nd ed.
p.      cm.
Rev. ed. of: The treasure hunter's gem & mineral guides to the U.S.A. c1999.
Includes index.
ISBN 0-943763-37-1 (NW)—ISBN 0-943763-40-1 (SE)—
ISBN 0-943763-38-X (SW)—ISBN 0-943763-39-8 (NE)
1.    Minerals—Collection    and    preservation—United    States—Guidebooks.
2.    Precious    stones—Collection    and    preservation—United    States—Guidebooks.
3. United States—Guidebooks. I. Pedersen, Stephen F., 1948– II. Rygle, Kathy J., 1955– Treasure hunter's gem & mineral guides to the U.S.A. III. Title.
QE375.R92 2003
549.973—dc21

2003040801

ISBNs for fourth edition:
ISBN-13: 978-0-943763-55-2(NW)          ISBN-13: 978-0-943763-56-9(SW)
ISBN-10: 0-943763-55-X(NW)              ISBN-10: 0-943763-56-8(SW)
ISBN-13: 978-0-943763-57-6(NE)          ISBN-13: 978-0-943763-58-3(SE)
ISBN-10: 0-943763-57-6(NE)              ISBN-10: 0-943763-58-4(SE )

Cover design by Bronwen Battaglia
Text design by Chelsea Dippel

10  9  8  7  6  5  4  3  2  1

Manufactured in the United States of America

Published by GemStone Press
A Division of LongHill Partners, Inc.
Sunset Farm Offices, Route 4, P.O. Box 237
Woodstock, VT 05091
Tel: (802) 457-4000          Fax: (802) 457-4004
www.gemstonepress.com

*Dedications, with love, to our parents and children:*

To my parents, Joe and Helen Rygle, who taught me the love of nature; my earliest remembrances of "rockhounding" are hikes with my dad in the fields, forests, and streams near our home. I also remember weekend trips with my mother to a shop that sold specimens of minerals from around the world. To my daughter, Annie Rygle, who has shared with me the wonders of nature. Also, thanks to Annie for helping me sort the information for the first three editions. —K. J. R.

To my parents, Cliff and Leone Pedersen, who taught me to value nature and to not quit. To my daughters Kristi and Debbie, who challenge me to keep growing. —S. F. P.

To our combined families, including Georgia Pedersen, and to family no longer with us.

*With special thanks:*

To all the owners of fee dig mines and guide services, curators and staff of public and private museums, mine owners, miners, and fellow lapidarists. Our thanks to all those individuals both past and present who share the wonders of the earth with us.

To our agent, Barb Doyen, and her childhood rock collection.

To our publisher, Stuart M. Matlins; editors Emily Wichland, Jessica Swift, and Michaela Powell; Production members Tim Holtz, Jenny Buono, Kristi Menter, and Melanie Robinson; and all the staff at GemStone Press for their guidance, assistance, and patience.

To Mrs. Betty Jackson for, in her own way, telling Kathy to write the books.

To God and the wonders He has given us.

And finally, to each other, with love and the perseverance to keep on trying.

# Volume 3—Southeast States

## CONTENTS

# All-American Gems

*by Antoinette Matlins, P.G.*

When Americans think of costly and fabled gems, they associate them with exotic origins—Asia, South Africa or Brazil. They envision violent jungle quests or secret cellars of a sultanate, perhaps scenes from a Jorge Amado novel or from *A Thousand and One Nights*, a voluptuous Indian princess whose sari is adorned with the plentiful rubies and sapphires of her land, or a Chinese emperor sitting atop a throne flanked by dragons carved from exquisitely polished jade.

Asked what gems are mined in the United States, most Americans would probably draw a blank. We know our country is paved with one of the finest highway systems in the world, but we don't know that just below the surface, and sometimes on top of it, is a glittering pavement of gemstones that would color Old Glory. The red rubies of North Carolina, the white diamonds of Arkansas, the blue sapphires of Montana—America teems with treasures that its citizens imagine come from foreign lands. These include turquoise, tourmaline, amethyst, pearls, opals, jade, sapphires, emeralds, rubies, and even gem-quality diamonds.

Not only does America have quantity, it has quality. American gems compare very favorably with gems from other countries. In fact, fine gemstones found in the U.S. can rival specimens from anywhere else in the world. Some gems, like the luxurious emerald-green hiddenite and steely blue benitoite, are found only in America. Others, like the tourmalines of Maine and California, rival specimens found in better-known locations such as Brazil and Zambia.

The discovery of gemstones in U.S. terrain has been called a lost chapter in American history. It continues to be a saga of fashion and fable that, like the stones themselves, are a deep part of our national heritage. Appreciation of our land's generous yield of sparkling colored stones reached a zenith at the end of the nineteenth century with the art nouveau movement and its utilization of them. When the Boer Wars ended, South Africa's diamonds and platinum eclipsed many of our own then so-called semiprecious stones. Not until the 1930s, and again starting with the 1960s, did economics and the yen for color make gems more desirable again.

In the late 1800s, the nation sought out and cherished anything that was unique to the land. The search for gemstones in America coincided with the exploration of the West, and nineteenth-century mineralogists, some bonafide and others self-proclaimed, fulfilled that first call for "Made in America." Their discoveries created sensations not only throughout America but in the capitals of Europe and as far away as China. The Europeans, in fact, caught on before the Americans, exhibiting some of America's finest specimens in many of Europe's great halls.

But the search for gemstones in this country goes back even further than the nineteenth century. In 1541, the Spanish explorer Francisco Coronado trekked north from Mexico in the footsteps of Cortés and Pizarro, searching not only for gold but also for turquoise, amethyst and emeralds. In the early 1600s, when English settlers reached Virginia, they had been instructed "to searche for gold and such jeweles as ye may find."

But what eluded the Spanish explorers and early settlers was unearthed by their descendants. Benitoite, which may be our nation's most uniquely attractive gem, was discovered in 1907 in California's San Benito River headwaters. A beautiful, rare gem with the color of fine sapphire and the fire of a diamond, benitoite is currently found in gem quality only in San Benito, California.

Like many of America's finest stones discovered during the "Gem Rush" of the nineteenth century, benitoite was held in higher regard throughout the rest of the world than it was on its native U.S. soil.

The gem occurs most commonly in various shades of blue. A fine-quality blue benitoite can resemble fine blue sapphire, but it is even more brilliant. It has one weakness, however: in comparison to sapphire, it is relatively soft. It is therefore best used in pendants, brooches and earrings, or in rings with a protective setting.

While benitoite is among the rarest of our gems, our riches hardly stop there. America is the source of other unusual gems, including three even more uniquely American stones, each named after an American: kunzite, hiddenite and morganite.

The story of all-American kunzite is inseparable from the achievements of two men: Charles Lewis Tiffany, founder of Tiffany & Co., and Dr. George Frederick Kunz, world-renowned gemologist. By seeking, collecting and promoting gems found in America, these two did more for the development of native stones than anyone else during, or since, their time.

While working for Tiffany in the late 1800s, Dr. Kunz received a package in the mail containing a stone that the sender believed to be an unusual tourmaline. The stone came from an abandoned mine at Pala Mountain, California, where collectors had found traces of spodumene—a gemstone prized by the ancients but which no one had been able to find for many years. Dr. Kunz was ecstatic to find before him a specimen of "extinct spodumene of a gloriously lilac color." A fellow gemologist, Dr. Charles Baskerville, named the find "kunzite" in his honor.

Kunzite has become a favorite of such designers as Paloma Picasso, not only because of its distinctive shades—lilac, pink, and yellow-green orchid—but because it is one of a diminishing number of gems available in very large sizes at affordable prices. It is a perfect choice for the centerpiece around which to create a very bold, dramatic piece of jewelry. Designer Picasso's creations include a magnificent necklace using a 400-carat kunzite. Although it is a moderately hard stone, kunzite is easily fractured, and care must be taken to avoid any sharp blows.

Kunzite's sister gem, hiddenite, is also a truly "all-American" stone. In 1879, William Earl Hidden, an engraver and mineralogist, was sent to North Carolina on behalf of the great American inventor and prospector Thomas Alva Edison to search for platinum. Hidden found none of the precious white metal but in his pursuit unearthed a new green gemstone, which was named "hiddenite" in his honor.

Less well known than kunzite, hiddenite is an exquisite, brilliant emerald-green variety of spodumene not found anyplace else in the world. While light green and yellow-green shades have been called hiddenite, the Gemological Institute of America—this country's leading authority on gemstones—considers only the emerald-green shade of spodumene, found exclusively in the Blue Ridge Mountains of Mitchell County, North Carolina, to be true hiddenite.

The foothills of the Blue Ridge Mountains also possess America's most significant emerald deposits. While output is minimal compared to Colombia, Zambia or Pakistan, the Rist Mine in Hiddenite, North Carolina, has produced some very fine emeralds, comparable to Colombian stones. The discovery was first made by a farmer plowing his field who found them lying loose on the soil. The country folk, not knowing what they had come across, called the stones "green bolts."

In August 1970, a 26-year-old "rock hound" named Wayne Anthony found a glowing 59-carat "green bolt" at the Rist Mine only two feet from the surface. It was cut into a 13.14-carat emerald of very fine color. Tiffany & Co. later purchased the stone and called it the Carolina Emerald. "The gem is superb," said Paul E. Desautels, then the curator of mineralogy at the Smithsonian Institution. "It can stand on its own merits as a fine and lovely gem of emerald from anywhere, including Colombia." In 1973, the emerald became the official state stone of North Carolina.

A California prize, the warm peach- or pink-shaded morganite, was named by Dr. Kunz for financier John Pierpont Morgan, who purchased the Bement gem collection for donation to the American Museum of Natural History in New York, where it can be viewed today. Morganite is a member of the beryl family, which gives us aquamarine (the clear blue variety of beryl) and emerald (the deep green variety of beryl). However, morganite is available in much larger sizes than its mineralogical cousins and is much more affordable.

Many consider the core of our national treasure chest to be gems like the tourmalines of Maine and California and the sapphires of Montana, gems that are mined in commercial quantities and have earned worldwide reputations. One day in the fall of 1820, two young boys, Ezekiel Holmes and Elijah Hamlin, were rock hunting on Mount Mica in Oxford County, Maine. On the way home, one of the boys saw a flash of green light coming from underneath an uprooted tree. The find was later identified as tourmaline, and Mount Mica became the site of the first commercial gem mine in the United States. The mine was initially worked by Elijah Hamlin and his brother Hannibal, who later became Abraham Lincoln's vice president.

The colors of the rainbow meld delicately in the tourmalines of Maine, producing some of the finest specimens in the world, rivaling in quality even those from Brazil. A 150-mile strip in central Maine provides shades of apple green, burgundy red and salmon pink, to mention just a few. Some stones are bi-colored.

Miners are kept busy in the Pala district of San Diego County, California, as well. California, in fact, is North America's largest producer of gem-quality tourmaline.

The hot-pink tourmalines, for which California is famous, began to come into greater demand in 1985, as pastel-colored stones became more and more coveted by chic women around the globe. Curiously enough, over one hundred years ago the Chinese rejoiced in the fabulous colors of this fashionable stone. The Empress Dowager of the Last Chinese Imperial Dynasty sent emissaries to California in search of pink tourmalines. She garnished her robes with carved tourmaline buttons and toggles, and started a fad which overtook China. Much of the empress's collection of fine carvings was lost or stolen when the dynasty fell around 1912, but artifacts made from California's pink tourmaline can be seen today in a Beijing museum. China's fascination with pink tourmalines lasted long after the empress. In 1985, a contingent of the Chinese Geological Survey came to California with two requests: to see Disneyland and the Himalaya Mine, original site of California pink tourmaline.

While the Chinese are mesmerized by our tourmalines, Americans have always been attracted to China's jade. But perhaps we ought to take stock of our own. Wyoming, in fact, is the most important producer of the stone in the Western Hemisphere. The state produces large quantities of good-quality green nephrite jade—the type most commonly used in jewelry and carvings. California also boasts some jade, as does Alaska. Chinese immigrants panning for gold in California in the late 1800s found large boulders of nephrite and sent them back to China, where the jade was carved and sold within China and around the world.

The U.S. is also one of the largest producers of turquoise. Americans mostly associate this stone with American Indian jewelry, but its use by mainstream designers has regularly come in and out of fashion.

Some of the most prized gems of America are the stunning sapphires from Yogo Gulch, Montana. These sapphires emit a particularly pleasing shade of pale blue, and are known for their clarity and brilliance.

The Montana mine was originally owned by a gold-mining partnership. In 1895, an entire summer's work netted a total of only $700 in gold plus a cigar box full of heavy blue stones. The stones were sent to Tiffany & Co. to be identified. Tiffany then sent back a check for $3,750 for the entire box of obviously valuable stones.

Once one can conceive of gem-quality sapphires in America, it takes only a small stretch of the mind to picture the wonderful diamonds found here. A 40.23-carat white gem found in Murfreesboro, Arkansas, was cut into a 14.42-carat emerald-cut diamond named Uncle Sam. Other large diamonds include a 23.75-carat diamond found in the mid-nineteenth century in Manchester, Virginia, and a greenish 34.46-carat diamond named the Punch Jones, which was claimed to have been found in Peterstown, West Virginia.

Each year, thousands of people visit Crater of Diamonds State Park in Arkansas, where, for a fee, they can mine America's only proven location of gem-quality diamonds. Among them is a group known as "regulars" who visit the park looking for their "retirement stone."

In 1983, one of the regulars, 82-year-old Raymond Shaw, came across a 6.7-carat rough diamond. He sold it for $15,000 uncut. According to Mark Myers, assistant superintendent of the state park, the stone was cut into an exceptionally fine, 2.88-carat gem (graded E/Flawless by the Gemological Institute of America). Myers says the cut stone, later called the Shaw Diamond, was offered for sale for $58,000.

Diamonds have also been found along the shores of the Great Lakes, in many localities in California, in the Appalachian Mountains, in Illinois, Indiana, Ohio, Kentucky, New York, Idaho and Texas. Exploration for diamonds continues in Michigan, Wisconsin, Colorado and Wyoming, according to the U.S. Bureau of Mines. The discovery of gem-quality diamonds in Alaska in 1986 initiated a comprehensive search there for man's most valued gem.

Many questions concerning this country's store of gems remain unanswered. "Numerous domestic deposits of semiprecious gem stones are known and have been mined for many years," wrote the Bureau of Mines in a 1985 report. "However, no systematic evaluations of the magnitude of these deposits have been made and no positive statements can be made about them." Even as the United States continues to offer up its kaleidoscopic range of gems, our American soil may hold a still greater variety and quantity of gems yet to be unearthed.

And here, with the help of these down-to-earth (in the best possible way!)

guides, you can experience America's gem and mineral riches for yourself. In these pages rockhounds, gemologists, vacationers, and families alike will find a hands-on introduction to the fascinating world of gems and minerals . . . and a treasure map to a sparkling side of America. Happy digging!

*T*

**Antoinette Matlins, P.G.** is the most widely read author in the world on the subject of jewelry and gems (*Jewelry & Gems: The Buying Guide* alone has almost 400,000 copies in print). Her books are published in six languages and are widely used throughout the world by consumers and professionals in the gem and jewelry fields. An internationally respected gem and jewelry expert and a popular media guest, she is frequently quoted as an expert source in print media and is seen on ABC, CBS, NBC and CNN, educating the public about gems and jewelry and exposing fraud. In addition, Matlins is active in the gem trade. Her books include *Jewelry & Gems: The Buying Guide; Jewelry & Gems at Auction: The Definitive Guide to Buying & Selling at the Auction House & on Internet Auction Sites; Colored Gemstones: The Antoinette Matlins Buying Guide—How to Select, Buy, Care for & Enjoy Sapphires, Emeralds, Rubies and Other Colored Gems with Confidence and Knowledge; Diamonds: The Antoinette Matlins Buying Guide—How to Select, Buy, Care for & Enjoy Diamonds with Confidence and Knowledge; Engagement & Wedding Rings: The Definitive Buying Guide for People in Love; The Pearl Book: The Definitive Buying Guide;* and *Gem Identification Made Easy: A Hands-On Guide to More Confident Buying & Selling* (all GemStone Press).

# Introduction

This is a guide to commercially operated gem and mineral mines (fee dig mines) within the United States that offer would-be treasure hunters the chance to "dig their own," from diamonds to thundereggs.

For simplicity, the term *fee dig site* is used to represent all types of fee-based mines or collection sites. However, for liability reasons, many mines no longer let collectors dig their own dirt, but rather dig it for them and provide it in buckets or bags. Some fee-based sites involve surface collection.

This book got its start when the authors, both environmental scientists, decided to make their own wedding rings. Having heard stories about digging your own gems, they decided to dig their own stones for their rings. So off to Idaho and Montana they went, taking their three children, ages 8, 13, and 15 at the time, in search of opals and garnets, their birthstones. They got a little vague information before and during the trip on where to find gem mines and in the process got lost in some of those "mosquito-infested lands." But when they did find actual "dig your own" mines (the kind outlined in this book), they found opals, garnets, and even sapphires. They have since made other trips to fee dig mines and each time have come home with treasures and some incredible memories.

Upon making their second collecting trip out west, the authors purchased some lapidary equipment, i.e. rock saw and rock polisher. They first used them to cut thundereggs collected from a mine in Oregon. The next project was to trim the many pounds of fossil fish rocks they acquired at a fee dig fossil site. A sequel to this guide series is proposed to cover authorized fossil collecting sites, educational digs, as well as museums on fossils and dinosaurs. It will include such topics as where to view and even make plaster casts of actual dinosaur tracks. There are even museums where kids of all ages can dig up a full-sized model of a dinosaur!

## Types of Sites

The purpose of this book is principally to guide the reader to fee dig mine sites. These are gem or mineral mines where you hunt for the gem or mineral in ore at or from the mine. At fee dig sites where you are actually permitted to go into the field and dig for yourself, you will normally be shown what the gem or mineral you are seeking looks like in its natural state (much different from the polished or cut stone). Often someone is available to go out in the field with you and show you where to dig. At sites where you purchase gem- or mineral-bearing ore (either native or enriched) for washing in a flume, the process is the same: there will usually be examples of rough stones for comparison, and help in identifying your finds.

Also included are a few areas that are not fee dig sites but that are well-defined collecting sites, usually parks or beaches.

Guided field trips are a little different. Here the guide may or may not have examples of what you are looking for, but he or she will be with you in the field to help in identifying finds.

For the more experienced collector, there are field collecting areas where you are on your own in identifying what you have found. Several fee areas and guided field trips appropriate for the experienced collector are available. Check out the listings for Ruggles Mine (Grafton, NH, volume 1); Harding Mine (Dixon, NM, volume 2); Poland Mining Camps (Poland, ME, volume 1); Perhams (West Paris, ME, volume 1); and Gem Mountain Quarry Trips (Spruce Pine, NC, volume 3).

## Knowing What You're Looking For

Before you go out into the field, it is a good idea to know what you are looking for. Most of the fee dig mines listed in this guide will show you specimens before you set out to find your own. If you are using a guide service, you have the added bonus of having a knowledgeable person with you while you search to help you find the best place to look and help you identify your finds.

Included in this guide is a listing of museums that contain rock and gem exhibits. A visit to these museums will help prepare you for your search. You may find examples of gems in the rough and examples of mineral specimens similar to the ones you will be looking for. Museums will most likely have displays of gems or minerals native to the local area. Some of the gems and minerals listed in this guide are of significant interest, and specimens of them can be found in museums around the country. Displays accompanying the exhibits might tell you how the gems and minerals were found, and their place in our nation's history. Many museums also hold collecting field trips or geology programs, or may be able to put you in touch with local rock and lapidary clubs.

For more information on learning how to identify your finds yourself—and even how to put together a basic portable "lab" to use at the sites—the book *Gem Identification Made Easy* by Antoinette Matlins and A. C. Bonanno (GemStone Press) is a good resource.

Rock shops are another excellent place to view gem and mineral specimens before going out to dig your own. A listing of rock shops would be too extensive to include in a book such as this. A good place to get information on rock shops in the area you plan to visit is to contact the chamber of commerce for that area. Rock shops may be able to provide information not only on rockhounding field trips but also on local rock clubs that sponsor trips. There are numerous listings on the Internet of rock and mineral clubs. Among these are the American Federation of Mineralogical Societies (www.amfed.org), which lists member clubs, and Bob's Rock Shop (www.rockhounds.com), which has a U.S. club directory (supplied information).

Through mine tours you can see how minerals and gems were and are taken from the earth. On these tours, visitors learn what miners go through to remove the ores from the earth. This will give you a better appreciation for those sparkly gems you see in the showroom windows, and for many of the items we all take for granted in daily use.

You will meet other rockhounds at the mine. Attending one of the yearly events listed in the guide will also give you the chance to meet people who share your interest in gems and minerals and exchange ideas, stories, and knowledge of the hobby.

## How to Use This Guide

To use this book, you can pick a state and determine what mining is available there, or pick a gem or mineral and determine where to go to "mine" it.

In this guide are indexes that will make the guide simple to use. If you are interested in finding a particular gem or mineral, go to the Index by Gem or Mineral in the back of the book. In this index, gems and minerals are listed in alphabetical order with the states and cities where fee dig sites for that gem or mineral may be found.

If you are interested in learning of sites near where you live, or in the area where you are planning a vacation, or if you simply want to know whether there are gems and minerals in a particular location, go to the Index by State, located in the back of the guide. The state index entries are broken down into three categories: Fee Dig Sites/Guide Services, Museums and Mine Tours, and Special Events and Tourist Information. Please note that the information provided in each individual listing is subject to availability.

There are also several special indexes for use in finding your birthstone, anniversary stone, or zodiac stone.

### Site Listings

The first section of each chapter lists fee dig sites and guide services that are available in each state. Included with the location of each site (if available) is a description of the site, directions to find it, what equipment is provided, and what you must supply. Costs are listed, along with specific policies of the site. Also included are other services available at the site and information on camping, lodging, etc. in the area of the site. Included in the section with fee dig sites are guide services for collecting gems and minerals.

In the second section of each chapter, museums of special interest to the gem/mineral collector and mine tours available to the public are listed. Besides being wonderful ways to learn about earth science, geology, and mining history (many museums and tours also offer child-friendly exhibits), museums are particularly useful for viewing gems and minerals in their rough or natural states before going out in the field to search for them.

The third section of each chapter lists special events involving gems and minerals, and resources for general tourist information.

A sample of the listings for fee dig mines and guide services (Section 1 in the guides) is on the next page.

---

## Tips for mining:

1. Learn what gems or minerals can be found at the mine you are going to visit.

2. Know what the gem or mineral that you're hunting looks like in the rough before you begin mining.

Visiting local rock shops and museums will help in this effort.

3. When in doubt, save any stone that you are unsure about. Have an expert at the mine or at a local rock shop help you identify your find.

---

# Sample Fee Dig Site Listing

**TOWN in which the site is located /** *Native or enriched[1]* • *Easy, moderate, difficult[2]*

---

Dig your own  *T*

*The following gems may be found:*
• List of gems and minerals found at the mine

Mine name
Owner or contact (where available)
Address
Phone number
Fax
E-mail address
Website address

**Open:** months, hours, days
**Info:** Descriptive text regarding the site, including whether equipment is provided
**Admission:** Fee to dig; costs for predug dirt
**Other services available**
**Other area attractions** (at times)
**Information on lodging or campground facilities** (where available)
**Directions**

Map (where available)

---

*Notes:*

1. Native or enriched. *Native* refers to gems or minerals found in the ground at the site, put there by nature. *Enriched* means that gems and minerals from an outside source have been brought in and added to the soil. Enriching is also called "salting"—it is a guaranteed return. Whatever is added in a salted mine is generally the product of some commercial mine elsewhere. Thus, it is an opportunity to "find" gemstones from around the world the easy way, instead of traveling to jungles and climbing mountains in remote areas of the globe. Salted mines are particularly nice for giving children the opportunity to find a wide variety of gems and become involved in gem identification. The authors have tried to indicate if a mine is enriched, but to be sure, ask at the mine beforehand. If the status could not be determined, this designation was left out.

2. Sites are designated as easy, moderate, or difficult. This was done to give

you a feel for what a site may be like. You should contact the site and make a determination for yourself if you have any doubts.

*Easy:* This might be a site where the gem hunter simply purchases bags or buckets of predug dirt, washes the ore in a flume or screens the gem-bearing gravel to concentrate the gems, and flips the screen. The gems or minerals are then picked out of the material remaining in the screen. A mine which has set aside a pile of mine material for people to pick through would be another type of site designated as "Easy."

*Moderate:* Mining at a "Moderate" site might mean digging with a shovel, then loading the dirt into buckets, followed by sifting and sluicing. Depending on your knowledge of mineral identification, work at a "Moderate" site might include searching the surface of the ground at an unsupervised area for a gem or mineral you are not familiar with (this could also be considered difficult).

*Difficult:* This might be a site requiring tools such as picks and shovels, or sledgehammers and chisels. The site may be out of the way and/or difficult to get to. Mining might involve heavy digging with the pick and shovel or breaking gems or minerals out of base rock using a sledge or chisel.

## Maps

Maps are included to help you locate the sites in the guide. At the beginning of each state, there is a state map showing the general location of towns where sites are located.

Local maps are included in a listing when the information was available. *These maps are not drawn to scale!* These maps provide information to help you get to the site but are not intended to be a substitute for a road map. Please check directly with the site you are interested in for more detailed directions.

---

## Special Note:

Although most museums and many fee dig sites are handicapped accessible, please check with the listing directly.

---

## Fees

Fees listed in these guides were obtained when the book was updated, and may have changed. They are included to give you at least a general idea of the costs you will be dealing with. Please contact the site directly to confirm charges.

Many museums have discounts for members and for groups, as well as special programs for school groups. Please check directly with the institution for information. Many smaller and/or private institutions have no fee, but do appreciate donations to help meet the costs of staying open.

Many sites accept credit cards; some may not. Please check ahead for payment options if this is important.

## Requesting Information by Mail

When requesting information by mail, it is always appreciated if you send a SASE (self-addressed stamped envelope) along with your request. Doing this will often speed up the return of information.

## Equipment and Safety Precautions

### Equipment

The individual sites listed in these guides often provide equipment at the mine. Please note that some fee dig sites place limitations on the equipment you can use at their site. Those limitations will be noted where the information was available. Always abide by the limitations; remember that you are a guest at the site.

On the following pages are figures showing equipment for rockhounding. Figures A and B identify some of the equipment you may be told you need at a site. Figure C shows material needed to collect, package, transport, and record your findings. Figure D illustrates typical safety equipment.

Always use safety glasses with side shields or goggles when you are hammering or chiseling. Chips of rock or metal from your tools can fly off at great speed in any direction when hammering. Use gloves to protect your hands as well.

Other useful tools not shown include an ultraviolet hand lamp, and a hand magnifier.

Not pictured, but something you don't want to forget, is your camera. You may also want to bring along your video camera to record that "big" find, no matter what it might be.

Not pictured, but to be considered: knee pads and seat cushions.

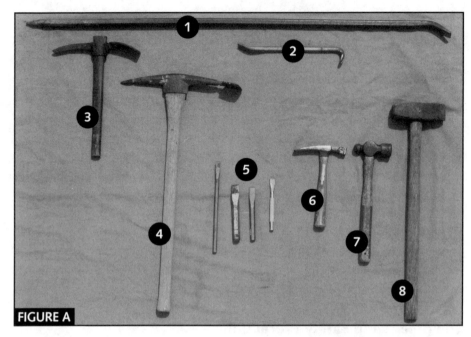

**FIGURE A**

1. Crowbar
2. Pry bar
3. Smaller pick
4. Rock pick
5. Various-sized chisels (*Note:* When working with a hammer and chisel, you may want to use a chisel holder, not shown, for protecting your hand if you miss. Always use eye protection with side shields and gloves!)
6. Rock hammer (*Note:* Always use eye protection.)
7. 3-pound hammer (*Note:* Always use eye protection.)
8. Sledgehammer (*Note:* When working with a sledgehammer, wear hard-toed boots along with eye protection.)

## *Other Safety Precautions*

- Never go into the field or on an unsupervised site alone. With protective clothing, reasonable care, proper use of equipment, and common sense, accidents should be avoided, but in the event of an illness or accident, you always want to have someone with you who can administer first aid and call for or seek help.
- Always keep children under your supervision.
- Never enter old abandoned mines or underground diggings!
- Never break or hammer rocks close to another person!

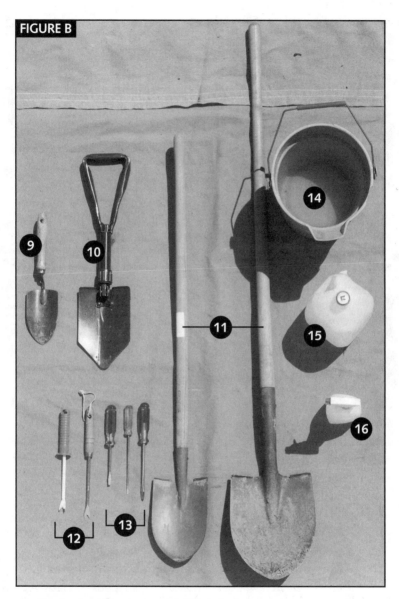

**FIGURE B**

9. Garden trowel
10. Camp shovel
11. Long-handled shovels
12. Garden cultivators
13. Screwdrivers
14. Bucket of water
15. (Plastic) jug of water
16. Squirt bottle of water; comes in handy at many of the mines to wash off rocks so you can see if they are or contain gem material

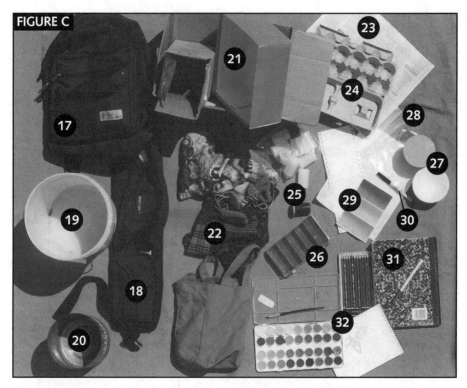

**FIGURE C**

17. Backpack
18. Waist pack to hold specimens
19. Bucket to hold specimens
20. Coffee can to hold specimens
21. Boxes to pack, transport, and ship specimens
22. Bags—various sized bags to carry collected specimens in the field
23. Newspaper to wrap specimens for transport
24. Egg cartons to transport delicate specimens
25. Empty film canisters to hold small specimens
26. Plastic box with dividers to hold small specimens
27. Margarine containers to hold small specimens

28. Reclosable plastic bags to hold small specimens
29. Gummed labels to label specimens (Whether you are at a fee dig site or with a guide, usually there will be someone to help you identify your find. It is a good idea to label the find when it is identified so that when you reach home, you won't have boxes of unknown rocks.)
30. Waterproof marker for labeling
31. Field log book to make notes on where specimens were found
32. Sketching pencils, sketchbook (waterproof notebooks are available), paint to record your finds and the surrounding scenery

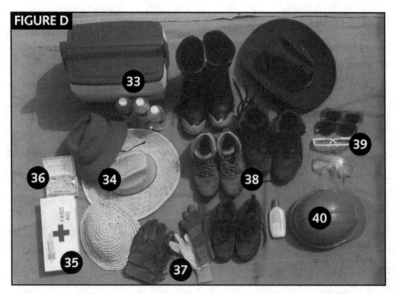

FIGURE D

33. Food and water—always carry plenty of drinking water (*Note:* many sites tell you in advance if they have food and water available or if you should bring some; however, it is always a good idea to bring extra drinking water. Remember—if you bring it in, pack it back out.)

34. Hats. Many of the sites are in the open, and the summer sun can be hot and dangerous to unprotected skin. Check with the site to see if they have any recommendations for protective clothing. Also, don't forget sunscreen.

35. First aid/safety kit

36. Snakebite kit. If the area is known to have snakes, be alert and take appropriate safety measures, such as boots and long pants. (*Note:* while planning our first gem-hunting trip, we read that the first aid kit should contain a snakebite kit. Just like rockhounds, snakes seem to love rocky areas!) In most cases, if you visit sites in the book, you will be either at a

flume provided by the facility, or with an experienced guide. At the first, you will most likely never see a snake; at the second, your guide will fill you in on precautions. For listings where you will be searching on a ranch or state park, ask about special safety concerns such as snakes and insects when you pay your fee. These sites may not be for everyone.

37. Gloves to protect your hands when you are working with sharp rock or using a hammer or chisel

38. Boots—particularly important at sites where you will be doing a lot of walking, or walking on rocks

39. Safety glasses with side shields, or goggles. Particularly important at hard rock sites or any site where you or others may be hitting rocks. Safety glasses are available with tinted lenses for protection from the sun.

40. Hard hats—may be mandatory if you are visiting an active quarry or mine; suggested near cliffs

## Mining Techniques

### *How to Sluice for Gems*

This is the most common technique used at fee dig mines where you buy a bucket of gem ore (gem dirt) and wash it at a flume.

1. Place a quantity of the gem ore in the screen box, and place the screen box in the water. Use enough gem ore to fill the box about a third.

2. Place the box in the water, and shake it back and forth, raising one side, then the other, so that the material in the box moves back and forth. What you are doing is making the stones move around in the screen box, while washing dirt and sand out of the mixture.

3. After a minute or two of washing, take the screen box out of the flume, and let it drain. Look through the stones remaining in the screen box for your treasure. If you're not sure about something, ask one of the attendants.

4. When you can't finding anything more, put the box back in the flume and wash it some more, then take it out and search again.

Clockwise from top: Gold pan; screen box used for sluicing; screen box used for screening.

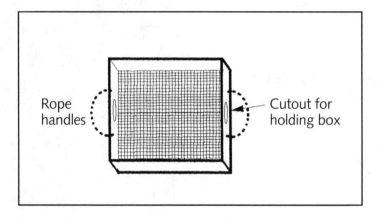

Rope handles

Cutout for holding box

## How to Build a Screen Box

1. A screen box that is easy to handle is generally built from 1" x 4" lumber and window screening.

2. Decide on the dimensions of the screen box you want, and cut the wood accordingly. Dimensions generally run from 12" x 12" up to 18" x 18". Remember that the end pieces will overlap the side pieces, so cut the end pieces 1½" longer.

3. There are two alternative methods of construction. In one, drill pilot holes in the end pieces, and use wood screws to fasten the end pieces to the side pieces. In the other, use angle irons and screws to attach the ends and sides.

4. Cut the screening to be ¼" smaller than the outside dimensions of the screen box, and use staples to attach the screen to the bottom of the box. Use metal screening rather than plastic if possible. For a stronger box, cut ¼" or ⅜" hardware cloth to the same dimensions as the screening, and staple the hardware cloth over the screening. The hardware cloth will provide support for the screening.

5. Cut ¼" wood trim to fit, and attach it to the bottom of the box to cover the edges of the screening and hardware cloth and staples.

6. If you like, add rope handles or cut handholds in the side pieces for easier handling.

5. If possible, move your screen box into bright light while you are searching, since the gems and minerals often show up better in bright light.

## How to Screen for Gems

This is another common technique used at fee dig mines where you buy a bucket of gem ore and screen it for gems. (The authors used this technique for garnets and sapphires in Montana.)

1. Place a quantity of the gem ore in the screen box, and place the screen box in the water. Use enough gem dirt to fill the box about a third.

2. Place the box in the water, and begin tipping it back and forth, raising one side, then the other, so that the material in the box moves back and forth. What you are doing is making the gemstones, which are heavier than the rock and dirt, move into the bottom center of the screen box while at the same time washing dirt and sand out of the mixture.

3. After a minute or two, change the direction of movement to front and back.

4. Repeat these two movements (Steps 2 and 3) three or four times.

5. Take the box out of the water and let it drain, then place a board on top and carefully flip the box over onto the sorting table. It may be helpful to put a foam pad in the box, then put the board over it. This helps keep the stones in place when you flip the box. If you have done it right, the gemstones will be found in the center of the rocks dumped onto the board. Use tweezers to pick the rough gemstones out of the rocks, and place them in a small container.

## How to Pan for Gold

The technique for panning for gold is based on the fact that gold is much heavier than rock or soil. Gently washing and swirling the gold-bearing soil in a pan causes the gold to settle to the bottom of the pan. A gold pan has a flat

bottom and gently slanting sides. Some modern pans also have small ridges or rings around the inside of the pan on these slanting sides. As the soil is washed out of the pan, the gold will slide down the sides, or be caught on the ridges and stay in the pan. Here's how:

1. Begin by filling the pan with ore, about ⅔ to ¾ full.

2. Put your pan in the water, let it gently fill with water, then put the pan under the water surface. Leave the pan in the water, and mix the dirt around in the pan, cleaning and removing any large rocks.

3. Lift the pan out of the water, then gently shake the pan from side to side while swirling it at the same time. Do this for 20–30 seconds to get the gold settled to the bottom of the pan.

4. Still holding the pan out of the water, continue these motions while tilting the pan so that the dirt begins to wash out. Keep the angle of the pan so that the crease (where the bottom and sides meet) is the lowest point.

5. When there is only about a tablespoon of material left in the pan, put about ½ inch of water in the pan, and swirl the water over the remaining material. As the top material is moved off, you should see gold underneath.

6. No luck? Try again at a different spot.

## Notes on Gem Faceting, Cabbing, and Mounting Your Finds

Many of the fee dig sites offer services to cut and mount your finds. Quality and costs vary. Trade journals such as *Lapidary Journal* and *Rock & Gem* (available at most large bookstores or by subscription) list suppliers of these services, both in the United States and overseas. Again, quality and cost vary. Local rock and gem shops in your area may offer these services, or it may be possible to work with a local jeweler. Your local rock club may be able to provide these services or make recommendations.

After their first gem-hunting trip, the authors had some of their finds faceted and cabochoned. They then designed rings and had them made using these stones, as shown in the photos below.

After saying for years that they would like to learn to cabochon and facet (and in the process learn how better to collect "usable" material), the authors were fortunate enough to meet a local gemologist at a gem and mineral show who taught classes in the lapidary arts. They have since cut their own cabo-

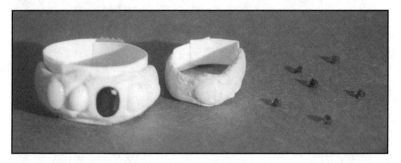

The authors sent their rough gems away for faceting. Using the faceted gems, they made crude mock-ups and sketches of the rings they wanted; then they sent the mock-ups, sketches, and gems to be made into rings.

The finished rings.

chons and faceted gemstones, getting a true appreciation for the art and knowledge of what to look for when field collecting.

Cutting your own finds can be a very rewarding hobby, and this hobby works two ways. You can cabochon, facet, and carve your special finds to your specifications, then make or have them made into jewelry. A cabochon is a highly polished convex-cut, but unfaceted gem. Facets are flat faces on geometric shapes which are cut into a rough gemstone in order to improve their appearance. The angles used for each facet affect the appearance of the gemstone. In learning the lapidary procedures, you also gain knowledge of what is a good find. You can look at a stone in the field and see if it is facetable, or if the pattern would make a spectacular cabochon.

Understanding what beautiful pieces you can make from your discoveries will amaze you, be they dug from a native mine, sluiced at a salted site, purchased from a local rock shop, or traded at a club meeting.

The first step to learning the lapidary arts is to do some research to see if it is for you. Search out books and articles on the topic and contact local club or rock shops to see if there are any classes near you.

A sample of the authors' lapidary work.

Taking sifted gravel to the jig at a sapphire mine in Montana. Pictured from left to right: Steve, Kathy, Annie Rygle, Debra Pedersen, Kristin Pedersen.

# ALABAMA

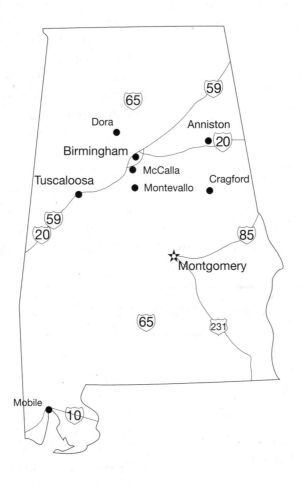

**State Gemstone:** Star Blue Quartz (1990)
**State Mineral:** Hematite (1967)
**State Stone/Rock:** Marble (1969)

## CRAGFORD / *Native · Easy to Moderate*

### Pan or Prospect for Gold

*The following gems or minerals can be found:*

- Gold

Alabama Gold Camp
1398 New Hope Road
Cragford, AL 36255
Phone: (256) 396-0389
E-mail: gold@alabamagoldcamp.com
www.alabamagoldcamp.com

**Open:** All year: winter, 7:00 A.M.–5:00 P.M.; summer, 7:00 A.M.–6:00 P.M.

**Info:** The camp is located in the heart of the Alabama gold fields, and has 10 miles of creek and 200 acres of gold-bearing land to explore.

**Rates:** With your own equipment: pan, sluice, or metal detector, $5.00/day; dredges, ranges from $15.00/day for a 2" dredge to $25.00/day for a 5" dredge; high-bankers range from $20.00/day. You must sign a disclaimer before entering the prospecting areas.

**Other services available:** Primitive camping, $5.00/night per person over 17; full hook-ups, $20.00/night or $125.00/week. General store sells all kinds of supplies. The gold camp plans to hold 4 common digs each year, call or check the website for more information.

**Directions:** Call or check the website for detailed directions.

## ALDRICH

### Museum 🏛

Aldrich Coal Mine Museum
137 County Road 203
Montevallo, AL 35115
Phone: (205) 665-2886

**Open:** Thursday–Saturday 10:00 A.M.–4:00 P.M., Sunday 1:00–4:00 P.M. or by appointment.

**Info:** Learn about the local coal mining history and history of the area. The museum is housed in the old Montevallo Coal Company company store, and includes a simulated coal mine.

**Rates:** Adults $5.00, children $3.00.

**Directions:** Take County Road 10 west in Montevallo to Aldrich, cross the railroad tracks, and turn left on County Road 203 and look for the museum.

## ANNISTON

## Museum

Anniston Museum of Natural History
P.O. Box 1587
800 Museum Drive
Anniston, AL 36207-1587
Phone: (256) 237-6766
Fax: (256) 237-6776
www.annistonmuseum.org

**Open:** September–May, Tuesday–Saturday 10:00 A.M.–5:00 P.M., Sunday 1:00–5:00 P.M.; June–August, Monday–Saturday 10:00 A.M.–5:00 P.M., Sunday 1:00–5:00 P.M. Closed major holidays.

**Info:** The Dynamic Earth exhibit details the processes and products of the formation of the earth as it traces the history of our ever-changing planet. Included in the exhibit are gemstones and a meteorite. The exhibit also features 25 mineral specimens from the collection of the Smithsonian Institute. The Underground World exhibit contains one of only a few person-made indoor caves in the Southeast.

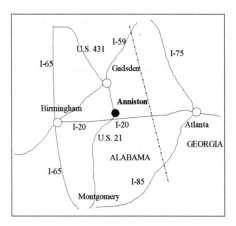

**Admission:** Adults $4.50, children 4–17 $3.50, discounts for seniors.

**Directions:** Anniston, in Calhoun County, is 60 miles northeast of Birmingham and 80 miles west of Atlanta, GA. Located in Lagarde Park, Anniston, Alabama, at the junction of Highways 431 and 21. From Interstate 20, exit 185, 7 miles north on Highway 21. Allow 1½ hours driving time from Birmingham or Atlanta.

## DORA

## Museum

Alabama Mining Museum
120 E. Street
Dora, AL 35062
Phone: (205) 648-2442

**Open:** All year, Tuesday–Friday, 8:30 A.M.–3:00 P.M.; Saturday, 10:00 A.M.–2:00 P.M. Open during the summer from 8:30 A.M.–1:00 P.M. Call ahead for changes.

**Info:** The museum has been designated by the Alabama Legislature as the official State Coal Mining Museum, and has a focus on coal mining between 1890 and 1940.

**Admission:** Free.

**Directions:** Call for directions.

## MCCALLA

## Museum

Tannehill Ironworks Historical State Park
12632 Confederate Parkway
McCalla, AL 35111

> Gold was discovered in the 1830s in the Piedmont Upland area of Alabama. When the California Gold Rush occurred the prospectors left and the Alabama gold fields were forgotten.

Phone: (205) 477-5711
Fax: (205) 477-6400
www.tannehill.org/museum.html

**Open:** Tuesday–Friday 8:30 A.M.–4:30 P.M., Saturday 9:30 A.M.–4:30 P.M., Sunday 12:30 P.M.–4:30 P.M.

**Info:** Some exhibits focus on geology, iron furnace fuels, and the Birmingham cast iron pipe industry.

**Admission:** Adults $2.00, children 6–11 and seniors 62+, $1.00, children 5 and under free.

## TUSCALOOSA

### Museum

Alabama Museum of Natural History
University of Alabama Main Campus
P.O. Box 870340
Tuscaloosa, AL 35487

Phone: (205) 348-7550
http://amnh.ua.edu

**Open:** Tuesday–Saturday, 10:00 A.M.–4:30 P.M.

**Info:** Museum has a variety of mineral specimens and the Hodges Meteorite—the only meteorite known to have struck a human.

**Admission:** Adults $2.00, seniors and students $1.00, children under 6 free.

**Directions:** Located at the corner of Capstone Drive and 6th Avenue on the university campus. From Highway 82, take the University Boulevard exit and drive west to Sixth Avenue. From I-59, take I-359 to the University Boulevard exit to 6th Avenue, then go north one block.

---

## SECTION 3: Special Events and Tourist Information

### TOURIST INFORMATION

### State Tourist Agency ☞

Alabama Bureau of Tourism and Travel
401 Adams Avenue, Suite 126
P.O. Box 4927
Montgomery, AL 36103-4927

Phone: (800) ALABAMA or
(800) 252-2262 or (334) 242-4169
www.touralabama.org

# ARKANSAS

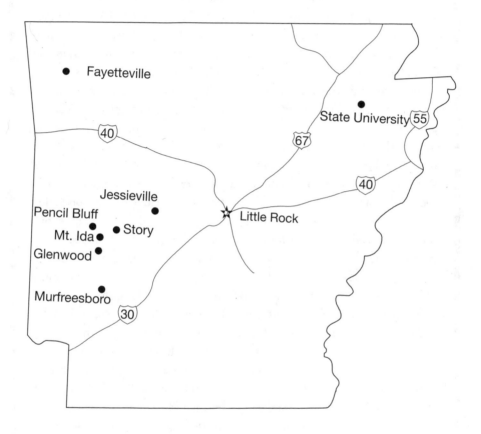

**State Gemstone:** Diamond
**State Mineral:** Quartz Crystal (1967)
**State Stone/Rock:** Bauxite (1967)

# Quartz Crystals

Although quartz makes up nearly 25% of the earth's surface, only three known places have enough high-quality crystal to warrant commercial mining. These are Brazil, Madagascar (a small island off the coast of Africa), and the Ouachita Mountain range of Arkansas. Quartz is the leading mineral mined in the Ouachita Mountains, which rank among the oldest mountain ranges in the U.S. Quartz is found in open crystal pockets formed in the sandstone, shale, and other rocks of the region. Crystals were once dug by Native Americans, who may have used and traded the crystals for religious and medicinal purposes.

Quartz crystals formed of silicon and oxygen are hexagonal structures that have the unique property of piezoelectricity, which means that they respond in a direct vibratory pattern when stimulated electrically or by pressure. Because of its piezoelectric qualities, quartz crystal can be used to amplify, transform, focus, and transfer energy. During World War II, quartz from Fisher Mountain was used by the U.S. Government for oscillators in radios.

There are several types of crystals, including single and double terminated, small to large clusters, and tabulars. Although a crystal can shatter, it is hard enough to cut glass (on the Mohs hardness scale a crystal is rated 7; a diamond 10). It is considered a semiprecious stone and is valuable to those who invest in and collect minerals.

Crystals are used in several fields, including industry, jewelry, and electronics. The piezoelectricity property makes quartz crystals indispensable to the international electronics industry for use in everything from radios and watches to Silicon Valley microcomputer chips, and thousands of products in between.

The use of quartz crystals in the metaphysical field to amplify, transform, focus, and transfer energy has led to a growing interest in them by groups and individuals who use the clear crystals for purposes generally described as healing. Quartz crystals are said to be dedicated healers that balance all elements needed to make a person whole. Quartz is claimed to be a purifier, which creates harmony and balance.

You can dig these quartz crystals in several mines located in the Mt. Ida area.

# SECTION 1: Fee Dig Sites and Guide Services

## JESSIEVILLE / *Native · Moderate*

### Dig Your Own Quartz Crystals *T*

*The following gems or minerals may be found:*

- Quartz crystals

Ron Coleman Mining, Inc.
211 Crystal Ridge Lane
Jessieville, AR 71949
Phone: (800) 291-4484
Fax: (501) 984-5443
E-mail: colemanquartz@hughs.net
www.colemanquartz.com

**Open:** Year round, 7 days/week. Winter, 8:00 A.M.–4:30 P.M.

**Info:** This is a working mine. Crystal digging is in 40 acres of mine tailings (material left over during mining operations) with fresh material routinely excavated, weather permitting. Keep all you find. Equipment is provided, including crystal washing stations.

**Admission:** Adults $20.00, seniors $15.00, students (7–16) $5.00, children under 7 free.

**Other services available:** Retail shop, wholesale showroom for dealers, gift shop, open 8:00 A.M.–5:00 P.M. daily.

**Campground:** Crystal Ridge RV Park (located on the grounds of Ron Coleman Mining, Inc.) has 26 quiet, shady sites on a paved circle. Services offered: modern restrooms, clean hot showers, washateria, dump station, water and electric hookups; $12.50 + tax/night. Call (888) 922-9601 for info.

**Directions:** Call for directions.

## JESSIEVILLE / *Native · Moderate*

### Dig Your Own Quartz Crystals *T*

*The following gems or minerals may be found:*

- Quartz crystals

Jim Coleman Crystal Mines and Rock Shop
5837 North Highway 7
Jessieville, AR 71949
Phone: (501) 984-5328
Fax: (501) 484-5457
E-mail: jimcoleman@
jimcolemancrystals.com
www.jimcolemancrystals.com

**Open:** Daily 8:00 A.M.–dusk; closed Christmas Day.

**Info:** This is a working mine. Simply dig in the piles brought up daily by the mine workers. Mine personnel will show you where to find crystals. Bring your own digging equipment and containers. Stay away from flagged areas and from machinery.

**Admission:** Adults $10.00, children under 10 free. You will get directions to the mine when you pay your fee.

**Other services available:** Primitive

## Digging Quartz

Bring a suitable digging tool such as a rock hammer, screwdriver, shovel, trowel, or anything to scratch around with. Wear old clothes, since the red clay stains anything it comes in contact with. On sunny days, a hat and sunscreen are suggested, along with drinking water. Hand tools are recommended to preserve the crystallography of the specimens.

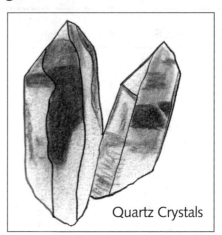

Quartz Crystals

## Cleaning Quartz

One process for cleaning quartz is to soak the crystals in a mild solution of oxalic acid. Use 1 pound of oxalic acid to 2½ gallons water. The cleaning procedure should be carried out only by an adult. Dissolve the oxalic acid in warm water in any container except aluminum. Soak crystals 4 to 5 days. Keep the solution properly labeled and in a secure place covered from the sun when in use or not. The solution can be reused up to three times. Be sure to follow the safety instructions when working with oxalic acid.

*(Information provided by Sonny Stanley's Mine)*

camping hookups are available for $4.00. Hookups with electricity are available for $10.00. Snacks and showers are available for a nominal fee.

**Directions:** The Rock Shop is located on Highway 7, approximately 15 miles north of Hot Springs.

**JESSIEVILLE /** *Native • Easy*

### Collect Quartz Crystals *T*

*The following gems or minerals may be found:*

- Quartz crystals

Ouachita National Forest
Crystal Mountain Quartz Collecting Site
Jessieville/Winona Ranger District
P.O. Box 189
Jessieville, AR 71949
Phone: (501) 984-5313
www.fs.fed.us/r8/ouachita/
natural-resources/minerals/crystal.shtml

**Open:** All year, weather permitting.

**Info:** This is a former small quartz crystal mine located near Lake Winona, in the Jessieville/Winona Ranger District, in central Arkansas. No digging is allowed at the site; collect only the crystals lying on the ground surface. A gravel forest service road goes past the site. *Note*: This is a primitive site. You must bring water and food with you, and take all trash out.

**Admission:** Free.

**Directions:** Call for directions.

## MOUNT IDA / *Native or Enriched* • *Easy to Moderate*

### Dig Your Own Crystals  *T*

*The following gems or minerals may be found:*

▪ **Quartz crystals, wavelite**

The Crystal Seen Trading Co.
Dennis & Julie Kincaid
2566 Highway 270 E
Mount Ida, AR 71957
Phone: (870) 867-4072
E-mail: ravenhawk@cebridge.net
http://crystalseen.tripod.com/

**Open:** Daily. Hours: 9:00 A.M.–6:00 P.M.; later in the summer.

**Info:** This site offers several options for digging. Option 1 is digging at the shop in more than 100 yards of mine tailings from a number of different crystal mines. A short orientation to crystal digging is given at the start. Some tools are available.

Option 2 is a 1-hour mini-workshop on crystal digging in the tailings at the shop. This includes a discussion of the area's geology, finding and identifying crystals, and some crystal uses. You receive a copy of a printed brochure on the area geology, a chart on crystal formations, and instruction and supplies for cleaning crystals.

Option 3 is a workshop on geology and fossils, geared toward children ages 7–15. This also includes a 45-minute dig for crystals and minerals in the mine tailings.

Option 4 is available from November through May. It consists of a 4-hour workshop on digging in the mines, and includes the basic geology, crystal identification, uses and cleaning, and printed material.

**Admission:** Option 1 is $8.00/hr. for one person, $15.00/hr. for two people, or $20.00/person for the day. Option 2 is $38.00/person. Option 3 is $15.00/person. Option 4 is $80.00 for the first person, $70.00 additional people up to a maximum of 10 people. Option 4 fees include mining fees. Children age 10 to 15 in a family are half price, and children under 9 in a family are free. Options 2, 3, and 4 are available by appointment only.

**Other services available:** Jewelry and gift shop; crystal workshops; jewelry design and repair.

**Directions:** On Highway 270 4 miles east of Mount Ida. Call for specific directions.

## MOUNT IDA / *Native ▪ Moderate*

### Dig Your Own Quartz Crystals *T*

*The following gems or minerals may be found:*

▪ Quartz crystals

Fiddler's Ridge Rock Shop &
Crystal Mines
Jim and Kathy Fecho
3752 Highway 270 E
Mount Ida, AR 71957
Phone: (870) 867-2127
E-mail: fecho@ipa.net
www.fiddlersridgecrystals.com/

**Open:** Year round, 9:00 A.M.–5:00 P.M., 7 days/week. Closed in January.
**Admission:** Adults $20.00/day, children 7–11 $10.00, children under 6 free.
**Other services available:** Gift shop. Get permit and instructions at gift shop. Supply your own tools, or small tools and gloves are sold at shop. Wear sturdy shoes. No sandals.
**Directions:** Located 7 miles east of Mt. Ida on U.S. 270 E.

## MOUNT IDA / *Native ▪ Easy*

### Collect Quartz Crystals *T*

*The following gems or minerals may be found:*

▪Quartz crystals

Ouachita National Forest
Crystal Vista Crystal Collecting Site
Womble Ranger District
P.O. Box 255, Highway 270 E
Mount Ida, AR 71957
Phone: (501) 867-2101
www.fs.fed.us/r8/ouachita/natural-resources/minerals

**Open:** All year, weather permitting.
**Info:** This is a former quartz crystal mine located at the end of a steep, mile-long hiking trail on top of Gardner Mountain in the Womble Ranger District in central Arkansas. No digging is allowed at the site; collect only the crystals lying on the ground surface
*Note*: This is a primitive site. You must bring water and food with you, and take all trash out.
**Admission:** Free.
**Directions:** South on Highway 27 3.8 miles from Mt. Ida, then turn left (east) on Owley Road (County Road 2237). The trailhead is 4.1 miles on Owley Road.

## MOUNT IDA / *Native ▪ Moderate*

### Dig Your Own Quartz Crystals—Open Pit Mining *T*

*The following gems or minerals may be found:*

▪ Quartz crystals

Sonny Stanley's Crystal Mine
P.O. Box 293
Mount Ida, AR 71957
Phone: (870) 867-3556 (day);
(870) 867-3719 (night)

**Open:** Year round, 6 days/week. 9:00 A.M.–5:00 P.M. Longer summer hours.

**Admission:** A key for access to the prospecting area may be obtained for a fee of $5.00/adult at the shop. Key can also be obtained from Judy's Crystal Shop, Rte. 270 E in Mount Ida. Group reservations requested, especially during tourist season.

**Directions:** Shop location is on the square in downtown Mount Ida.

## MOUNT IDA / *Native* ▪ *Moderate*

### Dig Your Own Quartz Crystals  𝑇

*The following gems or minerals may be found:*

▪ **Quartz crystals**

Starfire Crystal Mine
4503 Highway 270 E
Mount Ida, AR 71957
Phone: (870) 867-2431
Fax: (870) 867-0159
E-mail: crystals@ipa.net
www.starfirecrystals.com

**Open:** Year round; call for days and times. *Note:* This is now a recreational mine and is ideally suited for first time miners, children, and people who don't want to work too hard or get too dirty. Abundant material—nothing large, but bright and shiny!

**Admission:** $20.00/day, children under 12 $10.00, children under 5 free.

**Other services available:** Rock shop.

**Directions:** Located 12 miles east of Mt. Ida on U.S. 270.

## MOUNT IDA / *Native and Enriched* ▪ *Easy to Moderate*

### Dig Your Own Quartz Crystals or Pan for Gemstones  𝑇

*The following gems or minerals may be found:*

▪ **Quartz crystals; also rubies, emeralds, amethysts, and more**

Wegner Crystal Mines
82 Wegner Ranch Road
P.O. Box 205
Mount Ida, AR 71957
Phone/Fax: (870) 867-2309
www.wegnercrystalmines.com

**Open:** Seasonally, 8:00 A.M.–4:30 P.M., 7 days/week. Off-season, 5 days/week. Call for times/dates. Reservations required.

**Info:** Dig quartz crystals at one of three operating mines, or sluice for gemstones at a salted mine at a shaded lakeside location. Quartz crystals may be dug at one of three mines. Two of them, the world-famous Phantom Mine and the Crystal Mine, are located between 20 and 30 minutes' drive from the Visitors Center; transportation is provided to and from these mines.

**Admission:**

**Group Digs:**

▪ Phantom Mine $20.00/person, $200.00 minimum required per day.

▪ Crystal Forest Mine $20.00/person, $200.00 minimum required per day.

**Individual Activities:**

▪ Sluice area, easy for children and seniors, $13.50/two people, includes one free bucket of gem ore.

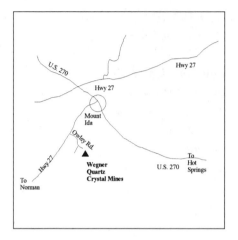

### Dig Your Own Diamonds and Other Gems $T$

*The following gems or minerals may be found:*

▪ Diamonds are the chief attraction; however, amethyst, agate, jasper, quartz, calcite, barite, peridot, and up to 40 other gems or minerals can also be found

Crater of Diamonds State Park
209 State Park Road
Murfreesboro, AR 71958
Phone: (870) 285-3113
Fax: (870) 285-4169
www.craterofdiamondsstatepark.com

**Open:** Year round except major winter holidays. Memorial Day–Labor Day, 8:00 A.M.–8:00 P.M.; rest of the year, 8:00 A.M.–5:00 P.M.

**Info:** Crater of Diamonds State Park offers a one-of-a-kind adventure—the chance to find and keep real diamonds. You can search a 37-acre field of lamproite soil, which is the eroded surface of

▪ Tailings area, dig all day, $9.50/adult, $6.00 seniors and children under 11.

**Other services available:** Rock shop with a variety of quartz quality and of other minerals, famous 10,000 square foot wholesale barn, tour showing the process of preparing quartz for shipment worldwide.

**Directions:** Located 6 miles south of Mt. Ida, off Owley Road, which comes off Highway 27. Take Route 27 south from Mount Ida. Travel approximately 3½ miles, then turn left on Owley Road (first paved road outside Mt. Ida city limits). Follow Owley Road to the warehouse.

## Diamond-Hunting Tips

Look for small, well-rounded crystals. A diamond weighing several carats may be no larger than a marble. Look for clean crystals, since diamonds have an oily, slick outer surface that dirt and mud don't stick to. The diamonds come in several colors. The most common found at the crater are clear, white, yellow, and brown.

an ancient gem-bearing volcanic pipe (lava tube). Prospectors enter the field through a visitors center that includes exhibits and an audiovisual program explaining the area's geology and providing tips on recognizing diamonds in the rough.

Since diamonds were first discovered there in 1906, more than 70,000 have been found. Since the crater became a state park in 1972, over 25,000 diamonds have been found by visitors, and on the average, more than 600 diamonds are found each year. Among the diamonds that have been found are the Uncle Sam (40.23 carats), the Star of Murfreesboro (34.2 carats), the Star of Arkansas (15.33 carats), and the Amarillo Starlight (16.37 carats).

The park consists of 911 pine-covered acres along the banks of the Little Missouri River. The first diamond was found in 1906; the property has changed hands several times over the years. Previous owners made several attempts to mine diamonds commercially. These attempts are mostly shrouded in mystery, and all ultimately failed; lawsuits, fires, or lack of capital are some of the reasons for failure. In 1972, the State of Arkansas bought the property and established Crater of Diamonds State Park.

Lamproite, a relatively rare rock of magmatic origin, is a source rock containing commercially viable concentrations of diamonds. The lamproite soil, very different from red Arkansas clay, is dark green to black, gummy when wet, and powdery

when dry. Wyoming and Colorado have several diamond deposits similar to those at Crater of Diamonds State Park and also similar to those mined in South Africa.

This is the only diamond field open to the public in North America. The field is plowed approximately monthly. The park staff at the park's Diamond Discovery Center will aid you in the identification of any stone you find.

Diamond mining tools, such as army shovels, trowels, gardening tools, and screen boxes, can be rented or purchased at the park. Two mineral-washing pavilions contain huge dumpsters filled with water to aid in screening for diamonds.

Any organized group may dig at one half the regular fee. Advance notice must be given to obtain the reduced rate.

The State Park offers a variety of orientation programs during the summer months: programs cover nature, geology, diamond-"hunting" methods, and history. **Admission:** Adults $6.50, children (6–12) $3.50, children under 6 free.

**Other services available:** Restaurant (seasonal), gift shop, restrooms, river trail, interpretive exhibits, historical structures, fishing.

A 1.2-mile-long river trail winds its way through the woods to the scenic Little Missouri River. This provides a relaxing 1-hour hike over level terrain.

**Campground:** Fifty-seven Standard B campsites in a secluded woodsview setting. Water and electric hookups are available on all campsites.

**Other services available:** Shady sites,

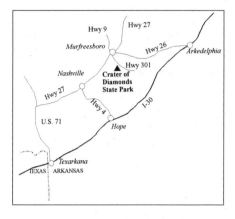

**Info:** Six acres of open pit are available for digging. There are also special tours available. Keep all you find; no weight limits.
**Admission:** Adults, $20.00/day, children under 9 free with paying adult. Special area digs available on certain days for $50.00 and up. Call ahead for dates.
**Directions:** Take U.S. 270 to Mt. Ida. Turn onto Route 27 S next to the Exxon gas station. Travel approximately 3½ miles, then turn left on Owley Road. Go 3 miles down Owley Road. Look for sign on right. Go 1 mile up mine road to mine.

modern restrooms, clean hot showers, laundry facilities, dump station, tent sites, nearby fishing.
**Directions:** The State Park is located 2 miles southeast from Murfreesboro on Arkansas Route 301.

## PENCIL BLUFF / *Native · Moderate*

### Dig Your Own Quartz Crystals

*The following gems or minerals may be found:*

- Quartz crystals

Arrowhead Crystal Mine
Matthew Price
P.O. Box 35
Pencil Bluff, AR 71965
Phone: (870) 326-4443
Cell: (501) 538-9627
E-mail: arrowheadcrystalmine@alltel.net
www.arrowheadcrystals.com

**Open:** Call ahead; appointment required. 9:30 A.M.–4:00 P.M., 7 days/week, weather permitting.

## STORY / *Native · Easy to Moderate*

### Dig Your Own Crystals

*The following gems or minerals may be found:*

- Quartz crystals

Gee & Dee Crystal
G. W. & Dolores Johnson
4764 Highway 27 N
Story, AR 71970
Phone: (870) 867-4561

**Open:** Daily. Hours: Summer Monday–Friday, 8:00 A.M.–5:00 P.M.; Saturday–

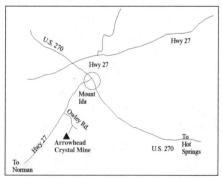

Sunday, 8:00 A.M.–4:00 P.M. Winter: Daily 8:00 A.M.–4:00 P.M.

**Info:** Dig in dirt excavated from the mine, or occasionally in the mine. This is an "old-fashioned mom & pop" mine. G. W. has more than 45 years experience digging crystals. Some tools are available, and there is a self-contained flush toilet at the mine. Bring food and beverages, appropriate clothing, and sunscreen.

**Admission:** Adults $20.00/day, seniors 59 and up $15.00/day, children 10–15 $10.00/day; 9 and under free.

**Other services:** Crystals can be purchased at the shop.

**Directions:** Take Highway 27 N from Mount Ida and drive 11½ miles until you see a green house with crystals and signs for the mine in the front yard.

STORY / *Native • Moderate*

## Dig Your Own Quartz Crystals

*The following gems or minerals may be found:*

- Quartz crystals

Sweet Surrender Crystal Mine
2608 Highway 27 N.
Story, AR 71970

Phone: (870) 867-0104
Cell: (870) 867-7014; (870) 867-7075
www.arcrystalmine.com
www.sweetsurrendercrystals.com

**Open:** 9:00 A.M.–4:00 P.M. weather permitting. Call at least 1 day ahead.

**Info:** This is a working mine. Dig in the walls and veins, or simply pick up crystals from the tailings (mine tailings are material left over during mining operations). Mine personnel will show you where to find crystals. This is a primitive area, with no facilities, services, or phones. Bring your own digging equipment and containers. Suggested tools for digging: an old screwdriver, hand garden tools, sometimes a rock hammer, old digging bar. Stay away from flagged areas and from machinery.

**Admission:** Adults $20.00, children 10–14 $10.00. Children under 10 free with paying adult.

**Directions:** From Mount Ida, take Highway 27 north for approximately 10½ miles until you reach Horseshoe Bend Road, about ½ mile past Washita, AR. Turn right onto Horseshoe Bend Road and travel for about ½ mile, and turn right just before the first mail box (Floyd Irons' mail box). Follow this road to the mine at the top of the hill.

In Benton, AR, there is a building constructed entirely from bauxite, which is aluminum ore. It was originally the medical office of Dr. Dewell Gann, built by his patients who were unable to pay him, and who built him an office, instead. It is the only known building in the world built from bauxite. It now houses the Gann Museum.

## FAYETTEVILLE

## Museum

The University Museum
The Museum Building
The University of Arkansas
Fayetteville, AR 72701

**Open:** All year, Monday–Saturday 9:00 A.M.–4:30 P.M.

**Info:** Exhibits on rocks and minerals include geology of the Fayetteville area, Arkansas' mineral wealth, and the quartz of Arkansas.

**Admission:** Adults $3.00, children $2.00.

**Directions:** On Garland Avenue (Highway 112) at the intersection with Maple Avenue.

## LITTLE ROCK

## Museum

Geology Learning Center
Arkansas Geological Commission
3815 W. Roosevelt Road
Little Rock, AR 72204
Phone: (501) 296-1877
Fax: (501) 663-7360

**Open:** All year between 8:00 A.M. and 4:30 P.M., by appointment only. Call one of the geologists at the Commission to make an appointment.

**Info:** The learning center is intended to give students of all ages who are interested in earth sciences direct exposure to rocks, minerals, fossils and fuels. Exhibits include the Arkansas Geological Commission, Arkansas' mineral wealth, fossil fuels in Arkansas, Arkansas gems and minerals, and Arkansas fossils.

**Admission:** Free.

**Directions:** Located at 1911 Thayer Street, just south of the intersection of West Asher and West Wright Avenues.

## MOUNT IDA

## Museum

Heritage House Museum of
Montgomery County, Alabama
P.O. Box 1362
819 Luzerne Street
Mount Ida, AR 71957-1362
Phone: (870) 867-4422
E-mail: museum@hhmmc.org
www.hhmmc.org

**Open:** Monday, Tuesday, Wednesday, Friday 9:00 A.M.–4:00 P.M., Saturday–Sunday, 1:00 P.M.–4:00 P.M., closed Tuesdays.

**Info:** The museum has a display on quartz crystals.

**Admission:** Call for rates.

**Other services available:** Gift shop.

**Directions:** Located in Mount Ida at the intersection of Highway 27 and Luzerne Street.

## STATE UNIVERSITY

## Museum

ASU Museum
Arkansas State University
Museum/Library Building
P.O. Box 490
State University, AR 72467
Phone: (870) 972-2074
http://museum.astate.edu

**Open:** All year, closed campus holidays. Tuesday–Friday 9:00 A.M.–4:00 P.M., Saturday and Sunday 1:00 P.M.–5:00 P.M.

**Info:** Exhibits include a chart showing relative lengths of the periods of the earth's formation, several fossils, and a variety of minerals, including a large number found in Arkansas. Arkansas minerals displayed include fluorite, bauxite, calcite clusters, halite, granite, gypsum, quartz and drusy quartz, smithsonite, golden dolomite and dolomite crystals, selenite, nepheline syenite and septarian concretions.

**Admission:** Free, donations appreciated.

**Directions:** ASU is on the eastern outskirts of Jonesboro. The museum occupies the west wing of the Dean B. Ellis Library building.

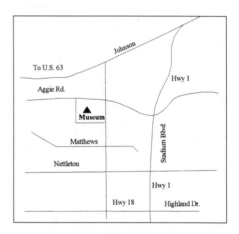

---

## SECTION 3: Special Events and Tourist Information

### ANNUAL EVENT

### Quartz Crystal Festival and World Championship Dig, Mount Ida  ☛

In Mount Ida (Quartz Crystal Capital of the World), dig in actual working quartz crystal mines in the heart of the Ouachita Mountains. The contest is held as part of the Annual Quartz, Quiltz, and Craftz

Festival. The festival includes a gem and mineral show and is held on the second Friday, Saturday, and Sunday in October.

The dig begins on Thursday, one day before the Festival. Diggers have three days to dig. The hours are 9:00 A.M. to 3:00 P.M. Prize money is awarded to the top five winners in each division; crystal trophies go to the first- and second-place winners in each division.

**Pre-registration fee:** $75.00/person.

Prizes, costs, and deadlines change from year-to-year, so call for details. Keep all you dig; use hand tools only (provide your own). Ages 10–16 permitted to dig with adult supervision. Primitive toilets are available at dig sites. At the festival, crystals, gems, minerals, jewelry, equipment, supplies, books, dealers, and exhibits are available. For further details and a registration form, write to:

Mt. Ida Chamber of Commerce
P.O. Box 6
Mt. Ida, AR 71957
Phone: (870) 867-2723
E-mail: director@mountidachamber.com
www.mtidachamber.com

The Chamber of Commerce can also provide information on the Ouachita National Forest, the South's oldest and largest national forest, covering 1.6 million acres. Features include Lake Ouachita, which offers fishing, scuba diving, water skiing, sailing, horseback riding, camping, and hiking; 480 miles of hiking trails run throughout the National Forest.

## TOURIST INFORMATION

### State Tourist Agency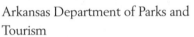

Arkansas Department of Parks and Tourism
One Capital Mall
Little Rock, AR 72201
Phone: (501) 682-7777; (800) NATURAL
http://www.arkansas.com

Mt. Ida Area Chamber of Commerce
P.O. Box 6
Mt. Ida, AR 71957
Phone: (870) 867-2723
E-mail: director@mountidachamber.com
www.mtidachamber.com
Hours: 9:00 A.M.–3:30 P.M.

Hot Springs Convention and Visitors Bureau
134 Convention Boulevard
Hot Springs National Park, AR 71902
Phone: (800) 543-2284
Fax: (501) 321-2135
E-mail: hscvb@hotsprings.org
www.hotsprings.org

# FLORIDA

**State Gemstone:** Moonstone
**State Stone/Rock:** Agatized coral

**FT. DRUM /** *Native • Easy to Moderate*

## Dig Your Own Calcite Crystals 𝖳

*The following gems or minerals may be found:*

•Calcite crystals on fossil shells, micropyrite, iridescent marcosite

Fort Drum Crystal Mine
Eddie Ruck
Mailing address:
28320 NE 55th Avenue
Okeechobee, FL 34972
Mine address:
6645 NE 304th Street
Okeechobee, FL 34972
Phone: (863) 634-4579
E-mail: fortdrumcrystalmine@yahoo.com

**Open:** Daily 8:00 A.M.–dark, by reservation only.

**Info:** This is an operating shell pit, which allows collecting. The quarry is excavating fossil clams from a sand layer and from a limestone layer; the fossil shells are encrusted with calcite crystals.

**Admission:** $30.00 per person, which allows collection of a 5-gallon pail of specimens. Bring your own tools and pail.

**Other services available:** Mr. Ruck has written a book describing the geology and paleontology of the Ft. Drum Crystal Mine. Camping is available, call for rates.

**Directions:** Take exit 193 on Florida Turnpike and look for signs. Call or e-mail for detailed directions.

# SECTION 2: Museums and Mine Tours

## DELAND

## Museum 🏛

Gillespie Museum
Stetson University
Physical address:
234 E Michigan Avenue
DeLand, FL 32723
Mailing address:
Stetson University, Unit 8403
421 N Woodland Boulevard
Deland, FL 32723
Phone: (386) 822-7330
http://gillespiemuseum.stetson.edu

**Open:** September–May, Tuesday–Friday, 10:00 A.M.–4:00 P.M.; Family Days on some Saturdays, July–August, by appointment.

**Info:** The mineral cases house an ever changing variety of minerals, including rare and historic minerals. The gemstone exhibit features both rough and faceted gemstones. Faceting equipment is on display, and demonstrations are frequently provided during special events and Family Days. There is also a replica mine, a cave, and a display that provides information on the 3 types of rocks, and the rocks and minerals used in our day-to-day lives.

**Admission:** Adults $2.00, students and

seniors $1.00. Group rates are available.
**Directions:** Call for directions.

## MULBERRY

## Museum

Mulberry Phosphate Museum
P.O. Box 707
Mulberry, FL 33860
Phone: (863) 425-2823
www.mulberrychamber.org/
attractions.htm

**Open:** All year, Tuesday–Saturday 10:00
A.M.–4:30 P.M. Special tours can be
arranged by calling.
**Info:** The museum houses educational
exhibits on the phosphate industry.
**Admission:** Donation requested.
**Directions:** One block south of State
Highway 60 on State Highway 37 in
downtown Mulberry.
*Note:* The phosphate deposits are rich in
fossils.

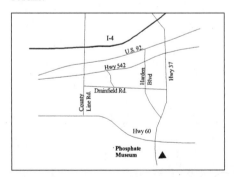

## TAMPA

## Museum

Ed and Bernadette Marcin Museum,
Department of Geology
University of South Florida
East Fowler Avenue, Room 534
Tampa, FL 33620
Phone: (813) 974-2236

**Open:** All year by appointment only,
Monday–Friday except holidays. Special
arrangements can be made for groups.
**Info:** Located in Room 534 of the Science
Center at the University of South Florida's
Tampa Campus. This is a small museum,
which includes minerals and gemstones
created through the donations of Dr. and
Mrs. Pious. They accumulated their collection over a period of about 20 years, large-
ly while traveling through the western U.S.
and Florida. The museum collection is aug-
mented and maintained through gifts to
the departmental collection and by collectors throughout Florida. Included in the
museum collections are an agatized wood
collection and a mineral collection.
**Admission:** Free.
**Directions:** The museum is located in
the Science Center at the University of
South Florida–Tampa campus.

## SECTION 3: Special Events and Tourist Information

**State Tourist Agency** 👉
http://visitflorida.com

# GEORGIA

**State Gemstone:** Amethyst
**State Mineral:** Staurolite
**State Stone/Rock:** Quartz

**CLEVELAND /** *Native and Enriched*
- *Easy to Moderate*

## Dig Your Own Minerals *T*

*The following gems or minerals
may be found:*

- Gold, sapphires, rubies, emeralds,
amethyst, topaz

Gold'n Gem Grubbin
75 Gold Nugget Lane
Cleveland, GA 30528
Phone: (706) 865-5454
E-mail: info@goldngrubbin.com
www.goldngem.com

**Open:** Daily all year, 9:00 A.M.–5:00 P.M.
**Info:** North Georgia's only commercially operating gold mine. Pan buckets of
concentrate taken from the strip mine.
Pan for gold in the mine's sluice buckets.
The gold ore has been concentrated to
increase the likelihood of finding gold.
Free panning lessons for first-timers. Buckets of gem ore can be purchased for sluicing. You can also dig your own gold and
gems from the stream.
**Admission:** Free. Gold buckets: $10.00
for 1-gallon standard bucket; 2-gallon
buckets available. Gem buckets: $8.00 for
standard 1-gallon bucket; $30.00 for 2-gal-
lon super bucket (includes $15.00 credit
for making jewelry); $60.00 for 5-gallon
pay dirt bucket; $100.00 for 5-gallon
Mother Lode bucket. Mining in the creek:
adults and children (7–12) half day
$15.00, full day $25.00.

**Other services available:** Gift shop,
gem cutting, mining equipment sales,
fishing on Golden Pond (small fee).
**Camping:** Campground with primitive
sites for tents, and full hook ups for
RVs. Tent sites are $18.00 and RV sites
are $28.00. Weekly rates available.
**Directions:** From Cleveland, take SR
400 to SR 52/115. Turn right onto SR
52/115 for 11½ miles, then turn left on
Town Creek Road (look for the sign),
and drive for 2 miles to the mine.

**DAHLONEGA /** *Native • Easy*

## Pan for Gold *T*

*The following gems or minerals
may be found:*
- Gold

Consolidated Gold Mine
185 Consolidated Gold Mine Road
Dahlonega, GA 30533
Phone: (706) 864-8473
E-mail: info@consolidatedgoldmine.com
www.consolidatedgoldmine.com

**Open:** All year, 7 days/week. Winter,
10:00 A.M.–4:00 P.M. Summer, 10:00 A.M.–
5:00 P.M.
**Info:** For further information on the Consolidated Gold Mine tour, see Section 2.
**Admission:** Adults $11.00, children
(4–14) $7.00. Varying rates on buckets.
Panning is included in the mine tour.
**Other services available:** Mine tour, shops.

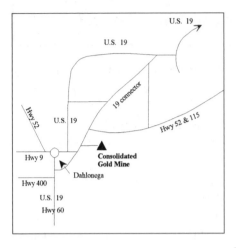 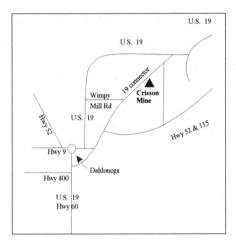

**Directions:** ¾ mile east of Dahlonega on Highway 52, where Highways 52, 60, 19, and 9 merge.

## DAHLONEGA / *Native and Enriched • Easy*

# Pan for Gold or Gemstones 𝑇

*The following gems or minerals may be found:*

• **Gold, rubies, emeralds, garnets, sapphires, and many more**

Crisson Gold Mine
2736 Morrison Moore Parkway East
Dahlonega, GA 30533
Phone: (706) 864-6363
www.crissongoldmine.com

**Open:** All year; 10:00 A.M.–6:00 P.M. April–October, 10:00 A.M.–5:00 P.M. November–March, 7 days/week.

**Info:** The mine offers indoor panning in winter; ore is also sold "to go."

**Rates:** One pan of gold ore $5.50, 5-gallon bucket of gold ore $10.50, 2-gallon bucket of gem dirt $5.50, 5-gallon bucket of gem dirt $10.50.

**Other services available:** Tour and demonstration of a 124-year-old stamp mill, picnic area, gift shop, restrooms. Trail ride and farm equipment display available during summer only.

**Directions:** On U.S. 19 Connector, 2½ miles from downtown Dahlonega.

## GAINESVILLE / *Native • Easy to Moderate*

# Pan for Gold 𝑇

*The following gems or minerals may be found:*
• Gold

Supervisor's Office:
Chattahoochee-Oconee National Forest
1755 Cleveland Highway
Gainseville, GA 30501
Phone: (770) 297-3000
Fax: (770) 297-3011
http://www.fs.fed.us/conf/rec/gold_panning.htm

## Dahlonega: Site of America's First Gold Rush

DAH-LON-E-GA is the word in the Cherokee language for the "precious yellow metal" found in these hills. In 1828, the cry "We've found gold" was heard far and near. With the discovery of gold in the foothills of the Blue Ridge Mountains, Dahlonega emerged in 1833 as a full-blown "hustle and bustle" town. Gold was mined into the early 20th century. Now, several attractions highlight the town's historic activities, including a gold museum, gold panning, and gold mine tours. Attend Gold Rush Days, or attend the gold panning championships.

Information on the area may be obtained by contacting the Dahlonega-Lumpkin County Chamber of Commerce, Dahlonega, GA 30533, Phone: (706) 864-3711.

**Open:** Monday–Friday, 8:00 A.M.–4:30 P.M. Recreational gold panning and rockhounding are both allowed within the Chattahoochee-Oconee National Forest. In-stream sluicing and dredging are not allowed. Significant surface excavation is not allowed, and no mechanical equipment can be used. In addition, there may be claims which affect where you can pan or collect. Check with the Forest Ranger's office for information.

**LA GRANGE /** *Native • Moderate to Difficult*

### Hunt for Your Own Crystals T

*The following gems or minerals may be found:*

- **Star rose quartz, aquamarine, beryl (rare), black tourmaline**

Hogg Mine
Dixie Euhedrals
Rodney Moore
1320 Chappell Mill Road
Jackson, GA 30233
Phone: (404) 975-8005 or (404) 520-5059
Fax: (770) 467-0472
E-mail: sio2ga@bellsouth.net
www.dixieeuhedrals.com
www.dixieeuhedrals.net

**Open:** All year, weather permitting; by prior reservation via e-mail only. The mine will be open the second Saturday of each month.

**Info:** This is a collecting site in Wilkes County, Georgia that offers the opportunity to search for star rose quartz crystals, as well as a variety of other gems and minerals. There is no guarantee of finding crystals. You must sign a release form and pay before going to the site.

**Rates:** Adults $35.00/day, children under 16 free. This allows collection of one 5-gallon bucket of specimens per paid admission.

**Directions:** E-mail or call for directions.

## LA GRANGE / *Native • Moderate to Difficult*

## Hunt for Your Own Crystals *T*
*The following gems or minerals may be found:*

▪Clear quartz crystals

La Grange Clear Quartz Crystals
Dixie Euhedrals
Rodney Moore
1320 Chappell Mill Road
Jackson, GA 30233
Phone: (404) 975-8005 or
(404) 520-5059
Fax: (770) 467-0472
E-mail: sio2ga@bellsouth.net
www.dixieeuhedrals.com
www.dixieeuhedrals.net

**Open:** All year, weather permitting, by prior reservation via e-mail only. The mine will be open the second Saturday of each month.

**Info:** This is a collecting site in Wilkes County, Georgia that offers the opportunity to search for clear quartz crystals. The crystals can be similar to those found in the mines around Hot Springs, AR. There is no guarantee of finding crystals. You must sign a release form and pay before going to the site.

**Rates:** Adults $15.00/day, children

under 18 $5.00/day. This allows collection of one 5-gallon bucket of specimens.

**Directions:** E-mail or call for directions.

## LINCOLNTON / *Native • Difficult*

## Dig Your Own Minerals *T*
*The following gems or minerals may be found:*

▪ Rutile, lazulite, pyrophyllite, kyanite, hematite, pyrite, ilmenite, muscovite, fuchsite, barite, sulfur, blue quartz, quartz crystals, and microcrystals such as woodhouseite, variscite, strengite, phosphosiderite, cacoxenite, crandallite

Graves Mountain
Junior Norman, caretaker
1717 Lewis Crook Road
Lincolnton, GA 30817
Phone: (706) 359-3862 (business);
(706) 359-2381 (home)

**Open:** The collecting area will be open to the public for a 3-day period twice each year. Call or check on the website for dates. 2008 dates are April 25–27 and October 3–5; hours will be 8:00 A.M.– 6:00 P.M.

**Info:** Dig in the soil or rocks, or simply pick up crystals from the tailings. Bring your own digging equipment and containers. Stay away from the highwalls and only collect in designated areas. Sign a liability release and leave a donation at the Hospitality Tent. Portable toilets will be provided. In addition, food and beverages will be available for purchase, and tables can be set up for a "Rock Swap."

**Admission:** Donations accepted for expenses in opening the mountain to the public and providing portable toilets.

**Other information:** The mountain will be open to collecting at other times only to colleges, universities, and gem and mineral societies. Contact the caretaker, Junior Norman for reservations. See the Georgia Mineral Society web page (http://www.gamineral.org/commercial-graves mountain.htm) for more information.

**Directions:** From I-285 in Atlanta, take I-20 east to the exit for Washington, which is Georgia Route 78 (Route 10 and Route 17). Turn left and travel north to Washington, and take Georgia Route 378 for 11 miles to the Graves Mountain area. If coming from Washington, turn left at the first road after the Lincoln County sign (Norman Road). Junior Norman's garage is about ½ mile up the road.

---

## SECTION 2: Museums and Mine Tours

---

### ATLANTA

## Museum

Fernbank Museum of Natural History
767 Clifton Road
Atlanta, GA 30307
Phone: (404) 929-6300
www.fernbank.edu/museum

**Open:** 10:00 A.M.–5:00 P.M. Monday–Saturday, 1:00 P.M.–5:00 P.M. Sunday. Closed Thanksgiving and Christmas.

**Info:** The Joachim Gem Collection on view within the Cultures of the World exhibition contains more than 400 cut and polished gemstones.

**Admission:** Adults $15.00, students and seniors (62+) $14.00, children (3–12) $13.00, children 2 and under free.

**Other services available:** Museum store.

**Directions:** Call for directions.

### ATLANTA

## Museum

Fernbank Science Center
156 Heaton Road NE
Atlanta, GA 30307
Phone: (678) 874-7102
Fax: (678) 874-7110
http://fsc.fernbank.edu/

**Open:** Days and hours vary throughout the year. Check website or call for hours.

**Info:** The Science Center has a meteorite collection and an outdoor rock and mineral walk.

**Admission:** Free.

**Directions:** Call or check website for directions.

## CARTERSVILLE

## Museum

Tellus Museum (formerly Weinman Mineral Museum)
P.O. Box 3663
Cartersville, GA 30120
Phone: (770) 386-0576
E-mail: info@tellusmuseum.org
www.tellusmuseum.org

**Open:** Call or check website for reopening date and hours of operations.

**Info:** The museum is currently under construction, with an anticipated opening date in 2008. The Weinman Mineral Gallery will showcase one of the largest and most comprehensive collections in the southeast.

**Admission:** Call for admission rates.

**Directions:** Take I-75 to Exit 293 (Highway 411), and turn left at the end of the exit ramp. Turn left immediately after the Holiday Inn, and the museum will be on your left.

## DAHLONEGA

## Mine Tour

Consolidated Gold Mine
185 Consolidated Gold Mine Road
Dahlonega, GA 30533
Phone: (706) 864-8473
www.consolidatedgoldmine.com

**Open:** All year, 7 days/week. Winter, 10:00 A.M.–4:00 P.M. Summer, 10:00 A.M.–5:00 P.M.

**Info:** Tour an actual underground gold mine as it appeared at the turn of the century. See displays of the actual equipment used, and discuss the excavating and mining techniques used. Learn the geology of the quartz and pyrite formations with which the early miners worked. Walk through the tunnel network complete with the original track system. The tour lasts 40 to 45 minutes. The mine is 60°F all year, so dress appropriately.

**Admission:** Adults $11.00, children (4–14) $7.00.

**Other services available:** Souvenir shop (offers a variety of rocks and minerals), restrooms.

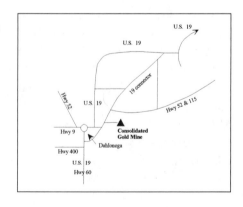

**Directions:** ¾ mile east of Dahlonega on Highway 52, where Highways 52, 60, 19, and 9 merge.

## DAHLONEGA

### Museum, State Historic Site

Dahlonega Courthouse Gold Museum
State Historic Site
1 Public Square
Dahlonega, GA 30533
Phone: (706) 864-2257
www.gastateparks.org/info/dahlonega

**Open:** Monday–Saturday, 9:00 A.M.–5:00 P.M. Sunday, 10:00 A.M.–5:00 P.M. Closed Thanksgiving, Christmas, and New Year's Day.

**Info:** The museum tells the story of the nation's first major gold rush. In 1828, 20 years before the discovery of gold in California, thousands of gold seekers flocked to the area inhabited by the Cherokee Nation in north Georgia. They were drawn by the first major gold rush in the U.S. For more than 20 years prospectors continued to arrive, and the gold towns of Auroria and Dahlonega

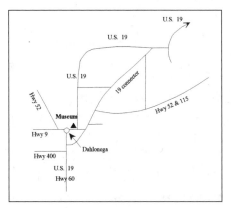

prospered. Between 1838 and 1861, more than $6 million in gold was coined by the U.S. Branch Mint in Dahlonega.

**Admission:** Adults $4.00, seniors $3.50, children (6–18) $2.50. Group discounts.

**Directions:** Inside the city limits of Dahlonega, on the Public Square.

## ELBERTON

### Mine Tour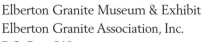

Elberton Granite Museum & Exhibit
Elberton Granite Association, Inc.
P.O. Box 640
Elberton, GA 30635
Phone: (706) 283-2551
Fax: (706) 283-6380

**Open:** Daily January 15–November 15, 2:00 P.M.–5:00 P.M. Closed Sunday. Limited schedule November 15–January 15; call for hours.

**Info:** The museum contains historical exhibits and artifacts, educational displays, and materials about the granite industry. Exhibit space on three levels graphically displays the unique granite products of the past, antique granite-working tools, and yesteryear's methods of quarrying, sawing, polishing, cutting, and sandblasting granite cemetery memorials. Exhibits also show how current quarrying methods and fabricating processes are carried out in Elberton's 35 different quarries and more than 100 manufacturing plants.

**Admission:** Free. Visitors may obtain a small specimen of granite for their collections.

**Directions:** Elberton is located in

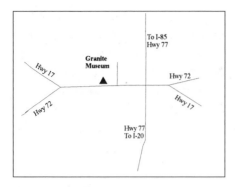

northeast Georgia, midway between I-85 and I-20. From the north, take State Highway 17 south from the Lavonia Exit on I-85 until you come to the granite museum. From the south, take State Highway 77 from the Union Point exit on I-20, to Elberton, then turn left on Highway 17 to the museum, or from the Washington exit on I-20, take State Highway 17/U.S. 78 north and follow State Highway 17 to Elberton, and the museum.

## MACON

## Museum 🏛

Museum of Arts and Sciences
4182 Forsyth Road
Macon, GA 31210

Phone: (478) 477-3232
Fax: (478) 477-3251
E-mail: info@masmacon.com
www.masmacon.com

**Open:** 10:00 A.M.–5:00 P.M. Monday–Saturday; 1:00 P.M.–5:00 P.M. Sunday; 10:00 A.M.–8:00 P.M. last Friday of each month.

**Info:** The museum has a collection of gems and minerals.

**Admission:** Adults $8.00, seniors $6.00, students $5.00, children under 12 $4.00.

**Directions:** Take exit 164 from Interstate 75, northbound take exit 172 from I-75 southbound or exit 9 from I-475. Turn toward the intersection of Vinerill Avenue and look for the fourth road.

## STATESBORO

## Museum 🏛

Georgia Southern Museum
Landrum Box 8061
Rosenwald Building
Statesboro, GA 30460
Phone: (912) 681-5444; (912) 681-0147
http:ceps.georgiasouthern.edu/museum

---

## Elberton Granite

Elberton is hailed as the Granite Capital of the World. While most granite quarries are less than 150 feet deep, geologists estimate the Elberton deposit to be 2 to 3 miles in depth. The physical properties and characteristics are perfect for the over 200,000 granite monuments, markers, and mausoleums made in Elberton each year.

**Open:** Year round; closed on major holidays. 9:00 A.M.–5:00 P.M. Monday–Friday, 2:00–5:00 P.M. Saturday–Sunday.

**Info:** The museum's Hall of Natural History contains a collection of rocks and minerals from Georgia's highland, Piedmont, and coastal regions.

**Admission:** Free.

**Directions:** On the campus of Georgia Southern University on Southern Drive.

## TALLAPOOSA

## Museum

West Georgia Museum of Tallapoosa
185 Mann Street

P.O. Box 725
Tallapoosa, GA 30176
Phone: (770) 574-3125
http://www.tallapoosaga.gov/museum/

**Open:** 9:00 A.M.–4:00 P.M. Tuesday–Friday, 9:00 A.M.–5:00 P.M. Saturday.

**Info:** The museum has a small collection of minerals from Haralson County.

**Admission:** Adults $2.00, children 4–12 $1.00, under 4 free.

**Directions:** From Interstate 20, take exit 5 (Highway 100), and go north on Highway 100 to Tallapoosa. In Tallapoosa, stay on Highway 100 to Mann Street; the museum is on the left.

---

# SECTION 3: Special Events and Tourist Information

## ANNUAL EVENTS

### Pickens County Marble Festival, Jasper, GA

First full weekend of October

*For more information:*
Pickens County Chamber of Commerce
500 Stegall Drive
Jasper, GA 30143
Phone: (706) 692-5600
Fax: (706) 692-9453
E-mail: info@pickenschamber.com
www.pickenschamber.com/

**Info:** Originally the Cherokee Indians' homeland, this part of north Georgia received its first white settlers in the 18th century. In 1834, Sam Tate purchased a large tract of land and opened a tavern. An enormous vein of marble, 2,000 feet wide, 4 miles long, and up to ½ mile deep was soon discovered in the area owned by Sam Tate. Sam's son Stephen began the mining industry, which placed Tate on the map. Through his efforts the railroad was built through Pickens County, and Georgia marble was shipped throughout the country as construction material for many important buildings and monuments.

The Georgia Marble Company currently operates the world's largest open-pit

marble quarry. It is open to the public by special tour only during the Marble Festival. Tours leave every 15 minutes from the festival grounds. Reservations are required.
**Tour:** Adults $7.00 plus festival admission $3.00, children $4.00, children under 4 free.

**Other services available:** Stephen Tate's son, Sam Tate, built a mansion in 1926 constructed of rare pink Etowah marble (the Tate House). This building has been renovated and is now a bed and breakfast. Tours of the mansion are available. Call (770) 735-3122.

**Directions:** Take I-575 to U.S. 515, which goes to the festival grounds.

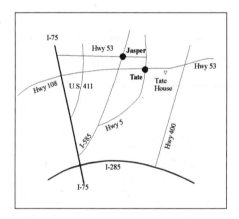

## Gold Rush Days, Dahlonega, GA

Third weekend of October

*For more information:*
Dahlonega Jaycees
P.O. Box 774
Dahlonega, GA 30533
Phone: (706) 864-7247
www.dahlonegajaycees.com

**Info:** This festival commemorates the first major gold rush in America, which occurred in 1828. Among the various arts and crafts activities is a gold panning contest.

**Directions:** Most of the activities are located on and around the Town Square.

## World Open Gold Panning Championship Dahlonega, GA

Held annually on the third Saturday of April

**Info:** Eight gold nuggets are placed in a gold pan filled with sand. The miner who pans the nuggets the fastest wins. The same pan and nuggets are used each

---

## World's Largest Open-Pit Marble Quarry

What is reported to be the world's largest open-pit marble quarry is located in Tate. A tract of land purchased in 1834 by Sam Tate was found to have a large deposit of marble. Mining began a few years later, and marble from this quarry has been used in building construction around the country. The Marble Festival is held in nearby Jasper, Georgia, every October; this is the only time when this quarry can be toured.

year, ensuring consistency of the contest. As a result, this is the only contest of its kind to be recognized by the *Guinness Book of World Records.*

For more information, contact:
Consolidated Gold Mine
185 Consolidated Gold Mine Road
Dahlonega, GA 30533
Phone: (706) 864-8473

## TOURIST INFORMATION

### State Tourist Agency

Georgia Department of Tourism
Phone: (404) 962-4087
www.georgia.org/travel/

# KENTUCKY

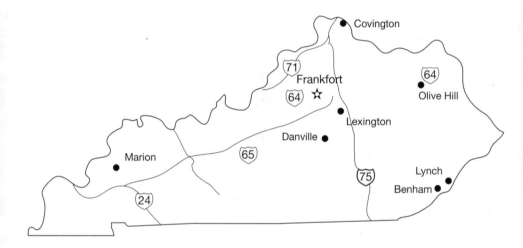

**State Gemstone:** Freshwater Pearl
**State Mineral:** Coal
**State Stone/Rock:** Kentucky Agate (2000)

**MARION /** *Native • Easy to Moderate*

---

## Collect Fluorite at an Old Open-Pit Mine *T*

*The following gems or minerals may be found:*

▪Fluorite and related minerals, fluorescent minerals

The Ben E. Clement Mineral Museum
205 N. Walker Street
Marion, KY 42064
Phone: (270) 965-4263
Fax: (270) 965-4263
www.marionkentucky.us/
clementmineralmuseum

**Open:** Day and night digs are scheduled once a month from April to October. Check the museum website for specific dates.

**Info:** Two digs are scheduled on the mine dumps once each month—one during the day, and a second that night. The night digs are for UV fluorescent minerals. Each person must bring his or her own equipment; suggested equipment includes rock hammers, small pick, small sledge hammer; pry bar, insect repellent, a 5-gallon bucket, and a UV light. You may want to bring food, water, and extra clothing as needed.

**Rates:** The fee for the day dig is $20.00, and for the night dig is $30.00. This allows you to collect one 5-gallon bucket of specimens; additional buckets are charged at the same rate. You must make a reservation, attendance is limited to 30 during the day digs, and 20 for the night digs. Private digs may be arranged for groups.

**Directions:** Contact the mineral museum for directions.

---

SECTION 2: **Museums and Mine Tours**

---

## BENHAM

---

## Museum

Kentucky Coal Mine Museum
221 Main Street + Highway 160
P.O. Box A
Benham, KY 40807

Phone: (606) 848-1530
Fax: (606) 848-1546
E-mail: kycoalmuseum@earthlink.net
www.kingdomcome.org/museum/

**Open:** Year round; closed some holidays. 10:00 A.M.–5:00 P.M. Monday–Saturday, 1:00 P.M.–4:00 P.M. Sunday.

**Info:** Benham was originally a company town owned by International Harvester; the museum is located in the former company commissary. Photographs, memorabilia, videos, and scale models are used to present the story of coal mining in Kentucky. See the floor plan of a typical underground coal mine, and view displays on the formation of coal. (A personal collection of country music legend Loretta Lynn is displayed on the third floor of the museum.) A walking mine tour is available in Lynch, 2 miles away. There is an opportunity for visitors to obtain a piece of coal for their personal collections.

**Admission:** Adults $5.00, students $2.00, seniors $4.00.

**Directions:** The museum is located in Benham, which is on State Highway 160, just off of U.S. 119, 2 miles east of Harlan and approximately 55 miles from 25 E.

# COVINGTON

## Museum

Behringer-Crawford Museum
Devou Park
1600 Montague Road
Covington, KY 41011
Phone: (859) 491-4003
Fax: (859) 491-4006

**Open:** 10:00 A.M.–5:00 P.M. Tuesday–Friday, 1:00–5:00 P.M. Saturday and Sunday.

**Info:** The museum has a display of gems and minerals that includes quartz, barite roses, gold, pyrite, and a large geode.

**Admission:** Adults $7.00, seniors $6.00, children $4.00.

**Other services available:** Museum store.

**Directions:** From Interstates 71/75, take exit 191 (Pike Street/12th St.) to Pike Street, and look for the signs to Devou Park. Turn right on Lewis Street, and at the third stop sign, bear right on Montague Road up the hill into the park. At the top of the hill, turn right, go through the intersection, and turn left into the parking lot.

# DANVILLE

## Museum

JFC Museum
1369 Stanford Avenue
Danville, KY 40422
Phone: (859) 236-7057
www.bellsouthpwp.net/r/o/rocktown/

**Open:** Saturday and Sunday 10:00 A.M.–5:00 P.M.

**Info:** The museum displays the private collection of Danny Curtsinger, who has been collecting rocks, fossils, currency, jewelry, and local phenomena for more than forty years.

**Admission:** Free.

**Directions:** The museum is a few miles south of Danville on Stanford Avenue (Rt. 150). Specific detailed directions are available on the website.

## LEXINGTON

## Museum

Headley-Whitney Museum
4435 Old Frankfort Pike
Lexington, KY 40510
Phone: (859) 255-6653
Fax: (859) 255-8375
www.headley-whitney.org

**Open:** Tuesday–Friday 10:00 A.M.–5:00 P.M.; Saturday–Sunday noon–5:00 P.M.

**Info:** The museum's Jewel Room exhibits George Headley's collection of jewelry, bibelots (trinkets), and mounted semi-precious stones.

**Admission:** Adults $7.00, seniors 62+ $5.00, students $5.00, children under 5 free. Group rates available.

**Other services available:** Gift shop.

**Directions:** Located 6 miles from downtown Lexington. Take New Circle Road (Rt. 4) to Exit 6, Old Frankfort Pike. At the end of the ramp follow signs to Frankfort. The museum is located 4 miles from the exit at 4435 Old Frankfort Pike.

## LYNCH

## Mine Tour

Portal #31 Walking Tour
221 Main Street + Highway 160
P.O. Box A
Benham, KY 40807
Phone: (606) 848-1530
Fax: (606) 848-1546
E-mail: kycoalmuseum@earthlink.net

www.kingdomcome.org/portal/index.html

**Open:** Year round; closed some holidays. 10:00 A.M.–5:00 P.M. Monday–Saturday, 1:00–4:00 P.M. Sunday.

**Info:** The mine tour is presented in association with the Kentucky Coal Mine Museum (see first listing). Lynch, located 2 miles from Benham, was originally a company town owned by U.S. Steel. The walking tour takes you through the surface buildings and structures built in Lynch to serve Mines 30, 31, and 32. The Exhibition Mine Tour features a ride into the mine on a mantrip car, an exhibit of the pony mine days, and features eight displays of mining technology at various time periods. The Louisville and Nashville RR station are open to the public with an exhibit on the UMW. Portal 31 RV park is located directly across from the Portal.

**Admission:** See listing for Kentucky coal mine.

**Directions:** Follow U.S. 119 to Cumberland and follow 160 on to Lynch.

## MARION

## Museum

The Ben E. Clement Mineral Museum
205 N. Walker Street
P.O. Box 391
Marion, KY 42064
Phone: (270) 965-4263
Fax: (270) 965-4263
www.marionkentucky.us/
clementmineralmuseum

**Open:** Wednesday–Saturday, 10:00 A.M.–3:00 P.M.

**Info:** The museum has a display of gems, minerals and mining artifacts collected by Ben E. Clement during a twenty-five year career in the fluorspar industry and sixty years of collecting. It also includes maps, letters, and records, as well as fluorite carvings, and fifty rare faceted fluorite gemstones cut by George O. Wild of Germany.

**Admission:** Adults $5.00, seniors $4.50, children (5–12) $3.00. Group rates and educational classes are available.

**Other services available:** Gift shop.

**Directions:** Call for directions.

## OLIVE HILL

## Museum

Northeastern Kentucky Museum
1385 Carter Caves Road
Olive Hill, KY 41164
Phone: (606) 286-6012
E-mail: nekymuseum@atcc.net
www.kymuseum.org

**Open:** Spring and fall, 9:00 A.M.–5:00 P.M.; summer, 9:00 A.M.–dark; winter, by appointment only.

**Info:** The museum has displays of rocks, minerals, jewelry, and fossils.

**Admission:** Free

**Other services available:** Gift shop

**Directions:** The museum is located just outside of Olive Hills, KY, near Carter Caves State Park.

---

## SECTION 3: Special Events and Tourist Information

---

## TOURIST INFORMATION

### State Tourist Agency

Kentucky Department of Tourism
Capital Plaza Tower, 22nd floor
500 Metro Street
Frankfort, KY 40601

Phone: (800) 225-8747;
(502) 564-4930
www.kentuckytourism.com

# LOUISIANA

**State Gemstone:** Agate
**State Stone/Rock:** Petrified Palm

## SECTION 1: Fee Dig Sites and Guide Services

No information available.

## SECTION 2: Museums and Mine Tours

### SHREVEPORT

## Museum

Louisiana State Exhibit Museum
P.O. Box 38356
3015 Greenwood Road
Shreveport, LA 71133
Phone: (318) 632-2020

**Open:** All year, closed holidays. Monday–Friday 9:00 A.M.–4:00 P.M., Saturday–Sunday 12:00–4:00 P.M.

**Info:** The museum has exhibits on mining and on salt domes.

**Admission:** Adults $5.00, children 6–17 $1.00, 5 and under free.

**Directions:** Take Interstate 20 to exit 6A; go north ¹/₁₀ mile to Greenwood Road. Turn west onto Greenwood.

## SECTION 3: Special Events and Tourist Information

### TOURIST INFORMATION

## State Tourist Agency

Louisiana Office of Tourism
Phone: (225) 342-8100
E-mail: free.info@crt.state.la.us
www.louisianatravel.com

# MISSISSIPPI

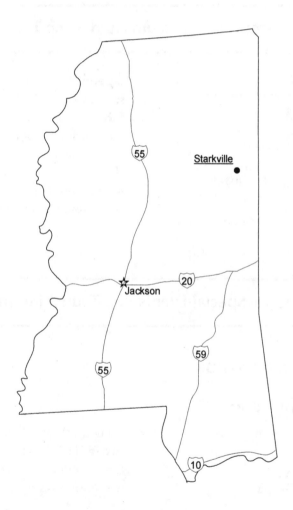

**State Stone/Rock:** Petrified Wood

# SECTION 1: Fee Dig Sites and Guide Services

No information available.

# SECTION 2: Museums and Mine Tours

## STARKVILLE

### Museum

Dunn-Seiler Museum
Mississippi State University
Mississippi State, MS 39762
Phone: (662) 235-3915
www.msstate.edu/dept/geosciences/
museum.htm

**Open:** By appointment during the school year.
**Info:** Extensive mineral and rock collections, including meteorites. Displays on mineral families and properties, the three classes of rocks, and plate tectonics.
**Admission:** Free.
**Directions:** Call for directions.

# SECTION 3: Special Events and Tourist Information

## TOURIST INFORMATION

### State Tourist Agency

Mississippi Division of Tourism
Development
P.O. Box 849
Jackson, MS 39205

Phone: (601) 359-3297; (866) 733-6477
Fax: (601) 359-5757
E-mail: tourdiv@mississippi.org
www.visitmississippi.org

# MISSOURI

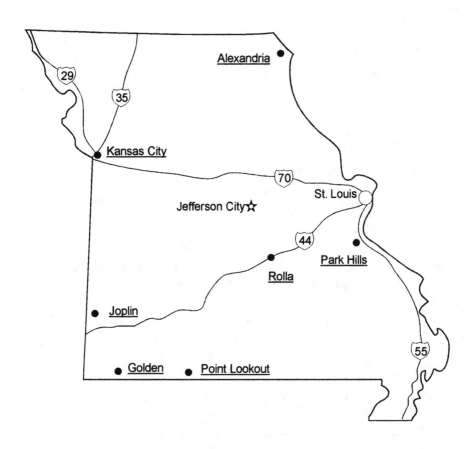

**State Gemstone:** Galena (1967)
**State Stone/Rock:** Mozarkite (1967)

# SECTION 1: Fee Dig Sites and Guide Services

## ALEXANDRIA / *Native • Easy to Moderate*

### Dig Your Own Geodes

*The following gems or minerals may be found:*

- **Crystal-lined geodes**

Sheffler Rock Shop
Tim Sheffler
R.R.1, Box 171
Alexandria, MO 63430
Phone: (660) 754-6443

**Open:** April 1–December 1 9:00 A.M.–5:00 P.M., 6 days/week (Closed Sundays.) (weather permitting). Call ahead for conditions at the mine, since weather affects digging at the mine.

**Info:** Geode mine digging; easily accessible strip mine. You can find geodes lined with minerals such as calcites, pyrites, barites, selenite needles, dolomite, sphalerite, kaoline, aragonite, goethite, and hematite. You must provide your own equipment; you will need a bucket, pry bar, pick, or rock hammer. A shovel may be useful.

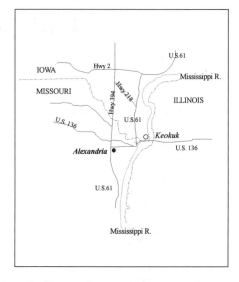

**Admission:** $20.00 per person for 50 pounds of geodes; $0.75/pound for over 50 pounds. Call to make reservations.

**Other services available:** Rock shop which includes display of opened geodes, mineral specimens, and fossils.

**Directions:** On U.S. 61, 6 miles west of Alexandria. Three miles south of Wayland. *Note:* Road construction may effect access to shop and fee dig. Contact the shop regarding this construction (shop can also be contacted via the web).

# SECTION 2: Museums and Mine Tours

## GOLDEN

### Museum 🏛

Golden Pioneer Museum

Highway 86 and "J"
P.O. Box 216
Golden, MO 65658
Phone: (417) 271-3300; (417) 217-3299

# Geodes

Geodes are round stones that have a crystal-filled hollow in the middle. They began as gas-filled bubbles in lava, or as soft areas in rock, which were eroded. Over time, water containing minerals seeped into the hollow and evaporated, leaving the minerals behind as crystals.

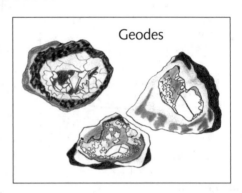

Geodes

The geodes from eastern Missouri are lined with a layer of chalcedony, a form of quartz, which holds the geode together. These geodes have clear and smoky quartz crystals inside, with different mineral buildups in them. The buildups could be clear or white calcite, iron pyrite, goethite, or pink dogtooth calcite with brown calcite crystals; some have fluorescent crystals.

**Open:** Tuesday–Saturday 10:30 A.M.–4:30 P.M.

**Info:** The museum displays minerals from around the world, including what is reported to be the world's largest turquoise carving, made from a 68-pound stone. The museum also contains what is reported to be the largest double terminated single quartz crystal (1,250 pounds), a single cluster of quartz crystals weighing over 4,000 pounds, a large display of amethyst, fluorite crystals, and selenite clusters.

**Admission:** Free.

**Directions:** Located at the intersection of Highway 86 and "J," on Table Rock Lake, between Branson, MO, and Eureka Springs, AR.

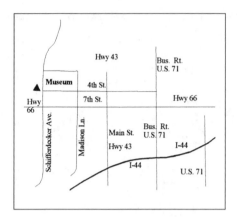

## JOPLIN

## Museum

Everett J. Ritchie Tri-State Mineral Wing
Schifferdecker Park
P.O. Box 555
Joplin, MO 64802
Phone: (417) 623-1180
Fax: (417) 623-6393
www.joplinmuseum.org

**Open:** Tuesday 10:00 A.M.–7:00 P.M.,
Wednesday–Saturday 10:00 A.M.–5:00
P.M., Sunday 2:00–5:00 P.M.

**Info:** The museum has exhibits of ore
specimens and mining artifacts depicting
the story of lead and zinc mining in the
Tri-State (Kansas, Missouri, and Oklahoma) area.

**Admission:** $2.00/person, 5 and under
free. $5.00 for family.

**Directions:** Located in the Joplin Museum

Complex. From I-44, take exit 4 north
(MO43) on Schifferdecker Avenue to
Schifferdecker Park.

## KANSAS CITY

## Museum 🏛

University of Missouri–Kansas City
Geosciences Museum
Rm. 271 Robert H. Flarsheim Hall
5110 Rockhill Road
Kansas City, MO 64110
Phone: (816) 235-1334
Fax: (816) 235-5535

**Open:** Monday–Friday, 8:30 A.M.–4:30
P.M., Saturday 10:00 A.M.–4:00 P.M.
when school is in session.

**Info:** The museum has the following displays: a large collection of petrified wood;
agates, including several dozen specimens
from the basalt lavas of Lake Superior; thirty crystals containing liquid inclusions;
more than 500 matched cabochons of
semiprecious stones and unusual stones;
selenite crystals, minerals from the Joplin
mining district; specimens from the Kansas
City area; and a spectacular fulgurite, several feet long, formed when lightning struck
the ground and fused the soil and shale.

**Admission:** Free.

**Directions:** On Rockhill Road in
Kansas City.

## PARK HILLS

## Museum

Missouri Mines State Historic Site
Highway 32, P.O. Box 492
Park Hills, MO 63601-0492
Phone: (573) 431-6226; (800) 334-6446
www.mostateparks.com/momines.htm

**Open:** All year. 10:00 A.M.–4:00 P.M.
Monday–Saturday. Noon–5:00 P.M. Sundays in winter; noon–6:00 P.M. Sundays in summer.

**Info:** The museum has 1,100 specimens of minerals, ores, and rocks on display. The collection is based on an original collection by Missouri's first great mineral collector, Fayette P. Graves. The mineral gallery has 27 cases, some of which are antique display cases built in the 1920s. Eleven of the cases contain a collection demonstrating the systematic classification of minerals. The museum also has a fluorescent mineral room, dominated by minerals from Franklin, N.J., zinc mines. There is also a display featuring Missouri minerals as well as specimens of other minerals easily collected in the state.

The museum has a gallery featuring some of the underground mining machinery used in area mines. In addition, some of the mining buildings at the museum complex are being restored, and historical interpretations and walking tour trails will be installed.

The area is known as the "Old Lead Belt." Big-company lead mining occurred between 1864 and 1972, and the area was the nation's leading producer of lead for 60 of those years.

**Admission:** Adults $2.50, children (6–12) $1.50, children under 6 free.

**Directions:** On the south side of Highway 32, 1½ miles west of the junction with U.S. 67 in Park Hills.

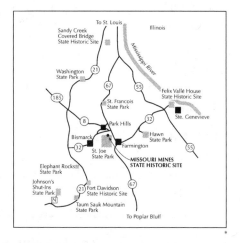

## POINT LOOKOUT

## Museum

Ralph Foster Museum
College of the Ozarks
Point Lookout, MO 65726
Phone: (417) 334-6411, ext. 3407
E-mail: museum@cofo.edu
www.rfostermuseum.com

**Open:** Monday–Saturday 9:00 A.M.–4:30 P.M. February–mid-December.

**Info:** The museum has several displays of minerals and rocks. These include a display of minerals in the Ozarks, which has varied types of quartz, jasper, graphite, mica, pyrite, copper, and others. There are also displays of many types of geodes, quartz crystals, and over 150 different minerals. There is a display of mineral spheres and of fluorescent minerals.

**Admission:** Adults $4.50, seniors $3.50, children free.

**Directions:** On the college campus in Point Lookout.

## ROLLA

### Museum

Mineral Museum—University of Missouri–Rolla
Department of Geology and Geophysics
125 McNutt Hall

Rolla, MO 65409-0410
Phone: (573) 341-4616
Fax: (573) 341-6935

**Open:** Monday–Friday 8:00 A.M.–4:30 P.M. when school is in session.

**Info:** The museum has about 3,500 specimens of minerals, ores, and rocks from 92 countries and 47 states on display. The collection is based on an original collection from the state of Missouri exhibit displayed at the 1904 Louisiana Purchase Exposition, along with minerals donated by Mexico and the Missouri geology collection from the 1893 Chicago World Fair. Displays of gemstones and gold specimens from Peru are among the museum highlights.

**Admission:** Free.

**Directions:** On the university campus in Rolla.

---

## SECTION 3: Special Events and Tourist Information

---

## TOURIST INFORMATION

### State Tourist Agency

Missouri Division of Tourism
P.O. Box 1055
Jefferson City, MO 65102

Phone: (800) 519-2100
Fax: (573) 751-5160
E-mail: tourism@ded.mo.gov
www.visitmo.com/

# NORTH CAROLINA

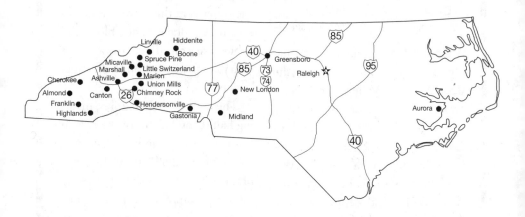

**State Gemstone:** Emerald (1973)
**State Stone/Rock:** Unakite/Granite

# Introduction to Gem Mining in North Carolina: Cowee Valley Mines

The list of gems and minerals native to this valley in Franklin is said to include the following:

| | |
|---|---|
| Rubies | Quartz crystal |
| Sapphires | Rutile |
| Rhodolite, almandite, and pyrope garnet | Kyanite |
| | Mica |
| Periodot | Feldspar |
| Sillimanite | Moonstone |

Although Native Americans probably collected gemstones in the Cowee Creek Valley long before 1800, gemstones found in the valley in the gravel of the Caler Fork of Cowee Creek, a tributary of the Tennessee River, soon after the Civil War resulted in a systematic search of the area. Rubies and sapphires were found in the gravels of the Caler Fork for a distance of 3 miles. These finds led to commercial exploration by two developers in particular, the American Mining and Prospecting Co. and the United States Ruby Mining Co. These developers searched for the source of the gems found in the creek gravels; however, to this day, this source has never been discovered. One theory is that the gem-bearing matrix has completely washed out of the ancient Appalachian Mountains, and consequently there is no mother lode in the range.

All that remains are the crystals that settled into the relatively protected beds of the valley.

There are only two places in the world where sandy gravel yields blood-red rubies. One is in the Mogok Valley in Burma, India, and the other is in the Cowee Valley of North Carolina. The blood-red rubies are considered to be more valuable than diamonds of equal quality.

The commercial ventures, meeting failure, pulled out of the area in the early 1900s, and the land was divided into small farms. The sands of the valley were never subjected to intensive commercial mining, thus leaving a wealth of material for the collector. In response, several mines opened to offer mining of gems from the Cowee Valley gravels.

Actually, calling them *mines* is somewhat misleading. There are no tunnels or shafts or any of the equipment associated with underground mining. The gem-bearing ore is located along the Caler Fork of Cowee Creek in a layer of mud, clay, and gravel, which varies from 2 to 10 feet in depth.

Most mine owners excavate the ore in a shallow surface mine and supply the excavated ore to collectors in buckets or bags; the collector washes the same dirt he or she would have dug, but without the work of digging and transporting the ore to the flume. At the time of this writing, the authors have located only one mine in the Franklin area where a collector can still dig his or her own gem ore from the source. There are also mines where prospectors can screen natural gravel which the mine owners/operators say has not been salted or enriched.

---

## SECTION 1: Fee Dig Sites and Guide Services

---

### ALMOND / *Enriched Ore · Easy*

#### Pan for Gems  *T*

*The following gems or minerals may be found:*

- Rubies, sapphires, amethyst, topaz, garnet, citrine, smoky quartz, emeralds

Nantahala Gorge Ruby Mine
P.O. Box 159
11900 US19-US74 West
Almond, NC 28702
Phone: (828) 488-3854
Fax: (828) 488-3854

**Open:** Mid-May through mid-October, 10:00 A.M.–6:00 P.M., 7 days/week, weather permitting.
**Info:** Enriched native ore is sold by the bag.
**Admission:** Free. Gem ore bags range from $10.00 to $300.00/bag.
**Other services available:** Gem cutting and mounting.
**Directions:** On U.S. 19/U.S. 74 midway between Bryson City and Andrews.

### BOONE / *Enriched · Easy*

#### Screen Your Own Gems and Minerals *T*

*The following gems or minerals can be found:*

- Topaz, garnet, aquamarine, peridot, ruby, star sapphire, amethyst, citrine, smoky quartz, tourmaline, emerald

Foggy Mountain Gem Mine
Dana Morace and Lucas Critcher, GG
4416 NC Highway 105 S
Boone, NC 28607
Phone: (828) 963-GEMS (4367)
www.foggymountaingems.com

**Open:** All year, 10:00 A.M.–5:00 P.M. Closed major holidays.
**Info:** Screen your own gems and minerals. Foggy Mountain provides buckets of gem ore that you screen in their flume. Indoor flume for use during bad weather. All equipment is provided.
**Admission:** Free. Buckets range in price from $12.50 to $250.00.

The Old Pressley Sapphire Mine is the source of the Star of the Carolinas, a 1,445-carat sapphire and the Southern Star, a 1,035-carat sapphire.

**Other services:** Gift shop, gem cutting.
**Directions:** Located on Highway 105, just south of Boone, NC.

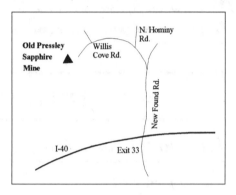

## CANTON / *Native Material • Easy*

### Sluice for Gems  *T*

*The following gems or minerals may be found:*

- Sapphires (pink, blue, gray, white, bronze), zircon, garnet, mica

Old Pressley Sapphire Mine
George and Brenda McCannon
240 Pressley Mines Road
Canton, NC 28716
Phone: (828) 648-6320

**Open:** Summer, 9:00 A.M.–5:00 P.M. Monday–Friday; 9:00 A.M.–6:00 P.M. Saturday–Sunday. Winter, 9:00 A.M.–4:00 P.M. Monday–Saturday. Closed Sunday.
**Info:** Buy buckets of ore from the mine (native stones only) or prospect in mine tailings.
**Admission:** $5.00; potluck bucket of gem ore, $10 (no guarantee). 3½-gallon family bucket, $45 (guaranteed to find gems).
    Prospecting: April–October $25.00, November–March $20.00. Group rates available.
**Other services available**: Refreshments, restrooms, picnic area, mountain scenery, rock shop, souvenirs.
**Directions:** From I-40, take exit 33 and travel north on New Found Road. Follow signs to the mine.

## CHEROKEE / *Enriched Native Ore • Easy*

### Pan for Gold or Gems  *T*

*The following gems or minerals may be found:*

- Rubies, sapphire, emerald, amethyst, topaz, garnet, citrine, smoky quartz, gold

Smoky Mountain Gold and Ruby Mine
Highway 441 North
Cherokee, NC 28719
Phone: (828) 497-6574
www.smgrm.com

**Open:** 7 days/week. May–October 9:00 A.M.–6:00 P.M.; November–April 10:00 A.M.–5:00 P.M.

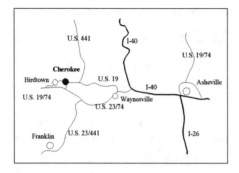

**Info:** Enriched native ore is sold by the bag or the bucket.

**Admission:** Gold bags $8.00–$200.00, mixed gems $6.00 (2 for $10.00), $12.00 emerald, ruby, and sapphire buckets (5-gallon bucket for $50.00).

**Other services available:** Gem, jewelry, and rock shop.

**Directions:** Highway 441 North, in downtown Cherokee across from Dairy Queen.

## CHIMNEY ROCK / *Enriched • Easy*

### Screen Your Own Gems and Minerals

*The following gems or minerals can be found:*

▪ Aquamarine, emerald, ruby, peridot, garnet, quartz, agate, hematite, amethyst, sodalite

Chimney Rock Gemstone Mine
397 Main Street
Chimney Rock, NC 28720
Phone: (828) 625-5524
www.chimneyrockgemmine.com

**Open:** All year, 7 days/week, 10:00 A.M.–6:00 P.M.; open later in the summer.

**Info:** Screen your own gems and minerals. Chimney Rock Gemstone Mine provides buckets of gem ore that you screen in their flume. All equipment is provided.

**Admission:** Free. Buckets range in price from $5.00–$50.00.

**Other services:** Gift shop, gem cutting.

**Directions:** Located in the village of Chimney Rock, NC, east of Asheville on Highway 74A.

## Mines in the Franklin Area:

### FRANKLIN / *Enriched Ore • Easy*

## Sluice for Gems  *T*

*The following gems or minerals may be found:*

▪ Rubies, sapphires, garnets, tourmaline, smoky quartz, amethyst, citrine, moonstone and topaz

Cowee Mountain Ruby Mine
6771 Sylva Road (441 North)
Franklin, NC 28734
Phone: (828) 369-5271
Fax: (828) 524-0633
E-mail: cowee@verizon.net

**Open:** 9:00 A.M.–dark or 6:00 P.M. 7 days/week, mid-March–mid-November.

**Info:** Soil containing gems native to the region and enriched material from elsewhere can be purchased and sluiced. Help is provided to beginners, and there is a covered, lighted flume for sluicing.

**Admission:** Free. Bags and buckets of gem ore range from $5.00 to $100.

**Other services available:** Gem cutting, rock and mineral shop, clean restrooms.

# Mining in North Carolina

Essential equipment is provided by the mine: the flume, a trough with running water, and the sluice box, a wooden tray with a wire mesh screen for a bottom.

Mining at North Carolina mines basically involves putting a small amount of the gem ore (soil) in the sluice box, and then holding and gently shaking the box in the flume so that the dirt is washed away and the stones are left. The stones are then examined, and gems or minerals or stones that the miner wants are removed and placed in a container or small bag. The remaining material is dumped out, and more ore placed in the box and sluiced.

When mining in the natural soil, you may not always find a large quantity of stones, and those found may not be of gem quality or worth cutting. But for the true rockhound, the thrill is in knowing there is always the *possibility* that one may find that special gem or mineral at a mine, and searching until it is found. Many mines in the area have begun "enriching" or "salting" their native soil to provide additional material to find. Gems and minerals of pretty colors from around the world are mixed in with the ore in the bucket or bag. Children especially enjoy finding and identifying these added materials. When looking for a mine, ask if the gem-bearing soil is native or enriched. (See page 23 for a definition of *enriched* or *salted* material.)

**Directions:** North of Franklin on Highway 441.

**FRANKLIN /** *Enriched Native Ore* ▪ *Easy*

## Sluice for Gems  𝑇

*The following gems or minerals may be found:*

▪ Rubies, sapphires, garnets, emeralds, tourmaline, smoky quartz, amethyst, citrine, moonstone, topaz, aquamarine, gold

Gold City Gem Mine
Curtis and Susan Rhoades
9410 Sylva Road, Highway 441 North
Franklin, NC 28734
Phone: (828) 369-3905; (800) 713-7767
E-mail: curt@goldcityamusement.com
www.goldcityamusement.com

**Open:** March–December 19, 9:00 A.M.–5:30 P.M., closed Wednesday and Thursday.

**Info:** Soil containing gems native to the region and enriched material from

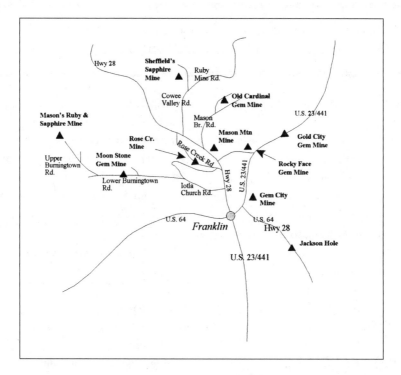

In the map:

Hwy 28

Sheffield's Sapphire Mine ▲

Ruby Mine Rd.

Cowee Valley Rd.

Old Cardinal Gem Mine ▲

U.S. 23/441

Mason's Ruby & Sapphire Mine ▲

Mason Br./Rd.

Rose Cr. Mine

Mason Mtn Mine ▲

Gold City Gem Mine ▲

Upper Burningtown Rd.

Moon Stone Gem Mine ▲

Rose Creek Rd.

Hwy 28

U.S. 23/441

Rocky Face Gem Mine

Lower Burningtown Rd.

Iotla Church Rd.

Gem City Mine ▲

U.S. 64

Franklin

U.S. 64

Hwy 28

Jackson Hole ▲

U.S. 23/441

---

elsewhere can be purchased and sluiced. Gold panning is offered. Help is provided, and there is a covered flume for sluicing, which has been specially constructed for handicapped needs.

**Admission:** Free, fee charged for dirt. Group and student rates are available.

**Other services available:** Clean restrooms, snacks and cold drinks, picnic tables.

The jewelry and gift shop offers gifts and souvenirs, custom jewelry made on the premises, and jewelry repair. The country general store offers antiques, crafts, and collectibles.

**Directions:** Six miles north of Franklin on Highway 441.

**FRANKLIN /** *Enriched and Native Ore • Easy*

---

## Sluice for Gems *T*

*The following gems or minerals may be found:*

• **Rhodolite garnets, rubies, sapphires, kyanite, crystal quartz, smoky quartz, moonstones**

Mason Mountain Mine and Cowee Gift Shop (The Johnson's Place)
Brown and Martha Johnson
5315 Bryson City Road
Franklin, NC 28734
Phone: (828) 524-4570
E-mail: brownj@standard.net

**Open:** April 1–November 15, 8:00 A.M.–5:00 P.M., 7 days/week.

**Admission:** Free. Buckets of gem dirt $5.00 each, special bags of gem dirt $10.00–$20.00 each, super buckets $30.00–$300.00 each. Dig your own pile: $25.00, 8:00 A.M.–5:00 P.M.

**Other services available:** Gift shop, gem cutting (cabbing and faceting), crafts and jewelry, restrooms.

**Directions:** From Franklin take Highway 28 north approximately 5½ miles and look for the mine.

**FRANKLIN /** *Native Only • Easy to Moderate*

## Dig and Sluice for Gems  *T*

*The following gems or minerals may be found:*
- Sapphires (all colors) and pink and red rubies

Mason's Ruby and Sapphire Mine
Christine Mason and Pete Civitello
6761 Upper Burningtown Road
Franklin, NC 28734
Phone: (828) 369-9742

**Open:** All year, 7 days/week, 9:00 A.M.–5:00 P.M.

**Info:** Only mine in the area where you can dig and sluice your own gem-bearing dirt. All equipment is furnished at no charge, and help is provided for beginners.

**Admission:** Adults $20.00, children (6–11) $10.00, 5 and under free.

**Other services available:** Picnic tables, modern bathroom facilities, free parking.

**Directions:** Take Highway 28 north from Franklin to Airport Road. Turn left, and follow signs to the mine.

**FRANKLIN /** *Native and Enriched Ore • Easy*

## Sluice for Gems  *T*

*The following gems or minerals may be found:*
- Rubies, sapphire, rhodolite, garnets, other precious stones

Moon Stone Gem Mine
Mr. Willard O. Holbrook
8312 Lower Burningtown Road
Franklin, NC 28734
Phone: (828) 524-7764

**Open:** April 1–October 31, daylight to dark, 7 days/week.

**Info:** Sluice buckets of enriched native gemstone ore. All equipment is furnished at no charge. Help is provided.

**Admission:** $5.00, children under 6 free. 2-gallon bucket of gem dirt $4.00.

**Directions:** Take NC 28 north to the Big D Store, turn left immediately after store on Iotla Church Road. Stay on blacktop road approximately 8 miles, following signs to the mine.

# Gems from the Cowee Valley and Around the World

The Cowee Valley remains a location where natural precious gemstones can be found, but is also a location where you can learn identification of gem specimens from around the world.

The lure of gems has brought people to the Cowee Valley for over 400 years, beginning with Spanish explorers in the 1500s. In recent times, the area has seen the growth of the tourism industry and many "salted" mines have sprung up. These "salted" locations may be actual mine sites or just a flume line set up alongside the road. At these "mines" you can sluice for gemstones from around the world. Besides the educational value of identifying these finds, some of the material can be cabbed or faceted. In addition, they provide practice for sluicing native materials.

On a trip to the Cowee Valley, after only two hours of sluicing, the author's daughter, Annie, found a 12-carat sapphire which could be cabbed to a 7½-carat gem. The authors also found several smaller facetable sapphires—proving to them, at least, that there are natural gems to be found at the mines. While mining, the authors saw another gentleman who had just found a beautiful pigeon-blood-red ruby.

---

**FRANKLIN /** *Enriched Native Ore* ▪
*Easy*

## Sluice for Gems  *T*

*The following gems or minerals may be found:*

▪ **Rubies, sapphires, rhodolite garnets, and many other varieties**

Rocky Face Gem Mine
260 Saundertown Road
Franklin, NC 28734
Phone: (828) 524-3148

E-mail: gemstone@dnet.net

**Open:** April–October, 10:00 A.M.–late, 6 days/week. Closed Sunday.

**Info:** Sluice 2-gallon buckets of enriched gem dirt. Sluicing is done at a covered concrete flume beside a tree-shaded creek.

**Admission:** Free. Buckets of gem dirt: $5.00–$50.00.

**Directions:** 3 miles north of Franklin on U.S. 441; 300 feet off the highway on Saunderstown Road.

> Large gems including a 1,200-carat ruby and a 3,000-carat sapphire were found at the Rocky Face Mine.

**FRANKLIN /** *Native and Enriched Ore* ▪ *Easy to Moderate*

## Dig and Sluice for Gems  𝘛

*The following gems or minerals may be found:*

▪ Rubies, sapphires, garnets, moonstones, amethysts, smoky quartz, citrine, rose quartz, topaz, emerald

Rose Creek Mine and Rock Shop
The Sterrett Family
115 Terrace Ridge Drive
Franklin, NC 28734
Phone/Fax: (828) 349-3774
E-mail: info@rosecreekmine.com
www.rosecreekmine.com

**Open:** April–October, 9:00 A.M.–5:00 P.M., 6 days/week. Closed Sunday.

**Info:** Dig your own gems in the gem tunnel.* Help is provided for beginners, and there is a covered flume for panning rain or shine.

*\* Gem tunnel: dirt from the mine is placed in covered shed for digging.*

**Admission:** Adults $6.00 (includes one free bucket), children $3.00 (includes one free bucket), additional buckets $3.00, super buckets and concentrates $10.00–$75.00. Group rates are available.

**Other services available:** Lapidary supplies and equipment, gem rough for cutting and specimens available. Clean restroom, snacks, picnic tables.

**Directions:** Take Highway 28 north from Franklin. Turn left on Bennett Road at the Little Tennessee River.

**FRANKLIN /** *Native and Enriched as Indicated* ▪ *Easy*

## Sluice for Gems  𝘛

*The following gems or minerals may be found:*

▪ Native rubies and sapphires, or enriched material from around the world

Sheffield Mine
385 Sheffield Farm Road
Franklin, NC 28734
Phone: (828) 369-8383
E-mail: ruby@sheffieldmine.com
www.sheffieldmine.com

**Open:** April–October 10:00 A.M.–5:00 P.M.

**Info:** Only native Star Ruby mine in all of the Americas, the mine has been in continuous operation for over 100 years.

**Admission:** Adults $10.00 (includes two buckets), children under 10 or seniors over 65 $8.00. Additional buckets: Native dirt $2.00, Enriched Rainbow dirt $4.00 or 2 for $6.00. Specialty buckets, such as Emerald buckets, available. Group discounts available, call for more information.

**Other services available:** Lapidary shop, gift shop, snacks, and cold drinks.

**Directions:** Take Highway 28 north

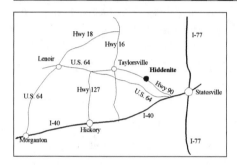

from Franklin to Cowee Creek Road. Take Cowee Creek Road to Leatherman Gap Road. Look for signs to mine.

## HIDDENITE / *Native or Enriched* • *Easy to Moderate*

## Dig and Sluice for Gems *T*

*The following gems or minerals may be found:*

• Sapphires, garnets, emeralds, hiddenite, smoky quartz, rutile, tourmaline, clear quartz, aquamarine, sillimanite, and others

Emerald Hollow Mine—Hiddenite Gems, Inc.
Dottie Watkins
P.O. Box 276
Hiddenite, NC 28636
Phone: (828) 632-3394; (866) 600-GEMS; (866) 600-4367
Fax: (828) 635-7986
E-mail: info@hiddenitegems.com
www.hiddenitegems.com

**Open:** All year, 8:30 A.M. to sunset or 7:30 P.M., 7 days/week; closed Thanksgiving, Christmas Eve, and Christmas Day.
**Info:** Sluice for gems in buckets of pre-dug dirt, dig your own, or search for gems in the creek. Help is provided, and there is a covered flume for sluicing.
**Admission:** Sluicing with one bucket of ore $5.00. Creekin'/ sluicing with one bucket of ore $8.00/day. Buckets of native ore $3.00, other buckets of ore from $2.00 to $100.00. Group and special student rates are available.

A "mother lode" bucket from the Blue Ridge Gemstone Mine yielded a rough sapphire that cut into a 300+-carat star sapphire plus 11 smaller cut stones.

**Other services available:** Beverages, picnic tables, lapidary shop, gift shop, restrooms.

The mine also offers special educational programs for students, guided by a former N.C. State geologist. The trip includes surface collection, searching creeks for gems, and sluicing a bucket of ore.

**Directions:** From Interstate 40, turn west on NC 90 toward Taylorville. Hiddenite is approximately 12 miles from I-40. In Hiddenite, turn right on Sulphur Springs Road (State Road 1001), and follow the green signs. Hiddenite Gems, Inc. is on the right.

## HIGHLANDS / *Native or Enriched Ore • Easy*

## Sluice for Gems  *T*

*The following gems or minerals may be found:*

▪ Rubies, sapphires, garnets, tourmaline, smoky quartz, amethyst, citrine, moonstone, topaz

Jackson Hole Gem Mine
9770 Highlands Road
Highlands, NC 28741
Phone: (828) 524-5850

**Open:** Summer 9:00 A.M.–5:00 P.M., 7 days/week. Winter 10:00 A.M.–4:00 P.M., closed Wednesday.

**Info:** Purchase soil containing gems native to the region and buckets of enriched material, and sluice for gems.

Help is provided, and there is a covered flume for sluicing.

**Admission:** Free. Buckets of ore: Small: $6.00 each, 2 for $10.00. Ultimate: $30.00 each, 2 for $50.00.

**Other services available:** Clean restrooms, gem shop, gem cutting.

**Directions:** East of Franklin on US 64 and Highway 28, halfway between Franklin and Highlands.

## LITTLE SWITZERLAND / *Enriched Native Ore • Easy*

## Sluice for Gems  *T*

*The following gems or minerals may be found:*

▪ Sapphire; emeralds; rubies; aquamarine; tourmaline; topaz; garnets; amethyst; clear, rose, rutilated, and smoky quartz; lepidolite; citrine; beryl; moonstone; and kyanite

Blue Ridge Gemstone Mine
Richard Johnson
P.O. Box 327, McKinney Mine Road
Little Switzerland, NC 28749
Phone: (828) 765-5264
Fax: (828) 765-2244
E-mail: blueridgegemston@bellsouth.net

**Open:** April 1–November 1, 9:00 A.M.–5:00 P.M., 7 days/week.

**Info:** Sluice enriched gem-bearing soil. All equipment is supplied, and help is available. Sluice at a 330-foot flume, which is enclosed and heated in spring and fall.

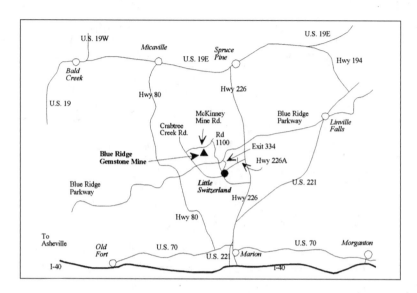

**Admission:** Free. Buckets $6.00–200.00 ("mother lode"). For a small fee ($30.00 or more), staff will cut, grind, and polish a stone you find and set it into handcrafted settings.

**Other services available:** Museum, picnic area, handicapped access. Rock and gift shop offering mining material, cut gems, finished jewelry, 14k gold and sterling silver mounts, chains and bracelets, lapidary equipment, services of a G.I.A.-trained gemologist.

**Directions:** Exit the Blue Ridge Parkway at Little Switzerland (exit 334). Take the first right (before the stop sign). Turn right onto Chestnut Grove Church Road, and go under the parkway, then drive for 1 mile. Turn left onto McKinney Mine Road. Blue Ridge Gemstone Mine is 2 miles down on the left.

## LITTLE SWITZERLAND / *Enriched*
*Native Ore • Easy*

## Sluice for Gems  𝑇

*The following gems or minerals may be found:*

• **45 different rocks, minerals, and gems, including rubies, sapphires, aquamarine, emeralds, garnets, smoky quartz, beryl, uranium, and fluorescent minerals**

Emerald Village
P.O. Box 98
McKinney Mine Road
Little Switzerland, NC 28749-0098
Phone: (828) 765-6463
Fax: (828) 765-6329
www.emeraldvillage.com

**Open:** April 1–November 15. April: Daily 10:00 A.M.–4:00 P.M. May: Daily 9:00

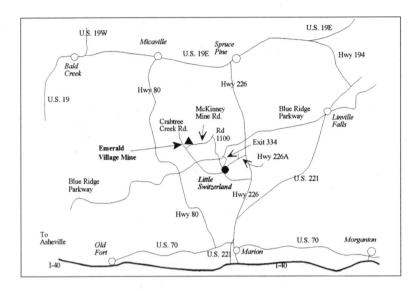

A.M.–5:00 P.M. Memorial Day–Labor Day: Daily 9:00 A.M.–6:00 P.M. September–October: Daily 9:00 A.M.–5:00 P.M. November 1–15: Daily 10:00 A.M.–4:00 P.M.

**Info:** Emerald Village is located at two gem mines: Big McKinney and Bon Ami Mines. See Section 2 on Mine Tours for more information. Sluice enriched gem-bearing soil at a shaded flume. All equipment is supplied, and help is available.

**Admission:** Free. Buckets range in price from $10.00 to $1000.00. Group rates available by reservation only.

**Other services available:** North Carolina Mining Museum; mine tour; picnic area; snacks and drinks; restrooms; cab and facet shop; gemstone identification; gem cutters at work; rock and gift shop offering mining material, cut gems, finished jewelry, rocks and minerals, souvenirs, lapidary equipment.

**Directions:** Take exit 334 (Little Switzerland) off the Blue Ridge Parkway. At the bottom of the exit ramp, turn right onto Chestnut Grove Road and go under the parkway. Drive approximately 1 mile then turn left onto McKinney Mine Road. The gemstone mine is at Emerald Village, 2 miles down the road, on the right.

## MARION / *Native • Moderate*

### Mine Your Own Gold and Gems  *T*

*The following gems or minerals may be found:*

▪ Gold, emeralds, aquamarine, moonstone, feldspar crystals, garnets, smoky quartz, rose quartz, blue quartz, quartz crystals, and tourmaline

Carolina Emerald Mine and Vein Mountain Gold Camp

Donald Davidson
1694 Polly Spout Road
Marion, NC 28752
Phone: (828) 738-9544
www.veinmountaingoldcamp.com

**Open:** April 1–November 5, 8:30 A.M.–6:00 P.M.; off-season by reservation.

**Info:** Pan for gold at this mine, and you may also discover gems. Gold recovery equipment can be rented, including high-bankers or a dredge. Gold can be found in the river gravel; gems can also be found there, or can be dug from the pegmatite.

**Admission:** Gem sluicing: $20.00 adults. Children under 11 half price. Gold panning and gem hunting in the creek (hand panning and digging only) $5.00.

**Other services available:** Fishing in their catch-and-release pond.

**Campground:** Campsites are available for $10.00/night for primitive sites, or $12.00/night for a site with hook-ups. $2.50 per each person more than three.

**Directions:** From Interstate 40, take exit 85, and drive south on Route 221 for 6½ miles. Turn left onto Polly Spout Road and drive 1¾ miles to the mine.

**MARION /** *Native and Enriched ▪ Easy to Moderate*

## Hunt for Gems and Minerals  𝑇

*The following gems or minerals may be found:*

▪ **Gold, variety of gems and minerals**

Heather Grove Gold and Gem Panning
43 Polly Spout Rd.
Marion, NC 28752
Phone: (828) 738-3573
E-mail: mikeandbrooke@
heathergrovegold.com
www.heathergrovegold.com

**Open:** March 21–December 8, Thursday–Monday 8:00 A.M.–6:00 P.M., closed Tuesday and Wednesday.

**Info:** Gold-bearing soils are excavated from an old creek bed on the property and bagged for panning, or spread for high banking. Enriched bags of gem dirt are sold for gem panning.

**Rates:** Bags of gold dirt range from $15.00 to $100.00. Bags of gem dirt range from $15.00 to $50.00. High banking: $40.00 for a front end bucket of gold dirt, $30.00 to rent the Heather Grove high bank machine. Dredging: up to 3" is $20.00/day. 3"–4" is $25.00/day; Heather Grove 2½" dredge rental is $60.00/day. Panning, hand-sluicing, and/or metal detecting in the creek: $5.00/day, sluice rental: $10.00/day.

**Other services available:** Miner's cabins range from $40.00 to $85.00/night; camping ranges from $12.00–$20.00/night.

**Directions:** From I-40, take exit 85 on Hwy. 221 South to Polly Spout Road, 5 to 6 miles on the left. Look for signs for the mine. From I-85, take U.S. Highway 221 North for about 45 miles. After crossing McDowell County line go about 2 miles. Heather Grove is on the right.

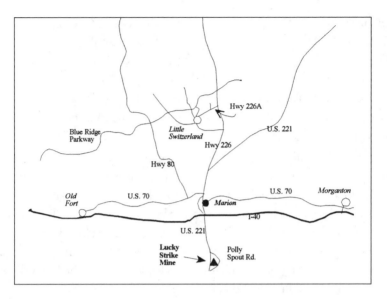

## MARION / *Enriched Ore* • *Easy*

### Sluice for Gems or Pan for Gold $T$

*The following gems or minerals may be found:*

- **Gold and gemstones**

The Lucky Strike
Liz McCormick
251 Lucky Strike Drive
Marion, NC 28752
Phone: (828) 738-4893
www.luckystrikegoldandgem.com

**Open:** All year, Monday–Saturday 9:00 A.M.–6:00 P.M., Sunday 1:00–5:00 P.M.

**Info:** All equipment is supplied, and help is available. Instructions on panning are provided. Dredges and sluice boxes are available for rent.

**Admission:** Free. Buckets: 1-gallon $5.00, 3-gallon $20.00. Gold bags $25.00–$100.00.

**Other services available at the mine:** Restaurant, campground. BBQ and Music Jamboree one or two times a month. Call for dates and cost.

**Directions:** 5.3 miles south of I-40 on Route 221, then turn left on Polly Spout Road.

## MARSHALL / *Native* • *Difficult*

### Take a Horseback Ride to an Old Garnet Mine or Dig Your Own $T$

*The following gems or minerals may be found:*

- **Garnets**

Little Pine Garnet Mine
Sandy Bottom Trail Rides
1459 Caney Fork Road
Marshall, NC 28753
Phone: (800) 959-3513 or (828) 649-3464; evenings (828) 649-3788
E-mail: info@sandybottomtrailride.net

**Open:** All year, closed Thanksgiving and Christmas. Rides normally leave at 10:00 A.M., noon, and 2:00 P.M., but other times can be arranged.

**Info:** Rides of three or more hours can go to the Little Pine Garnet Mine, where you can dig for gem quality garnets, and keep all that you find. Those who prefer can go directly to the mine for garnets. Horse and wagon rides to the mine can be arranged.

**Rates:** 3-hour trail ride, $75.00; 4-hour ride, $120.00. Fee-digging only $25.00.

**Directions:** From Asheville, NC, take Highway 19-23 north, then take Highway 25-70 west at Exit 19A. Travel 12.6 miles, then turn left on Little Pine Road, and travel 3.8 miles to Caney Fork Road. Signs are provided.

## MICAVILLE / Native · Moderate

## Dig Your Own Gems 𝑇

*The following gems or minerals may be found:*

▪ Emeralds, aquamarine, golden beryl, feldspar, pink feldspar, star garnets, biotite, olivine, moonstone, thulite, and black tourmaline

Rock Mine Tours
P.O. Box 877
Micaville, NC 28755
Phone: (828) 675-0004

**Open:** Monday–Saturday all year, weather permitting. Digging tours leave at 10:00 A.M. and 2:00 P.M. Reservations required.

**Info:** Dig your own gem material. You will go to the mining claim, where you will learn mining techniques for this mine. Then you will be taken to one of the mine pits and can dig your own gems. Keep everything you find. All equipment is provided.

**Admission:** Adults $50.00, children under 17 $25.00, under 5 free. Group discount available.

**Other services available:** Gift shop.

**Directions:** Get directions when you make reservations.

## MIDLAND / Native · Easy

## Pan for Gold 𝑇

*The following gems or minerals may be found:*

▪ Gold

Reed Gold Mine State Historic Site
9621 Reed Mine Road
Midland, NC 28107
Phone: (704) 721-4653
Fax: (704) 721-4657
E-mail: reedmine1799@msn.com
www.reedmine.com

**Open:** April 1–October 31, Tuesday–Saturday 9:00 A.M.–5:00 P.M. November 1–March 31, Tuesday–Saturday 10:00 A.M.–4:00 P.M. Closed Sunday and Monday year-round.

**Info:** Gold panning is available only during the summer months (April through October) and closes at 4:00 P.M. See full entry in Section 2 for details on the Reed Gold Mine State Historic Site.

**Panning fees:** $2.00/pan of ore. Instruction included.

**Directions:** From I-85 or I-77 in Charlotte, take I-485 to the NC 24/27 (Albemarle) exit, #41. Turn left at the top of the ramp to take NC 24/27 east. Go 11 miles east through the community of Midland and across the Rocky River. Watch for the large brown Reed Gold Mine, NC Historic Site signs. Just across the Rocky River, turn left onto Reed Mine Road. Follow this road for 2½ miles. Entrance is on the right.

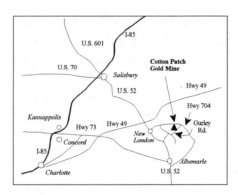

## NEW LONDON / *Placer Material* ▪ *Easy to Moderate*

## Pan for Gold *T*

*The following gems or minerals may be found:*

▪ Gold

Cotton Patch Gold Mine
41697 Gurley Road
New London, NC 28127
Phone: (704) 463-5797
www.cottonpatchgoldmine.com

**Open:** Mid-February–mid-November each year, 9:00 A.M.–5:00 P.M., Wednesday–Sunday.

**Info:** Much of the work conducted at the Cotton Patch Mine involved recovery of gold from placer material. In 1958 a trench was opened on the property, and in 1961 the mine was opened to the public for panning and mineral collecting. In 1987 one of the shafts dug on a large quartz vein was reopened. This material is occasionally mixed with the placer material, and visitors usually have good results when panning.

**Panning fee:** Call for prices on buckets of dirt. Fee entitles one to washed ore,

panning equipment, and instruction. Group rates are available. Sluicing for gold also an option; call for fees. Enclosed and heated panning area available in winter.

**Other services available:** General store, sandwiches and snacks, complete line of prospecting equipment, souvenirs, picnic area.

**Campground:** Call for rates.

**Directions:** From New London, take State Highway 740 east toward Badin. Gurley Road will be on the right, shortly after leaving New London. Turn right on Gurley Road to get to the mine.

## NEW LONDON / *Native* ▪ *Easy to Moderate*

## Pan for Gold *T*

*The following gems or minerals may be found:*

▪ Gold

Mountain Creek Gold Mine
38805 Smokeridge Road
New London, NC 28127
Phone: (704) 463-7749

**Open:** All year 7:30 A.M.–dark.

**Info:** Originally part of the Crowell Mine, you can pan washed or unwashed dirt, or use a highbanker or dredge to look for gold.

**Fees:** Panning—$10.00/day for unwashed material. Sluicing in creek, $10.00; sluicing washed material (one full backhoe scoop), $75.00; highbanking in creek, $15.00/two people; dredging, $20.00/two people. (Your own dredge; 4-inch output nozzle max.) Dredge rental, $55.00 (3-inch output nozzle).

**Other services available:** Camping—$8.00/night for tent, $12.00/night for camper.

**Directions:** From I-85 take the Southmont exit, and go south on Highway 8 for 28 miles, to Highway 49. Go south on Highways 8/49 4 miles, then follow Highway 8 when it splits from Highway 49. Drive 2 miles to Baldwin Road, turn left on Baldwin Road, and follow it to the end at Highway 740. Turn left on Highway 740 and travel 1½ miles to Gurley Road (first right). Turn right on Gurley Road, travel 2 miles to the sign for the mine, and follow the signs to the creek.

## SPRUCE PINE / *Enriched Native Ore • Easy*

## Sluice for Gems  *T*

*The following gems or minerals may be found:*

- Sapphire, crabtree emeralds, Wiseman and Brushy Creek aquamarine, rubies, tourmaline, topaz, garnets, amethyst, citrine, moonstone

## Spruce Pine Area Mines

Another major gem-hunting area in North Carolina is Spruce Pine in Mitchell County. Just as the Cowee Valley is known for rubies and sapphires, the Spruce Pine area is known for emeralds and aquamarine. The only working emerald mine in North America is in Mitchell County. Approximately 250 different kinds of minerals and gems are found there. About 46% of the feldspar used in the production of porcelain, china, and glass in the U.S. comes from Mitchell County. The following gems and minerals are said to be found in mines in the Spruce Pine area:

| | |
|---|---|
| Beryl (including emerald) | Oligoclase |
| Hyalite | Moonstone |
| Autunite | Apatite |
| Torbernite | Uranium minerals |
| Tourmaline | Kyanite |
| Garnet | Quartz, rose and smoky |
| Columbite | Actinolite |
| Sphalerite | Spodumene |
| Thulite | Talc |
| Epidote | Aquamarine |
| Amethyst | Citrine |
| Hiddenite | |

Gem Mountain Gemstone Mine
Charles and Kay Buchanan
P.O. Box 488, Highway 226
Spruce Pine, NC 28777
Phone: (828) 765-6130; (888) 817-5829
E-mail: info@gemmountain.com
www.gemmountain.com

**Open:** All year except January and February. 9:00 A.M.–5:00 P.M. until Memorial Day, 9:00 A.M.–7:00 P.M. until Labor Day, 6 days/week. Closed Christmas Day.

**Info:** Sluice enriched gem-bearing soil provided in buckets. All equipment is furnished.

**Admission:** Free. 2-gallon bucket of ore:

start at $10.00 each, other sizes and prices of buckets available up to $110.00. Two stones cut free with $110.00 bucket.

The mine also offers "dig your own" tours at 10:00 A.M. every Saturday from June 1 to August 31. This is a 4-hour trip to the Brushy Creek Aquamarine Mine. Look for stones such as golden beryl, tourmaline, garnet, and aquamarine, and keep what you find. Each trip is headed by a trained guide. Transportation, safety glasses, and pick hammer are furnished and are included in the trip fee. By reservation only.

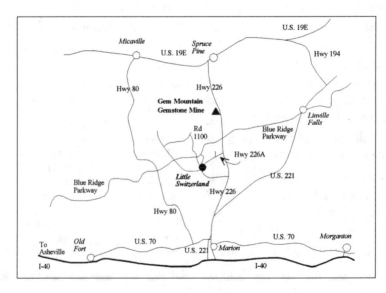

**Tour fee:** Adults $55.00, children under 12 $30.00.

**Other services available:** Displays of local minerals and specimens from all over the U.S. and the world, gem cutting, jewelry making, gift shop, sandwich and ice cream shop, picnic area.

Gem Mountain General Store featuring quilts, crafts, candies, gifts, and more. Open 6 days/week from March through December. Groups welcome.

**Directions:** Located between Spruce Pine and the Blue Ridge Parkway, 1 mile north of the North Carolina Mineral Museum.

## SPRUCE PINE / *Enriched Native Ore • Easy*

## Sluice for Gems  *T*

*The following gems or minerals may be found:*

▪ Emeralds; rubies; aquamarine; tourmaline; topaz; garnets; amethyst; rose, clear, rutilated, and smoky quartz; citrine; and beryl

Rio Doce Gem Mine
Jerry Call, Inc.
P.O. Box 296
Little Switzerland, NC 28749
Phone: (828) 765-2099
E-mail: jerrycallinc@bellsouth.net

**Open:** Easter–October 31, 9:00 A.M.–5:00 P.M., 7 days/week.

**Info:** Sluice enriched gem-bearing soil. The gem material is from local area mines and from famous mines in Brazil.

All equipment is supplied, and help is available.

**Admission:** Free. Buckets $10.00–$100.00 each; with $50.00 five-gallon bucket one gem cut free; with $100.00 eight-gallon bucket two gems cut free.

**Other services available at the mine:** Picnic area, free stone identification, gem and gift shop, mineral specimens, gem cutting school, rough stones, gem cutting, jewelry.

**Directions:** On Highway 226, ½ mile north of the Blue Ridge Parkway.

## SPRUCE PINE / *Enriched Native Ore • Easy*

## Sluice for Gems  *T*

*The following gems or minerals may be found:*

▪ 31 different gems, including emeralds, rubies, sapphires, aquamarine, tourmaline, topaz, garnets, amethyst, smoky quartz, citrine, and beryl

Spruce Pine Gem and Gold Mine
Intersection of Blue Ridge Parkway and Highway 226
15090 Highway 226 S
Spruce Pine, NC 28777
Phone: (828) 765-7981
www.sprucepinegemmine.com

**Open:** All year; hours vary seasonally.

**Info:** Use an indoor flume in heated water to sluice enriched native gem-bearing soil provided in buckets. All equipment is furnished, and experienced help is available.

**Admission:** Free. Buckets $10.00, $20.00, $40.00, $60.00, $80.00, $100.00, and $500.00.

**Other services available:** Gem cutting and setting, gift shop.

**Directions:** Exit 331 off the Blue Ridge Parkway on Highway 226 (next to the North Carolina Museum of Minerals).

**UNION MILLS /** *Native and Enriched • Easy*

## Pan for Gold and Gemstones T

*The following gems or minerals may be found:*

▪ **Gold, gemstones**

Thermal City Gold Mine
Lloyd Nanny, Owner
5240 U.S. 221 N. Highway
Union Mills, NC 28167
Phone: (828) 286-3016
www.HuntForGold.com

**Open:** March 1–November 30, 7 days/week, 8:30 A.M.–5:00 P.M.

**Info:** Site of a family-operated 1830s-era gold mine. Fine gold and an occasional nugget are found; a 7.26-ounce nugget was found in 1993. The site consists of a 1-mile section of the Second Broad River and about 60 acres of placer gravel deposits. Material for gold panning is brought up from the river using a backhoe, and this panning material is not enriched or salted. Gemstone panning material is enriched with native material.

**Panning fee:** $5.00/day per person for gold panning. Gem buckets: $5.00–$50.00.

**Common dig:** A backhoe-fed wash plant will be used to extract gold from placer gravel. All concentrates will be hand panned. You receive clean gold in a bottle and black sands separately. All gold recovered will be split among participants according to GPAA (Gold Prospectors Association of America) methods.

**Common dig schedule:** Memorial Day, July 4th, Labor Day. Cost: $100.00/miner. Dig may be conducted for private groups. Call for info and specific dates.

**The Annual Miners Meet** is held Memorial Day weekend, with panning, a treasure hunt, vendors, equipment demonstration, and other activities.

**Other services available:** Complete line of prospecting equipment, on-site gem flume and rock shop, campground (cabin rentals available), riverside camping, hot showers, some sites have electricity.

**Rates:** $12.00/night for primitive sites, $12.00/night for full hookup sites.

**Directions:** Take U.S. 221, exit 85 off I-40 at Marion, and go south toward Rutherfordton for approximately 9 miles. Look for the sign on the left and follow the signs to the mine.

## ASHEVILLE

## Museum

Colburn Earth Science Museum
2 South Pack Square
P.O. Box 1617
Asheville, NC 28802
Phone: (828) 254-7162
Fax: (828) 257-4505
www.colburnmuseum.org

**Open:** Tuesday–Saturday, 10:00 A.M.–5:00 P.M.; Sunday 1:00–5:00 P.M.; all year.

**Info:** The Colburn Earth Science Museum's mission is to foster an appreciation of the earth and its mineral resources through exhibits, educational programming, and the collection and care of specimens. The Colburn Earth Science Museum serves as a repository for gifts of mineral specimens. The museum opened in 1960 as a bequest of mineral collector Burnham Standish Colburn. Until 1982 it was operated by the Southern Appalachian Mineral Society; it is now a nonprofit organization.

Collections include mineral specimens from North Carolina and the world and include gemstones, rocks, fossils, micromounts, minerals, and related artifacts. On view are a 229-carat cut blue topaz and a 376-pound aquamarine crystal; mineral treasures from North Carolina include the rare gem hiddenite.

The museum's library contains over 500 volumes, publications, and manuscripts.

The museum hosts an annual Gem Fest each June featuring gem and mineral dealers from all over the U.S. The museum hosts an after-school Junior Rockhounds Club.

**Admission:** Adults $4.00, children, students, and seniors $3.00.

**Directions:** From Interstate 240, take exit 5A/Merrimon Avenue, and follow the signs for Highway 25 South for three blocks to Pack Square. From Interstate 40, take exit 50 (Highway 25, South Asheville) and continue on Highway 25 north through Biltmore Village for three miles. Parking is available streetside or in the parking garage adjacent to Pack Square. Handicapped accessible.

## AURORA

## Museum

Aurora Fossil Museum
400 Main Street, P.O. Box 352
Aurora, NC 27806-0352
Phone: (252) 322-4238
Fax: (252) 322-2220
E-mail: aurfosmus@yahoo.com
www.aurorafossilmuseum.com

**Open:** Labor Day–March 15, Monday–Saturday, 9:00 A.M.–4:30 P.M.; March 16–Labor Day, Saturday, 9:00 A.M.–4:30 P.M.; Sunday, 1:00 P.M.–4:30 P.M.

**Info:** The goal of the museum is to increase knowledge of the geology and paleontology of the North Carolina coastal plain.

**Admission:** Free, donations are gladly accepted.

**Directions:** Call for directions.

## FRANKLIN

## Museum

Franklin Gem and Mineral Museum
(The Old Jail Museum)
25 Phillips Street
Franklin, NC 28734
Phone: (828) 369-7831
http://fgmm.org

**Open:** May–October, noon–4:00 P.M., Monday–Friday. Saturday, 11:00 A.M.–3:00 P.M. November 1–April 30 Saturday 11:00 A.M.–3:00 P.M.

**Info:** The museum is located in the old Macon County Jail behind Rankin Square. It is operated by the Gem and Mineral Society of Franklin, N.C., Inc.

Collections include mineral specimens from North Carolina and the world and feature gemstones, rocks, minerals, Indian artifacts, and related items.

**Admission:** Free.

**Directions:** At the intersection of Main Street and Phillips Street in Franklin take a left and the museum is behind Rankin Square or left off of Palmer Street onto Phillips Street. Parking on Phillips Street or in museum parking lot.

## FRANKLIN

## Museum

Ruby City Gems & Minerals
130 E. Main Street
Franklin, NC 28734
Phone: (828) 524-3967
Fax: (828) 369-2678
www.rubycity.com

**Open:** April 1–December 26, 9:00 A.M.–5:00 P.M., Monday–Saturday.

**Info:** The museum is located in the Ruby City Gem and Mineral Store on East Main Street, and can be entered from the shop.

The museum features a collection of 500 spheres, cut, ground, and polished by the original owner of the Gem Shop. In addition, there is a collection of fluorescent minerals, local minerals, as well as worldwide specimens, boasting the world's largest sapphire and an extensive pre-Columbian artifacts collection.

**Admission:** Free.

**Directions:** On East Main Street in Franklin.

## GASTONIA

## Museum

Schiele Museum
1500 East Garrison Boulevard
Gastonia, NC 28054-5199
Phone: (704) 866-6900
Fax: (704) 836-6900

**Open:** 9:00 A.M.–5:00 P.M. Monday–Saturday, 1:00–5:00 P.M. Sunday; closed

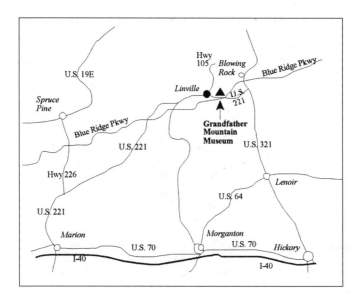

major holidays.

**Info:** The museum has a number of displays, including North Carolina gems and minerals, gold, properties of minerals, examples of gem and mineral classification systems, and gem cabbing and faceting.

**Admission:** Adults $4.00, students and seniors $2.00.

**Directions:** Call for directions.

**Open:** All year, Monday–Saturday 9:00 A.M.–5:00 P.M., Sunday 12:30–5:00 P.M.

**Info:** The collection of minerals is located in the Gem and Mineral Gallery. There are over 50 faceted N.C. mineral specimens on display.

**Admission:** Adults $8.00, children 3–13 and seniors $7.00.

**Directions:** Off U.S. 220, on the north side of the city.

## GREENSBORO

## Museum 🏛

Natural Science Center of Greensboro
4301 Lawndale Drive
Greensboro, NC 27455
Phone: (336) 288-3769
Fax: (336) 288-2531
E-mail: info@natsci.org
www.natsci.org

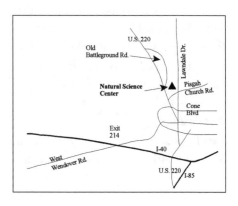

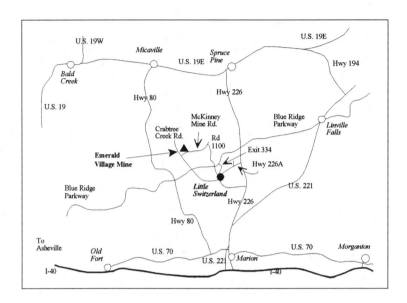

## HENDERSONVILLE

## Museum 🏛

Mineral & Lapidary Museum of
Henderson County, Inc.
400 N. Main Street
Hendersonville, NC 28792
Phone: (898) 698-1977
E-mail: mineralmuseum@cytechusa.com
www.mineralmuseum.org

**Open:** All year, Monday–Friday 1:00–
5:00 P.M., Saturday 10:00 A.M.–5:00 P.M.
**Info:** Exhibits cover mineralogy, geology,
paleontology, and associated lapidary art.
Geode cracking service available for a
moderate fee.
**Admission:** Free.
**Directions:** Corner of North Main
Street and 4th Avenue, Hendersonville.

## LINVILLE

## Museum 🏛

Grandfather Mountain Nature
Museum
P.O. Box 129
Linville, NC 28646
Phone: (800) 468-7325
Fax: (828) 733-2608
E-mail: nature@grandfather.com
www.grandfather.com

**Open:** Spring and fall 9:00 A.M.–6:00
P.M., winter 9:00 A.M.–5:00 P.M., April–
Labor Day 9:00 A.M.–7:00 P.M., 7 days/
week. Closed Thanksgiving and Christmas.
**Info:** Grandfather Mountain has been
singled out by the United Nations as a
biosphere reserve because of its significance to the biodiversity of the planet. It
is a privately owned and protected
wildlife sanctuary, which is home to 42

rare or endangered species.

The nature museum exhibits represent most of the historically important mines and miners of the last 100 years. Through these exhibits the history of rockhounding in N.C. is traced. Each specimen is identified as to where and by whom it was found.

Displays include most of the gems and minerals found in NC, organized by common mineral families and location. Families include quartz, garnet, radioactives, kyanite, beryl, and corundum; locations include the Foote Mineral Co. in Kings Mt. and the Hiddenite area. The exhibit includes choice N.C. specimens with a focus on emeralds and the largest amount of N.C. gold on display to the public in the state.

**Admission:** Adults $14.00, seniors 60+ $12.00, children 4–12 $6.00, children under 4 free. Group rates available.

**Other services available:** Gift shop, family restaurant, hiking and picnicking, highest suspension footbridge in America, hourly nature films.

**Directions:** Off U.S. 221 one mile south of the Blue Ridge Parkway, and two miles north of Linville.

## LITTLE SWITZERLAND

## Museum/Mine Tour

North Carolina Mining Museum and Mine Tour
Emerald Village, Inc.
P.O. Box 98
Little Switzerland, NC 28749-0098

Phone: (828) 765-6463
Fax: (828) 765-6329
www.emeraldvillage.com

**Open:** April 1–November 15. April: Daily 10:00 A.M.–4:00 P.M. May: Daily 9:00 A.M.–5:00 P.M. Memorial Day–Labor Day: Daily 9:00 A.M.–6:00 P.M. September–October: Daily 9:00 A.M.–5:00 P.M. November 1–15: Daily 10:00 A.M.–4:00 P.M.

**Info:** Take a walking tour of a now-closed feldspar mine. The mine was originally developed by the Bon Ami Company to mine feldspar as an ingredient for its polishing cleaner. Quartz and mica were also found in the mine, along with a complex uranium mineral known as samarskite, specimens of which can be seen in the mine ceiling. Because of the presence of uranium minerals in the mine, many of the rocks contain trace amounts of uranium, making them highly fluorescent when exposed to ultraviolet light.

The museum tells the story of the miners, the mining, the ores and minerals found in the mine, the equipment used, and the Bon Ami Mining Company. There are displays of antique equipment, with explanations of how they operated. The displays are in the visitors center, at the entrance to the mine, and inside part of the mine as well. Also included is a replica of a 1920s mining store.

**Admission:** Adults $6.00, seniors $5.50, students, $5.00.

**Directions:** Take exit 334 (Little

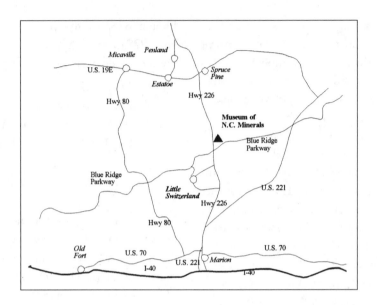

Switzerland) off the Blue Ridge Parkway. At the bottom of the exit ramp, turn right onto Chestnut Grove Road and go under the parkway. Drive approximately 1 mile then turn left onto McKinney Mine Road. The museum is at Emerald Village, 2 miles down the road, on the right.

## MIDLAND

## Mine Tour/State Historic Site 🏛

Reed Gold Mine State Historic Site
9621 Reed Mine Road
Midland, NC 28107
Phone: (704) 786-8331
E-mail: reedmine1799@msn.com
www.ah.dcr.state.nc.us/sections/hs/reed/reed.htm

**Open:** April 1–October 31, Tuesday–Saturday 9:00 A.M.–5:00 P.M. November 1–March 31, Tuesday–Saturday 10:00 A.M.–4:00 P.M. Closed Sunday and Monday year-round.

**Info:** Site of the first documented discovery of gold and the first intensive mining operation in the United States as part of the nation's first gold rush. The mine was in operation from 1803 to 1912. It was noted for the large size and purity of its gold nuggets. Gold discovery spread to nearby counties and into other southern states. North Carolina maintained a leadership in gold production until 1848, when it was eclipsed in importance by the great rush to California. Reed Gold Mine Historic Site is operated by the N.C. Department of Cultural Affairs, Resource Division of Archives and History, Historic Sites Section.

The site's visitors center features an introductory film and exhibits on historical events, gold mining processes, and equipment. Other features include:

*Mine tour:* A guided tour is conducted through a restored section of the old underground mine.

*Equipment tour:* A tour is available of the 19th-century stamp mill used to crush ore (a mechanical engineering landmark).

*Walking trails:* Trails wind through the historic mining area past several shafts and tunnels and an exhibit interpreting the 1850s Engine House.

**Admission:** Free.

**Directions:** From Charlotte, take N.C. routes 24/27 (Albemerle Road) into Cabarrus County, and travel until you cross Route 601. After crossing 601, look for Reed Mine Road; turn left and travel approximately 3 miles to the site on the right.

## SPRUCE PINE

# Museum  🏛

Museum of North Carolina Minerals
79 Parkway Maintenance Road
Milepost 331 on the Blue Ridge
Parkway
Spruce Pine, NC 28777
Phone: (828) 765-2761

**Open:** All year, 9:00 A.M.–5:00 P.M. In summer, 7 days/week; in winter, closed from noon–1:00 P.M. Closed Thanksgiving, Christmas Eve, Christmas Day, New Year's Day.

**Info:** The museum is operated by the National Park Service; specimens have been provided by local individuals and commercial enterprises.

The museum provides an introduction to the region's wealth of mineral resources. The primary focus is on minerals mined in the Spruce Pine district. Included are gemstones, fluorescent minerals, and rare radioactive rocks. Featured are quartz, local gold, and several commercial rocks and minerals, including famed feldspar. Various stages of refinement and everyday objects made from end products are displayed. The facing of the museum building itself is made of quartzite from a quarry on nearby Grandfather Mountain.

A visitors center operated by the Mitchell Chamber of Commerce located at the museum provides visitors with information about nearby attractions in western N.C.

**Admission:** Free.

**Directions:** Located on State Highway 226 where it crosses under the Blue Ridge Parkway.

## ANNUAL EVENTS

### Macon County Gemboree, Franklin, NC

Second-oldest gem and mineral show in the southeast.

Held for 4 days in July

**Admission:** Adults $2.00, children under 12 free. Run-of-show ticket $5.00 (good for all days).
Phone: (800) 336-7829

### "Leaf-Looker" Gemboree, Franklin, NC

Held for 4 days in October

**Admission:** Call for prices.
**Info:** Both events are sponsored by the Gem and Mineral Society of Franklin, NC, Inc., and by the Franklin Area Chamber of Commerce. Both are held at:

Macon County Community Building
U.S. 441 South
Franklin, NC

Both events offer rough and cut gems, minerals, jewelry, equipment, supplies, books, dealers, and exhibits.

*For more information:*
Franklin Area Chamber of Commerce
425 Porter Street
Franklin, NC 28734
Phone: (866) 372-5546
www.franklin-chamber.com/

### Original North Carolina Mineral and Gem Festival, Spruce Pine, NC

Retail shows held for 4 days at the end of July and/or the beginning of August. For information on the festival and on gem mines in Mitchell County, contact:

Mitchell County Chamber of Commerce
PO Box 858
Spruce Pine, NC 28777
Phone: (828) 765-9033; (800) 227-3912
www.mitchell-county.com

## TOURIST INFORMATION

### State Tourist Agency

North Carolina Travel and Tourism Division
Department of Commerce
301 N. Wilmington Street
Education Building
Raleigh, NC 27601
Mailing address:
4301 Mail Service Center
Raleigh, NC 27699-4301
Phone: (800) VISIT NC or (800) 847-4862
Fax: (919) 715-3097
www.visitnc.com

# SOUTH CAROLINA

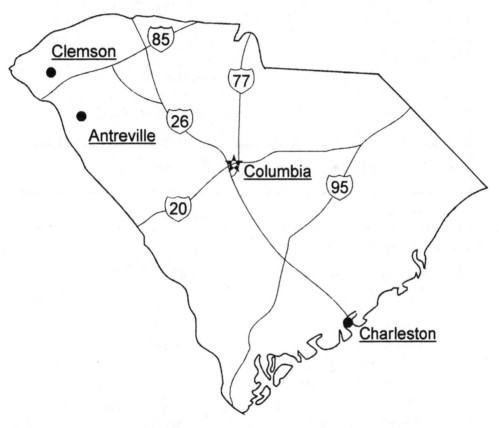

**State Gemstone:** Amethyst (1969)
**State Stone/Rock:** Blue Granite (1969)

# SECTION 1: Fee Dig Sites and Guide Services

**ANTREVILLE /** *Native · Moderate*

## Dig Your Own Quartz  *T*

*The following gems or minerals may be found:*

- White quartz crystals, skeletal quartz, amethyst (less common), smoky quartz (less common)

Diamond Hill
Chester Karwoski
1040 Sweet Gum Way
Watkinsville, GA 30677
Phone: (706) 769-8163
Fax: (706) 769-9589
E-mail: gailkarwoski@hotmail.com

**Open:** Daily; call for reservations.
**Info:** This is an old open-pit mine. In order to collect at this site, you must contact the owner, sign a release, and pay the fee. Bring your own tools, such as a pick and shovel, rock hammer, chisels, etc. Also bring food and water; there are no services at the mine.
**Admission:** Adults $15.00, children under 16 $6.00, children under 6 free.
**Directions:** Call for directions.

# SECTION 2: Museums and Mine Tours

## CHARLESTON

## Museum

The Charleston Museum
360 Meeting Street
Charleston, SC 29403
Phone: (843) 722-2996
www.charlestonmuseum.org

**Open:** All year, closed major holidays. Monday–Saturday 9:00 A.M.–5:00 P.M., Sunday, 1:00–5:00 P.M.
**Info:** The museum has a small display of gems and minerals, including some from Russia.
**Admission:** Adults $10.00, children (3–12) $5.00.
**Directions:** The museum is located in Charleston on Meeting Street at John Street.

## CLEMSON

## Museum  🏛

Bob Campbell Geology Museum
Clemson University
103 Garden Trail
Clemson, SC 29634
Phone: (864) 656-4600
Fax: (864) 656-6230
www.clemson.edu/geomuseum

**Open:** Wednesday, Saturday 10:00 A.M.–5:00 P.M.; Sunday 1:00–5:00 P.M., except university holidays and home football games. Call for information.
**Info:** Exhibits feature the southeast's only mounted skeleton of a saber-toothed cat, a world-class fluorescent mineral display, and an extensive faceted gemstone collection.

The displays also include rocks, minerals, and fossils from the region and around the world. There is a reference collection of minerals, and a library is available to researchers and museum friends.

**Admission:** Adults $3.00, children $2.00, $25.00 for an annual pass.

**Directions:** The museum is located in the South Carolina Botanical Garden, on the east side of Clemson University's campus, off Perimeter Road.

## COLUMBIA

## Museum

McKissick Museum
College of Arts and Sciences
University of South Carolina Campus
816 Bull Street
Columbia, SC 29208
Phone: (803) 777-7251
Fax: (803) 777-2829
www.cas.su.edu/mcks/

**Open:** All year, closed holidays. Monday–Friday 8:30 A.M.–5:00 P.M., Saturday 11:00 A.M.–3:00 P.M.

**Info:** The museum has exhibits on natural history study, geology, and gemstones.

**Admission:** Free.

**Directions:** The museum is located at the head of the Horseshoe area on the USC Campus, near Bull and Pendleton Streets.

## COLUMBIA

## Museum

South Carolina State Museum
301 Gervais Street, P.O. Box 100107
Columbia, SC 29202-3107
P.O. Box 100107
Phone: (803) 898-4921
www.museum.state.sc.us/

**Open:** All year, closed major holidays. Tuesday–Saturday 10:00 A.M.–5:00 P.M., Sunday 1:00–5:00 P.M.

**Info:** The museum has displays of gems and minerals, mostly as part of other exhibits. Others are found as part of a hands-on natural history exhibit called "NatureSpace."

**Admission:** Adults 13–61 $5.00, seniors 62+ $4.00, children (3–12) $3.00, infants under 2 free.

**Directions:** The museum is located at 301 Gervais Street, beside the historic Gervais Street Bridge and just a few blocks west of the state capitol in downtown Columbia.

---

# SECTION 3: Special Events and Tourist Information

## TOURIST INFORMATION

## State Tourist Agency

South Carolina Department of Parks, Recreation and Tourism

1205 Pendleton Street
Columbia, SC 29201
Phone: (803) 734-1700
www.discoversouthcarolina.com

# TENNESSEE

**State Gemstone:** Tennessee River Pearls
**State Stone/Rock:** Limestone and Tennessee Marble

**DUCKTOWN** / *Native* • *Moderate*

## Collect Minerals in Tailings

*The following gems or minerals may be found:*

- **Garnets, pyrite, chalcopyrite, pyrrhotite, and actinolite**

Burra Burra Mine
Ducktown Basin Museum
P.O. Box 458
Ducktown, TN 37326
Phone: (423) 496-5778

**Open:** Monday–Saturday; 9:30 A.M.–4:00 P.M. November–April; 10:00 A.M.–4:30 P.M. May–October. Collecting by appointment only. Call ahead.

**Info:** This is an old deep mine which was closed in 1987, and has subsequently been flooded. The Ducktown Basin was mined for copper, iron, sulfur, and zinc from the 1820's first by Native Americans, later by the settlers. The gems and minerals can be collected in the mine dump, which can only be reached through the museum. Bring your own tools, such as a small sledgehammer, chisels, rock hammer, and safety glasses.

**Admission:** (Museum) Adults $3.00, seniors $2.00, children 13–18 $1.00, children 6–12 $0.50, children under 6 free.

**Other services available:** Gift shop, mine overlook.

**Directions:** Take Interstate 575 north from I-75. I-575 will turn into SR 5, then into U.S. 76-SR 5-SR 515. Stay on SR 5 through McCaysville, and at Copperhill, SR 5 becomes SR 68; stay on SR 68 to Ducktown. The museum is on the right hand side of the road, about ¾ miles past the intersection with U.S. 64.

## DUCKTOWN

## Museum 🏛

Ducktown Basin Museum
212 Burra Burra Hill
Ducktown, TN 37326
Phone: (423) 496-5778

**Open:** Monday–Saturday; 9:30 A.M.–4:00 P.M. November–April; 10:00 A.M.–4:30 P.M. May–October.

**Info:** The Cherokee Indians mined copper from the Ducktown basin in the early 1800's. In 1850, the first copper mine was opened. The Ducktown Basin was mined for copper, iron, sulfur, and zinc. The museum preserves and presents the area's mining heritage.

**Admission:** Adults $3.00, seniors $2.00, children 13–18 $1.00, children 6–12 $0.50, children under 6 free.

**Other services available:** Gift shop, mine overlook.

**Directions:** Take Interstate 575 north from I-75. I-575 will turn into SR 5, then into U.S. 76-SR 5-SR 515. Stay on SR 5 through McCaysville, and at Copperhill, SR 5 becomes SR 68; stay on SR 68 to Ducktown. The museum is on the right hand side of the road, about ¾ miles past the intersection with U.S. 64.

## JOHNSON CITY

## Museum

Hands On! Regional Museum
315 E. Main Street
Johnson City, TN 37601
Phone: (423) 928–6508
www.handsonmuseum.org

**Open:** Tuesday–Friday 9:00 A.M.–5:00 P.M., Saturday 10:00 A.M.–5:00 P.M., Sunday 1:00–5:00 P.M.; Monday 9:00 A.M.–5:00 P.M. June–August only.
**Info:** The museum is aimed at children. As part of its exhibits, it has a simulated coal mine.
**Admission:** Adults and children 3 and up $8.00, children 2 and under free.
**Directions:** Take the Market Street exit off I-26 and drive west 1½ blocks to the museum.

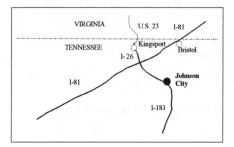

## KNOXVILLE

## Museum

The Frank H. McClung Museum
The University of Tennessee
1327 Circle Park Drive
Knoxville, TN 37996-3200
Phone: (865) 974-2144
Fax: (865) 974-3827
mcclungmuseum.utk.edu

**Open:** Monday–Saturday 9:00 A.M.–5:00 P.M., Sunday 1:00–5:00 P.M.; closed major holidays.
**Info:** Exhibits explore Tennessee's geologic history, including the rock cycle, crystals—the building blocks of rocks—and videos explaining geologic processes.
**Admission:** Free.
**Directions:** Call for directions.

## MEMPHIS

## Museum

Memphis Pink Palace Museum
c/o Pink Palace Family of Museums
3050 Central Avenue
Memphis, TN 38111-3399
Phone: (901) 320-6320
www.memphismuseums.org
**Open:** Monday–Saturday 9:00 A.M.–5:00 P.M., Sunday noon–5:00 P.M.
**Info:** A geology exhibit with two parts: physical geology and historical geology. The physical geology exhibit covers meteorites, including the Allende meteorite, which predates our solar system; earthquakes; seismology; and mineral exhibits. The mineral exhibit includes

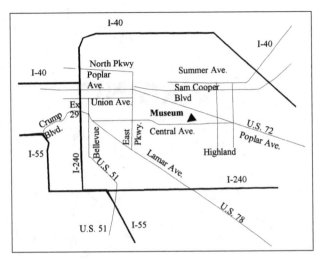

minerals from around the world and cases of minerals from famous mid-South localities, and spectacular geodes.

**Admission:** Adults $8.25, seniors $7.75, children 3–12 $5.75.

**Directions:** Take exit 29 off I-240 and drive east on Lamar Avenue. Take the left branch at the Y onto Central Avenue, and follow Central Avenue for several blocks. The museum will be on the left.

## MURFREESBORO

## Museum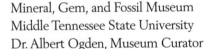

Mineral, Gem, and Fossil Museum
Middle Tennessee State University
Dr. Albert Ogden, Museum Curator

Department of Geosciences
MTSU Box 9,
Murfreesboro, TN 37132
Phone: (615) 898-4877
E-mail: aogden@mtsu.edu

**Open:** Saturdays and by appointment.
**Info:** The museum offers displays of exquisite calcite, fluorite, barite, and sphalerite specimens from the Tennessee Elmwood zinc mine; displays of birthstones: polished, faceted, and in the rough; black light room filled with fluorescent specimens; a display on mineral properties; and posters on plate tectonics, volcanism, earthquakes, caves, sinkholes, and groundwater pollution.
**Rates:** Call for rates
**Directions:** Call for directions

---

## SECTION 3: Special Events and Tourist Information

---

## TOURIST INFORMATION

### State Tourist Agency

Tennessee Tourism
Phone: (615) 741-9001
www.tnvacation.com

# VIRGINIA

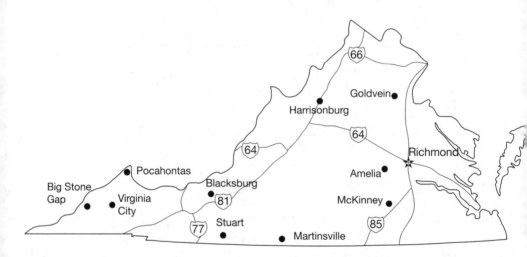

**AMELIA /** *Native · Easy to Difficult*

## Dig for Gems and Minerals *T*

*The following gems or minerals may be found:*

· Beryl, amazonite, calcite, fluorite, pyrite, quartz, topaz, tourmaline, mica, feldspar, phenakite, minerals in the tantalite/columbite series, and micro-crystals

Morefield Gem Mine, Inc.
13400 Butlers Road
Amelia, VA 23002
Phone: (804) 561-3399
Fax: (804) 561-4799

**Open:** Call or check website for schedule.
**Info:** Mine dump collecting, outcrop digging, and sluicing can all be done at the Morefield Mine. A collection from the Morefield Mine is on exhibit at the Smithsonian Institute.

Wear sturdy footwear to the mine and bring a container to carry your treasures home.
*Note:* This 79-year-old mine is currently for sale.
**Admission:** Adults, $12.00; children: preschool through 2nd grade, $7.00; grades 3 through 6, $8.00; grade 7 through high school, $10.00.
**Other services available:** Gift shop, gem cutting, vending machines, restrooms, picnic area.
**Directions:** Get on U.S. 360 west into Amelia County. 4.9 miles after crossing the Appomattox River, turn left onto County Road 628, and continue 1 mile south to the mine.

**MCKENNEY /** *Native and Enriched · Easy*

## Dig or Sluice for Gems and Minerals *T*

*The following gems and minerals may be found:*

· **Garnet, citrine, topaz, smoky quartz, tourmaline (rare), plus other gems and minerals from around the world**

Lucky Lake Gem and Mineral Mine of Virginia
4125 Harpers Road
McKenney, VA
Phone: (804) 478-5468
Fax: (804) 478-5469
E-mail: luckylakegems@yahoo.com
www.luckylakeva.com

**Open:** April–October, Monday–Saturday, 9:00 A.M.–6:00 P.M., Sunday 12:00–6:00 P.M.; September, Monday–Saturday, 9:00 A.M.–4:00 P.M., Sunday, 12:00–4:00 P.M.; November and December, Saturday 9:00 A.M.–4:00 P.M., Sunday, 12:00–4:00 P.M.
**Info:** Material excavated from the mine is placed in a pile for digging and sluicing, or sold in buckets enriched with gems and minerals from around the world. The mine owners hope to open a pit for additional material by blasting.

# Fairy Stones

Fairy Stone State Park takes its name from the amazing little crystals called fairy stones. Formed and found within the park boundaries, these stone crosses are composed of iron aluminum silicate, which is called staurolite. Single crystals are hexagonal and often intersect at right angles to form Roman or Maltese crosses, or at other angles to form St. Andrew's crosses.

The formation of staurolite crystals involves an exact combination of heat and pressure such as that provided by the folding and crumpling of the earth's crust during the formation of the Appalachian Mountains. Certain types of rock that have been folded and crumpled in this manner are called schists. The staurolite crystals are usually harder than the surrounding schist and less easily weathered. As the staurolite-bearing schist is weathered away, the more resistant crystals are uncovered and come to lie on the surface. Occasionally staurolites can be found still embedded in their schist matrix.

The crystals are found in various schist bodies from New England southward through Virginia and into Alabama and Georgia. Staurolite is also reported to have been found in Montana. Colors range from light brown to dark brownish-black, and sometimes even a deep red. Staurolite has the habit of forming cross-like twinned crystals; 60° twins are most common; and exceptional 90° crosses are the most prized. Also found are staurolite rosettas, unusual specimens found when three crystals grow together to form a common center.

**Rates:** Admission is free. Dig a bucket and sluice of native gem ore from the pile: $10.00. Buckets of enriched native gem ore range from $10.00–$100.00. A $50.00 bucket includes cutting one stone, a $100.00 bucket includes cutting 2 stones. The flume is partially covered.

**Other services available:** Cutting and mounting of gems, picnic area, gift shop, snacks.

**Directions:** The mine is located 3.3 miles on Harpers (Old Beaver Pond) Road from Route 40. Route 40 can be reached by taking Exit 42 from Highway 85.

**STUART /** *Native ▪ Easy to Moderate*

## Hunt for Fairy Stones  *T*

*The following gems or minerals may be found:*

▪ **Staurolite crystals, also called fairy stones**

Fairy Stone State Park
967 Fairystone Lake Drive
Stuart, VA 24171
Phone: (276) 930-2424
Fax: (276) 930-1136
E-mail: fairystone@dcr.virginia.gov
www.dcr.virginia.gov/state_parks/fai.shtml

**Open:** All year, daylight hours.
**Info:** No digging equipment is permitted. Bring a small container for your finds.
**Admission:** Free. Can take a small number of crystals for personal use; no commercial digging is permitted.
**Other services available:** Picnic area; hiking trails; restrooms; boat dock and rentals; swimming Memorial Day to Labor Day (weather permitting).

State Park campground and cabins are available for use; to get more information or make a reservation, call (800) 933-7275.
**Directions:** Park is located off Highway 57 between Stuart and Bassett. To get to the fairy stone area, leave the park

(Route 346) and turn left onto Route 57. Travel approximately 3 miles to the first service station (Haynes 57) on the left. The land on the left of the station is park property, and fairy stones may be hunted in that area.

## VIRGINIA CITY / *Enriched · Easy*

### Find Your Own Gems and Gold *T*

*The following gems or minerals may be found:*

▪Quartz, ruby, sapphire, garnet, gold

Virginia City Gem Mine and Museum
Virginia City, LLC
P.O. Box 542
Wytheville, VA 24382
Phone: (276) 223-1873
E-mail: info@vacity.com
www.vacity.com

**Open:** April 15–October 31, 10:00 A.M.–6:00 P.M., 7 days/week.
**Info:** Pan for gems at two covered sluices. Guides are available to show you how to pan, and to help you identify the stones that you find. Gold panning may also be done.
**Rates:** Buckets of ore cost between $10.00 (medium) and $25.00 (large), $50 (deluxe), $100 (rockhound bonanza). Group discounts are available.
**Directions:** On Highway 52, 10 miles north of Wytheville.

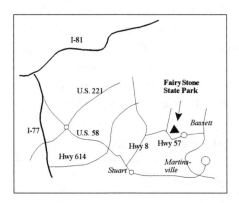

## The Legend of Fairy Stones

It is said that long, long, ago fairies inhabited a certain quiet and remote region in the foothills of the Blue Ridge Mountains. The fairies roamed freely and enjoyed the beauty and serenity of that enchanted place.

One day they were playing in a sunny glade when an elfin messenger arrived from a city far, far away bearing the sad news of the death of Christ. When the fairies heard the terrible details of the crucifixion, they wept. As

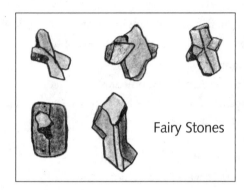

Fairy Stones

their tears fell to the earth, they crystallized into little stone crosses. Though the fairies are no longer to be found there, the fairy stones remain in that enchanted spot as mementos of that day. *(Information courtesy of Fairy Stone State Park)*

## SECTION 2: Museums and Mine Tours

### BIG STONE GAP

## Museum 🏛

Harry W. Meador, Jr., Coal Museum
East Third and Shawnee Avenue
Big Stone Gap, VA 24219
Phone: (276) 523-9209

**Open:** Wednesday–Saturday 10:00 A.M.–5:00 P.M., Sunday 1:00–5:00 P.M.

**Info:** Displays in the museum include a collection of photographs, mining equipment and tools, office equipment, and coal company items.

**Admission:** Free

**Directions:** The museum is located in the building that once served as the library and study of John Fox, Jr., author of *The Trail of the Lonesome Dove* and other folk tales, at the intersection of East Third and Shawnee Avenues.

### BLACKSBURG

## Museum 🏛

Virginia Tech Geosciences Museum
Department of Geosciences

2062 Derring Hall
Virginia Tech
Blacksburg, VA 24061
Phone: (540) 231-6894
www.outreach.geog.vt.edu/museum/

**Open:** 8:00 a.m.–4:00 p.m. Monday–Friday.

**Info:** The museum features gemstones, a seismograph, the largest display of state minerals in Virginia, and area mining history exhibits.

**Admission:** Call for prices.

**Directions:** Located in the center section on the second floor of Derring Hall —Virginia Polytechnic Institute and State University, Blacksburg, VA.

## GOLDVEIN

## Mining Camp

Monroe Park
P.O. Box 219
14421 Gold Dust Parkway
Goldvein, VA 22720
Phone: (540) 752-5330
Fax: (540) 752-5325
E-mail: southparks@fauquiercounty.gov
www.goldvein.com

**Open:** Tuesday, Wednesday, Friday, and Saturday, 9:00 A.M.–5:00 P.M.; closed major holidays.

**Info:** At one time, there were 18 gold mines in Fauquier County. The park presents the history of the search for gold in

Virginia, shows everyday life in a gold camp, and demonstrates gold panning. Development of the park is ongoing.

**Admission:** Museum is free. Call ahead for gold panning costs.

**Directions:** On U.S. 17, approximately 20 miles north from I-95, near Pine View, VA.

## HARRISONBURG

## Museum 🏛

The James Madison University Mineral Museum
Memorial Hall, Room 6139
James Madison University
Curator: Dr. Lance E. Kearns
Harrisonburg, VA 22807
Phone: (540) 568-6421
Fax: (540) 568-8058
E-mail: kearnsle@jmu.edu
http://csm.jmu.edu/minerals/

**Open:** Monday–Friday, 8:00 A.M.–4:30 P.M. when the university is in session.

**Info:** Has approximately 500 minerals and gems from around the world, including specialty collections of Virginia minerals; Elmwood, TN; and Franklin Sterling Hill fluorescent display.

**Admission:** Free.

**Directions:** Memorial Hall is located at the intersection of Route 42 and Contrell Avenue. Enter building at entrance on the south side.

## MARTINSVILLE

## Museum

Stone Cross Mountain Museum
Don Hopkins
17529 A.L. Philpot Highway
Martinsville, VA 24112
Phone: (276) 957-4873 (after 6:00 P.M.)
www.stonecrossmountain.com/
museum.htm

**Open:** May 1–December 31, Monday, Tuesday, and Thursday–Saturday, 10:00 A.M.–4:00 P.M.; closed Wednesday and Sunday. By appointment only, January 1–April 30.
**Info:** A museum of "Fairy Crosses," specimens of staurolite, a mineral often found as twinned crystals, with the twins at an angle to each other. The museum has specimens from Virginia, North Carolina, Georgia, New Mexico, Russia, and Australia.
**Admission:** Adults $4.00, children $2.00.
**Directions:** On Highway 58, west two miles from Highway 220 bypass.

## MARTINSVILLE

## Museum

Virginia Museum of Natural History
21 Sterling Avenue
Martinsville, VA 24112
Phone: (276) 634-4141
Fax: (276) 634-4199
www.vmnh.net

**Open:** All year; closed major holidays.

Monday–Saturday 9:00 A.M.–5:30 P.M., Sunday noon–3:00 P.M.
**Info:** The museum has a large collection of rocks and minerals, and exhibits on mining. The Rock Hall of Fame presents the rocks of Virginia and the world and discusses their uses in daily life.
**Admission:** Voluntary contribution. Recommended amounts: Adults $9.00/person per day, seniors $7.00, children (13–18) $5.00, children (3–12) $2.00, children 2 and under free.
**Directions:** The museum is located at the corner of U.S. 58 and U.S. 220 in Martinsville.

## POCAHONTAS

## Mine Tour

Pocahontas Exhibition Coal Mine and Museum
Town of Pocahontas
300 Centre Street
P.O. Box 128
Pocahontas, VA 24635-0128
Phone: (276) 945-2134 or 945-9522
Fax: (276) 945-9904
E-mail: pocahontasva@comcast.com
http://wvweb.com/www/pocahontas_mine/

**Open:** April–September, Monday–Saturday, 10:00 A.M.–5:00 P.M.; Sunday, 1:00 P.M–5:00 P.M.
**Info:** The mine was originally opened as an exhibition mine in 1938, reportedly the first in the country. The mine is in a

13-foot high coal seam.

**Admission:** Mine—adult $7.00, child 6–12 $4.50, under 6 free. Museum—free.

**Directions:** Call or e-mail for directions.

## RICHMOND

## Museum 🏛

University of Richmond Museums
Lora Robins Gallery of Design by Nature
Richmond, VA 23173
Phone: (804) 289-8276
Fax: (804) 287-1894
E-mail: museums@richmond.edu

**Open:** When school is in session, Tuesday–Friday, 11:00 A.M.–5:00 P.M.; Saturday–Sunday, 1:00 P.M.–5:00 P.M.

**Info:** Displays include a wide variety of Virginia minerals, amethyst geode, and a 2,400-carat blue topaz.

**Admission:** Free.

**Directions:** From I-64, take exit 183/Glenside Drive south to Three Chopt Road. Turn left onto Three Chopt for one mile, and turn right onto Boatwright Drive, to the main entrance to the University. At the main entrance, turn left onto Campus Drive, and after a ¼ mile, turn right onto Gateway Road, then turn right onto Richmond Way. Take Richmond Way down the hill, and the museum is the last building on the left before the lakefront turn, across from Thomas Hall. Limited parking is available on Richmond Way.

# SECTION 3: Special Events and Tourist Information

## TOURIST INFORMATION

## State Tourist Agency

Virginia Tourism Corp.
901 East Byrd Street
Richmond, VA 23219
Phone: (800) 847-4882
www.VIRGINIA.org

# WEST VIRGINIA

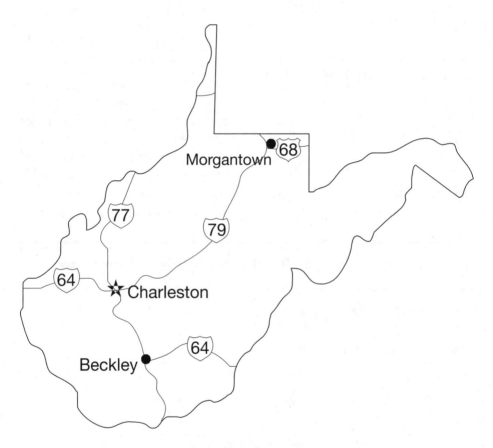

**State Gemstone:** Silicified Mississippian Limestone
(*Lithostrotionella*)

# SECTION 1: Fee Dig Sites and Guide Services

No information available.

# SECTION 2: Museums and Mine Tours

## BECKLEY

### Mine Tour

The Beckley Exhibition Coal Mine
New River Park
P.O. Box 2514
Beckley, WV 25801
Phone: (304) 256-1747
Fax: (304) 256-1798
www.beckleymine.com

**Open:** The Exhibition Mine is closed for renovations, and is scheduled to reopen in April, 2008. Call or check the website to be sure the mine has opened. When open, tours run from April 1–November 1, 10:00 A.M.–5:30 P.M.

**Info:** Listed on the National Register of Historical sites, and now part of New River Park, is the restored mine operated by the Phillips family in the late 1800s. Visitors ride a "man trip" car guided through the mine by veteran miners for an authentic view of low seam coal mining from its earliest manual stages to modern mechanized operation. (Bring a jacket—the temperature in the mine is always 58°.)

Visit a company house and a super's (mine superintendent's) house, both of which have been moved to the park and restored. The super's house also has reproductions of the company doctor's offices, the company post office, and the company barbershop. The museum features displays of mining photographs and artifacts from the mining era.

**Admission:** Adults $20.00, seniors 55+ $15.00, children 4–12 $12.00, children under 4 free.

**Other services available:** The craft and souvenir shop is open from 10:00 A.M.–6:00 P.M. A 17-site campground at the park provides full hookups.

**Directions:** From I-77 take exit 44. Turn east on Route 3 (Harper Road). Go 1½ miles to Ewart Avenue, then make a left by Sambino's Pizza. Drive 1 mile to New River Park entrance.

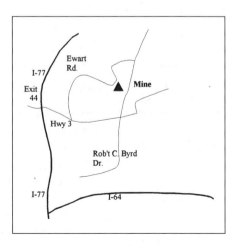

## CHARLESTON

### Museum

The Avampato Discovery Museum at the Clay Center
300 Leon Sullivan Way
Charleston, WV 25301
Phone: (304) 561-3575
Fax: (304) 347-2313
E-mail:
info@avampatodiscoverymuseum.org
www.avampatodiscoverymuseum.org

**Open:** All year, Wednesday–Saturday, 10:00 A.M.–5:00 P.M.; Thursday, 10:00 A.M.–7:00 P.M.; Sunday, noon–5:00 P.M., July–August. No Thursday evening sessions.

**Info:** Earth City provides a variety of exhibits which show the story behind West Virginia's geology.

**Admission:** Adults $12.50, or $6.50 for galleries only, seniors and children $10.00, or $5.00 galleries only.

**Directions:** Take Exit 100 on I-64 to Leon Way; quickly get into the left lane for parking.

## MORGANTOWN

### Museum / Visiting Geologist Program

Museum of Geology and Natural History
West Virginia Geological and Economic Survey
Mont Chateau Research Center
1 Mont Chateau Road
Morgantown, WV 26508-8079
Phone: (800) 984-3656,
(800-wv-geology), or (304) 594-2331
Fax: (304) 594-2575
www.wvgs.wvnet

**Open:** Monday–Friday, 8:00 A.M.–5:00 P.M.

**Info:** Small display of geologic specimens and geologic processes relating to West Virginia. Repository for specimens, books, maps, manuscripts, and artifacts. The survey also has a geology outreach program in which survey geologists present lectures at different West Virginia state parks in the evening, and then conduct a guided geologic walk in the park the next morning. Check the WVGES website for a schedule.

**Admission:** Free.

**Directions:** Call for directions.

---

## SECTION 3: Special Events and Tourist Information

### TOURIST INFORMATION

### State Tourist Agency

West Virginia Travel
Phone: (800) 225-5982
www.westvirginia.com

# Index by State

## ALABAMA

### Fee Dig Mines and Guide Services
**Cragford**    Alabama Gold Camp—Pan or prospect for gold

### Museums and Mine Tours
**Aldrich**    Aldrich Coal Mine Museum—Artifacts and simulated coal mine

**Anniston**    Anniston Museum of Natural History—Gemstones, meteorite, artificial indoor cave

**Dora**    Alabama Mining Museum—Focus on coal mining

**McCalla**    Tannehill Ironworks Historical State Park—Geology relevant to the iron industry

**Tuscaloosa**    Alabama Museum of Natural History—Minerals, meteorite

## ALASKA

### Fee Dig Mines and Guide Services
**Anchorage**    Alaska DNR—Pan, prospect, excavate, limited suction dredging for gold

**Chicken**    Chicken Gold Camp and Outpost—Pan or dig for gold

**Chugach National Forest**    Chugach National Forest—Pan for gold

**Copper Center**    Wrangell-St. Elias National Park and Preserve—Pan for gold, hunt for rocks and minerals (see exceptions in listing)

**Fairbanks**    El Dorado Gold Mine—Gold panning
    Faith Creek Camp—Pan, sluice, dredge for gold
    Gold Dredge No. 8—Gold panning

**Girdwood**    Crow Creek Mine—Pan, dredge, or use metal detectors for gold

**Juneau**    Alaska Gastineau Mill and Gold Mine—Pan or dig for gold or garnets

**McGrath**    Moore Creek Mining, LLC—Camp and prospect or dredge for gold

**Nome**    Nome Beaches—Pan for gold

**Skagway**    Klondike Gold Dredge Tours—Pan for gold
    Liarsville Gold Rush Trail Camp and Salmon Bake—Pan for gold

| Talkeetna | Clark/Wiltz Mining—Camp and prospect (with metal detectors) for gold |

## Museums and Mine Tours

| Chicken | The Chicken Gold Camp & Outpost—Gold dredge tour |
| Fairbanks | El Dorado Gold Mine—Gold mine tour and gold nugget display |
| | Gold Dredge No. 8—Gold dredge tour |
| | University of Alaska Museum—Minerals and gems from Alaska, Arctic Canada, and the Pacific Rim; includes gold and meteorites |
| Juneau | Alaska Gastineau Mill and Gold Mine—Mine tour |
| | Juneau-Douglas City Museum—History of gold mining |
| | Last Chance Mining Museum—Hard-rock gold mining museum |
| Nome | The Carrie N. McLain Memorial Museum—History of area gold mining |
| Skagway | Klondike Gold Dredge Tour—Gold dredge tour |
| | Liarsville Gold Rush Trail and Salmon Bake—Tour of gold rush camp |
| | Klondike Gold Rush National Historic Park—History of area gold mining |
| Wasilla | Independence Mine State Historical Park—Guided mine tour |

## ARIZONA

### Fee Dig Mines and Guide Services

| Apache Jct. | Apache Trail Tours—Gold panning jeep tours |
| Glendale | William Gardner III—Guide service; collect aragonite, fluorite, chrysocolla, quartz, galena, amethyst, fluorescent minerals, smithsonite, wulfenite (in a variety of forms), willemite, calcite, barite |
| Goldfield | Goldfield Ghost Town, Scenic Railroad, and Mine Tours—Gold panning |
| Prescott | Lynx Creek Mineral Withdrawal Area, Prescott National Forest—Pan for gold |
| Safford | Black Hills Rockhound Area—Dig for fire agates |
| | Round Hill Rockhound Area—Search for fire agates, chalcedony, small geodes. |
| Tempe | Fat Jack Mine—Collect amethyst scepters, quartz, garnet, tourmaline, limonite |
| Wickenburg | Robson's Mining World—Pan for gold (open for special events only) |

### Museums and Mine Tours

| Apache Jct. | Superstition Mountain Museum—Geology, minerals, and mining |
| Bisbee | Bisbee Mining and Historical Museum—Displays on local mining |
| | Queen Mine Tour—Tour an underground copper mine |
| Flagstaff | Meteor Crater Enterprises, Inc.—View a meteor crater, museum of astrogeology |

| | Museum of Northern Arizona—History of Colorado Plateau, geologic models, mineral specimens |
|---|---|
| **Goldfield** | Goldfield Ghost Town, Scenic Railroad, and Mine Tours—Gold mine tour, museum, ghost town |
| **Morenci** | Phelps Dodge Morenci Copper Mine—Tour an open-pit mine |
| **Phoenix** | Arizona Mining and Mineral Museum—3,000 minerals on exhibit including gemstones, lapidary arts, minerals from Arizona copper mines, meteorite, rock from the moon, geodes, fluorescent mineral display |
| **Quartzsite** | Quartzsite Historical Society—Displays of mining equipment |
| **Sahuarita** | ASARCO Mineral Discovery Center—Geology, mining, minerals, and tour of open-pit mine |
| **Sun City** | The Mineral Museum—3,000 rocks and minerals from the U.S. and the world, with emphasis on minerals from Arizona. Over 150 fluorescent rocks and minerals, most from Franklin and Sterling Hill, NJ |
| **Tempe** | Robert S. Dietz Museum of Geology—Mineral displays, seismograph |
| **Tombstone** | Good Enough Mine—Gold mine tour |
| **Tucson** | Arizona-Sonora Desert Museum—Mineral collection from Sonora desert region |
| | Flandreau: University of Arizona Science Center—2,100 of 15,000 minerals on display; Arizona minerals, meteorites, fluorescents, borate minerals |
| **Wickenburg** | Robson's Mining World—Tour old gold mining village (special events only) |
| | Vulture Gold Mine—Self-guided mine tour |

Annual Events

| | |
|---|---|
| **Quartzsite** | Gem and Mineral Shows—Mid-January–mid-February |
| **Scottsdale** | Minerals of Arizona—Symposium one day in March/April |
| **Tucson** | Gem and Mineral Shows—End of January through mid-February |

## ARKANSAS

Fee Dig Mines and Guide Services

| | |
|---|---|
| **Jessieville** | Jim Coleman Crystal Mines and Rock Shop—Dig for quartz crystals |
| | Ron Coleman Mining, Inc.—Dig for quartz crystals |
| | Ouachita National Forest, Crystal Mt. Quartz Collecting Site—Collect quartz crystals on the ground, no digging permitted |
| **Mt. Ida** | The Crystal Seen Trading Co.—Dig quartz crystals |
| | Fiddler's Ridge Rock Shop and Crystal Mines—Dig for quartz crystals |
| | Ouachita National Forest, Crystal Vista Quartz Collecting Site—Collect quartz crystals on the ground, no digging permitted |
| | Sonny Stanley's Crystal Mine—Dig for quartz crystals |
| | Starfire Crystal Mine—Dig for quartz crystals |

|               | Wegner Crystal Mine—Dig, sluice, or pick through tailings for quartz crystals |
|---------------|---|
| **Murfreesboro** | Crater of Diamonds State Park—Dig and screen for diamonds, amethyst, agates, barite, calcite, jasper, quartz, other gems |
| **Pencil Bluff** | Arrowhead Crystal Mine—Dig for quartz crystals |
| **Story** | Gee and Dee Crystal—Dig for quartz crystals |
|  | Sweet Surrender Crystal Mine—Dig for quartz crystals |

## Museum and Mine Tours

| **Fayetteville** | The University Museum—Quartz and other Arkansas minerals |
|---------------|---|
| **Little Rock** | Geology Learning Center—Arkansas gems, minerals, fossil fuels |
| **Mt. Ida** | Heritage House Museum of Montgomery County—Quartz and Mineral Exhibits |
| **State University** | ASU Museum—Minerals, many from Arkansas |

## Annual Events

| **Mt. Ida** | Quartz Crystal Festival and World Championship Dig—Second weekend in October |
|---------------|---|

## CALIFORNIA

### Fee Dig Mines and Guide Services

| **Coalinga** | Benitoite Gem Mine—Hunt for benitoite and other gems and minerals |
|---------------|---|
| **Coloma** | Marshall Gold Discovery State Historic Park—Gold panning |
| **Columbia** | Hidden Treasures Gold Mine Tours—Pan for gold and garnets |
| **Jackson** | Kennedy Gold Mine—Gold panning |
| **Jamestown** | Gold Prospecting Adventures, LLC—Sluice, pan, and prospect with metal detectors for gold |
| **Lucerne** | Lake County Visitors Information Center—Rockhounding for Lake County "diamonds" or "moon tears" |
| **Mariposa** | Little Valley Inn at the Creek—Gold panning |
| **Mesa Grande** | Himalayan Tourmaline Mine, High Desert Gems and Minerals—Look for California tourmaline in mine tailings |
| **Nevada City** | Malakoff Diggins State Historical Park—Gold panning |
| **Pala** | Oceanview Mine—Hunt for tourmaline (pink, green, bicolor), smoky crystals, garnets, book mica, smoky crystals, cleavelandite, kunzite, morganite, gossanite (clear beryl), purple lepidolite, muscovite mica, aquamarine |
| **Pine Grove** | Roaring Camp Mining Co.—Pan for gold, rockhounding for quartz crystals, jade, jasper, and river rubies |

| Placerville | Hangtown's Gold Bug Park and Mine—Learn gold panning |

**Museums and Mine Tours**

| Allegany | Underground Gold Miners Tours and Museum—Tour an active gold mine |
| Angels Camp | Angels Camp Museum and Carriage House—Museum features rocks and minerals, gold stamping mill, mining equipment |
| Avalon | Catalina Island Museum Society, Inc.—Exhibits on mining on Catalina Island |
| Boron | Borax Visitors Center—Story of borax |
| | Boron Twenty Mule Team Museum—History of area borate mining |
| Coloma | Marshall Gold Discovery State Historic Park—Gold mining exhibit/museum |
| Columbia | Hidden Treasure Gold Mine—Tour of active gold mine |
| Death Valley | Furnace Creek Borax Museum—Rocks and minerals, featuring borax minerals |
| El Cajon | Heritage of the Americas Museum—Rocks, minerals, and meteorites |
| Fallbrook | Fallbrook Gem & Mineral Society Museum—Features of minerals from San Diego County |
| Grass Valley | Empire Mine State Historic Park—Hard-rock gold mine |
| Independence | Eastern California Museum—Regional gem and mineral collection |
| Jackson | Amador County Museum—Collection of mineral spheres from California, Utah, and Nevada |
| | Kennedy Gold Mine Tours—Surface tour of gold mine |
| Julian | Eagle and High Peak Gold Mine Tours—Hard-rock gold mine tour |
| | Julian Pioneer Museum—Rock and mineral display, gold mining tools and equipment displays |
| Lakeport | Historic Courthouse Museum—Minerals and gems found in Lake County |
| Los Angeles | Natural History Museum of Los Angeles County—52,000 specimens, minerals of California, native gold, gems, and minerals |
| Mariposa | California State Mining and Mineral Museum—Gold from California, gems and minerals from around the world |
| Needles | Needles Regional Museum—Collection of Needles blue agate, Colorado River pebble terrace stones |
| Nevada City | Malakoff Diggins Park Association—History of hydraulic gold mining |
| Pacific Grove | Pacific Grove Museum of Natural History—Monterey County rocks, fluorescent minerals |

| Paso Robles | El Paso des Robles Area Pioneer Museum—Display of local minerals |
| Placerville | Hangtown's Gold Bug Park and Mine—Tour hard-rock gold mine |
| Quincy | Plumas County Museum—Exhibits on gold and copper mining in Plumas County |
| Rancho Palos Verdes | Point Vicente Interpretive Center—Exhibits on area geology |
| Red Bluff | Gaumer's Mineral and Mining Museum—Minerals from around the world |
| Redlands | San Bernardino County Museum—45,000 rocks, minerals, and gems |
| Ridgecrest | Maturango Museum—Small but well-rounded regional gem and mineral collection |
| Riverside | Jurupa Mountains Cultural Center—Crestmore minerals display, minerals from around the world on display and for sale, family education programs |
| | World Museum of Natural History—Fluorescent minerals, meteorites, tektites, over 1,300 mineral spheres |
| San Diego | San Diego Natural History Museum—26,000 mineral specimens, includes minerals found in San Diego County mines |
| Santa Barbara | Department of Earth Sciences, UCSB—Gem and mineral collection, minerals and their tectonic settings |
| Shoshone | Shoshone Museum—Rock collection reflecting the geology of the area |
| Sierra City | Kentucky Mine and Museum—Exhibits of local gold and mercury mining |
| Sonora | Tuolomne County Museum—Gold from local mines |
| Vallecito | Sutters Gold Mine—Hard-rock gold mine tour |
| Yermo | Calico Ghost Town—Explore a silver mine |
| Yreka | Siskiyou County Courthouse—Gold exhibit |
| Yucca Valley | Hi-Desert Nature Museum—Rock and mineral collection, includes fluorescent minerals |

Annual Events

| Boron | Rock Bonanza—Weekend before Easter |
| Coloma | Marshall Gold Discovery State Historic Park: Gold Rush Live—End of September–beginning of October |

## COLORADO

Fee Dig Mines and Guide Services

| Breckenridge | Country Boy Mine—Pan for gold |

| Granite | Gold Basin Mine—Prospect for gold |
| **Idaho Springs** | Argo Gold Mill—Pan for gold and gemstones |
| | Phoenix Mine—Pan for gold |
| **Ouray** | Bachelor-Syracuse Mine Tour—Learn to pan for gold |
| **Silverton** | Old Hundred Gold Mine Tours, Inc.—Pan for gold |

## Museums and Mine Tours

| **Breckenridge** | Country Boy Mine—Hard-rock gold mine tour |
| **Central City** | Gilpin History Museum—Displays of local minerals |
| **Colorado Springs** | Western Museum of Mining and Industry—Displays of mining and demonstrations on gold panning |
| **Creede** | Creede Underground Mining Museum—Displays of rocks, minerals, and mining equipment |
| **Cripple Creek** | Cripple Creek District Museum—Mineral displays |
| | Molly Kathleen Gold Mine—Gold mine tour |
| **Denver** | Denver Museum of Nature and Science—2,000 specimens; includes gold, topaz, aquamarine, amazonite, and other Colorado minerals |
| **Georgetown** | Lebanon Silver Mine—Ride a narrow-gauge train, then take a walking tour of the silver mine |
| **Golden** | Geology Museum, Colorado School of Mines—50,000 specimens, minerals from Colorado and from around the world, gemstones and precious metals, cave exhibit |
| **Idaho Springs** | Argo Gold Mill—Historic gold mill, mining museum, Double Eagle Gold Mine |
| | Edgar Experimental Mine—Tour an experimental mine (silver, gold, lead, copper) |
| | Phoenix Mine—See a working underground hard-rock mine (gold, silver) |
| **Lake City** | Hard Tack Mine—Gold mine tour |
| **Lakewood** | Hidee Gold Mine—Gold mine tour and gold ore sample |
| **Leadville** | Matchless Mine—Tour a symbol of the financial hazards of silver mining. |
| | National Mining Hall of Fame and Museum—Story of the American mining industry from coal to gold |
| **Ouray** | Bachelor-Syracuse Mine—Underground tour of gold and silver mine |
| | Ouray County Historical Society—Mineral and mining displays |
| **Salida** | Lost Mine Tour—Tour a closed manganese mine |
| **Silverton** | Mayflower Gold Mill—Tour a gold mill |
| | Old Hundred Gold Mine Tour, Inc.—Gold mine tour |

San Juan County Historical Society Museum—Minerals and gems from the Silverton area

**Victor**　　　Mine View—View of Colorado's largest open-pit gold mine

## CONNECTICUT

### Fee Dig Mines and Guide Services

**Roxbury**　　　Green's Farm Garnet Mine—Search for garnets

### Museums and Mine Tours

**East Granby**　Old New-Gate Prison and Copper Mine—Tour an old copper mine
**Greenwich**　　Bruce Museum of Arts and Sciences—Exhibits of minerals and rocks
**Kent**　　　　Museum of Mining and Mineral Science—Local minerals
**New Haven**　Peabody Museum of Natural History, Yale University—Minerals of New England and the world

## DELAWARE

### Fee Dig Mines and Guide Services

**Wilmington**　Woodlawn Quarry—Look through tailing piles for feldspar, quartz, mica, garnet, beryl

### Museums and Mine Tours

**Newark**　　　Iron Hill Museum—Natural history of Delaware, rock and mineral collections

University of Delaware, Mineralogical Museum—5,000 specimens (1,000 on display), crystals, gems, minerals

## DISTRICT OF COLUMBIA

### Fee Dig Mines and Guide Services

None

### Museums and Mine Tours

Smithsonian Institution, National Museum of Natural History—Gems and minerals (over 375,000 specimens and a research collection)

## FLORIDA

### Fee Dig Mines and Guide Services

**Ft. Drum**　　Ft. Drum Crystal Mine—Collect calcite encrusted fossil shells, micropyrite, irridescent marcosite

## Museums and Mine Tours

| | |
|---|---|
| **Deland** | Gillespie Museum, Stetson University—Minerals, gemstones, faceting, replica mine and cave |
| **Mulberry** | Mulberry Phosphate Museum—Exhibits on the phosphate industry |
| **Tampa** | Ed and Bernadette Marcin Museum, University of Florida—Minerals and gemstones, mainly from Florida and the western U.S. |

## GEORGIA

### Fee Dig Mines and Guide Services

| | |
|---|---|
| **Cleveland** | Gold'n Gem Grubbin—Dig and pan for gold, sapphires, rubies, emeralds, amethyst, topaz |
| **Dahlonega** | Consolidated Gold Mine—Gold panning |
| | Crisson Gold Mine—Pan gold sands or enriched gemstone ore |
| **Gainesville** | Chattahoochee-Oconee National Forest—Gold panning, rockhounding (restrictions apply) |
| **LaGrange** | Hogg Mine, Dixie Euhedrals—Collect star rose quartz, aquamarine, beryl (rare), black tourmaline |
| | LaGrange Clear Quartz Crystals, Dixie Euhedrals—Collect clear quartz crystals |
| **Lincolnton** | Graves Mountain—Search for audite, lazulite, pyrophyllite, kyanite, hematite, pyrite, ilmenite, muscovite, fuchsite, barite, sulfur, blue quartz, quartz crystals, microcrystals (such as woodhouseite), variscite, strengite, phosphosiderite, cacoxenite, crandallite (collecting allowed on special dates only) |

### Museums and Mine Tours

| | |
|---|---|
| **Atlanta** | Fernbank Museum of Natural History—Joachim Gem Collection containing 400 cut and polished gemstones |
| | Fernbank Science Center—Gems, carved opals, meteorites |
| **Cartersville** | Tellus—2,000 specimens, gems and minerals from the state, simulated cave |
| **Dahlonega** | Consolidated Gold Mine—Mine tour |
| | Dahlonega Courthouse Gold Museum—Tells the story of the Georgia gold rush |
| **Elberton** | Elberton Granite Museum & Exhibit—Granite quarry and products |
| **Macon** | Museum of Arts and Sciences—Display of gems and minerals |
| **Statesboro** | Georgia Southern Museum—Collection of rocks and minerals from Georgia's Highlands, Piedmont, and Coastal regions |
| **Tallapoosa** | West Georgia Museum of Tallapoosa—Small collection of local minerals |

## Annual Events

**Dahlonega**    Gold Rush Days—Third weekend in October
World Open Gold Panning Championship—Third Saturday of April
**Jasper**    Pickens County Marble Festival—First weekend in October

## HAWAII

### Fee Dig Mines and Guide Services
None

### Museums and Mine Tours

**Hawaii National Park**    Thomas A. Jaggar Museum—Museum on vulcanology and seismology, tour of volcano
**Hilo**    Lyman House Memorial Museum—Rocks, minerals, gems

## IDAHO

### Fee Dig Mines and Guide Services

**Moscow**    3-D's Panhandle Gems and Garnet Queen Mine—Guide service, star garnet screening
**Spencer**    Spencer Opal Mine—Pick through a stockpile for fire opal, prearranged digging at the mine on specified dates
**St. Maries**    Emerald Creek Garnet Area—Screen for star garnets

### Museums and Mine Tours

**Boise**    Museum of Mining and Geology—Exhibits on mining and geology
**Caldwell**    The Glen L. and Ruth M. Evans Gem and Mineral Collection, Orma J. Smith Museum of Natural History—Extensive collection of minerals, agate, jasper, other gemstones, 2,000 cabochons
**Kellogg**    Crystal Gold Mine—Mine tour
Staff House Museum—Rocks, minerals, mining equipment
**Pocatello**    Idaho Museum of Natural History—Displays of specimens from Idaho and the intermountain west
**Wallace**    Sierra Silver Mine Tour—Mine tour
Wallace District Mining Museum—Story of mining in northern Idaho

## ILLINOIS

### Fee Dig Mines and Guide Services

**Hamilton**    Jacobs Geodes—Hunt for geodes containing calcite, barite, quartz, kaolinite

| Roisclaire | American Fluorite Museum—Dig for fluorite in mine ore |

**Museums and Mine Tours**

| Carbondale | University Museum—Displays on geologic history |
| Chicago | The Field Museum—92-year-old exhibit |
| | Museum of Science and Industry—Simulated coal mine |
| Elmhurst | Lizzadro Museum of Lapidary Art—1,300 pieces of cut and polished gems, fluorescent rocks, a birthstone display |
| Rockford | Burpee Museum of Natural History—Displays of rocks, minerals, and gems |
| Rock Island | Augustana Fryxell Geology Museum—Rock and mineral museum |
| Rosiclare | The American Fluorite Museum—Story of fluorospar industry |
| Shirley | The Funk Gem and Mineral Museum—Gem and mineral collection |
| Springfield | Illinois State Museum—Gems and minerals, Illinois specimens, birthstones, fluorescent minerals, copper |

## INDIANA

**Fee Dig Mines and Guide Services**

| Knightstown | Yogi Bear's Jellystone Park Camping Resort—Midwestern gold prospecting |

**Museums and Mine Tours**

| Bedford | Land of Limestone Exhibition—History of Indiana limestone industry |
| | Lawrence County Museum of History—Exhibit on limestone, geological specimens from Lawrence County. |
| Fort Wayne | Indiana Purdue University at Fort Wayne—Hallway displays of minerals, meteorites, and rocks |
| Indianapolis | Indiana State Museum—Indiana and regional minerals |
| Richmond | Joseph Moore Museum of Natural History, Earlham College—Geology exhibit from local Ordovician limestone |

## IOWA

**Fee Dig Mines and Guide Services**

*(See annual event—Rocktober Geode Fest)*

**Museums and Mine Tours**

| Danville | Geode State Park—Display of geodes |
| Iowa City | University of Iowa—Displays on state geology |
| Sioux City | Sioux City Public Museum—Mineralogy exhibit |

| Waterloo | Grout Museum of History and Science—Displays of rocks and minerals |
| West Bend | Grotto of the Redemption—Grotto made of precious stones and gems |
| Winterset | Madison County Historical Society—Rock and mineral collection |

### Annual Events
| Keokuk | Rocktober Geode Fest—Three-day weekend in early October; field trips for geodes |

## KANSAS

### Fee Dig Mines and Guide Services
None

### Museums and Mine Tours
| Ashland | Pioneer Krier Museum—Mineral exhibit |
| Emporium | Johnston Geology Museum—Tri-state mining display, geological specimens from Kansas |
| Galena | Galena Mining and Historical Museum—Focus on local lead mining and smelting industry |
| Greensburg | Pallasite Meteorite at the Big Well Museum—Meteorite strike site and 1,000-pound meteorite |
| Hays | Sternberg Museum of Natural History—Displays of gems and minerals |
| Hutchinson | Kansas Underground Salt Museum and Mine Tour—Explains the underground mining of rock salt |
| McPherson | McPherson Museum—Meteorites |

## KENTUCKY

### Fee Dig Mines and Guide Services
| Marion | The Ben E. Clement Mineral Museum—Fluorite and fluorescent mineral collecting |

### Museums and Mine Tours
| Benham | Kentucky Coal Mine Museum—Displays on coal mining and formation of coal |
| Covington | Behringer-Crawford Museum—Display of gems and minerals |
| Danville | JFC Museum—Display of gems and minerals |
| Lexington | Headley-Whitney Museum—Display of gems and minerals |
| Lynch | Lynch Portal #31 Walking Tour—Walking tour of coal mining facilities |
| Marion | The Ben E. Clement Mineral Museum—Display of gems and minerals |
| Olive Hill | Northeastern Kentucky Museum—Displays of gems and minerals |

## LOUISIANA

**Fee Dig Mines and Guide Services**
>                     None

**Museums and Mine Tours**
**Shreveport**    Louisiana State Exhibit Museum—Displays on mining and salt domes

## MAINE

**Fee Dig Mines and Guide Services**
**Auburn**    City of Auburn/Feldspar and Greenlaw Quarries—Hunt for apatite, tourmaline, and quartz

Mt. Apatite Farm/Turner Quarry—Hunt for tourmaline, garnet, graphic granite, clevelandite, autenite, mica, beryl

**Bethel**    Maine Mineralogy Expeditions-Bumpus Quarry—Collect albite, almandine garnet, beryl, rose, and other quartz, black tourmaline, biotite, autunite, zircon

Songo Pond Mine—Collect tourmaline and other Maine gems and minerals

**Poland**    Poland Mining Camp—Collect tourmaline and other Maine gems and minerals

**West Paris**    Perham's of West Paris—Collect tourmaline and other Maine gems and minerals

**Museums and Mine Tours**
**Augusta**    Maine State Museum—Gems and minerals of Maine
**Bethel**    Maine Mineral Museum/Mt. Marin Jeweler's Gallery—Examples of gems from local and worldwide sources, crystal cave for kids
**Caribou**    Nylander Museum—Minerals of Maine
**Presque Isle**    Northern Maine Museum of Science—Display of Maine minerals, fluorescent minerals, Maine slate
**West Paris**    Perham's of West Paris—Maine gems and minerals, model of a feldspar quarry, model of a gem tourmaline pocket, fluorescent minerals

**Annual Events**
**Augusta**    Maine Mineral Symposium—Second full weekend in May
**Poland**    Maine Pegmatite Workshop—Week-long program at the end of May or beginning of June

## MARYLAND

### Fee Dig Mines and Guide Services
     None

### Museums and Mine Tours
**Kensington**    Great Falls Tavern Visitor's Center—Gold Mine Trail tours scheduled periodically

## MASSACHUSETTS

### Fee Dig Mines and Guide Services
     None

### Museums and Mine Tours
**Cambridge**    Harvard Museum of Natural History—Gems, minerals, ores, meteorites
**Springfield**    Springfield Science Museum—Minerals from around the world

## MICHIGAN

### Fee Dig Mines and Guide Services
**Grand Marais**    Woodland Park Campground—Search beaches for agates
**Mohawk**    Delaware Copper Mine—Search for souvenir copper
**Ontonagon**    Caledonia Copper Mine—Collect copper specimens, silver, epidote, calcite, datolite, quartz

### Museums and Mine Tours
**Ann Arbor**    Exhibit Museum of Natural History, University of Michigan—Exhibits of rocks and minerals
**Bloomfield Hills**    Cranbrook Institute of Science—5,000 minerals and crystals from around the world (including hiddenite), gold
**Calumet**    Coppertown, U.S.A.—Exhibits on copper mining
**Caspian**    Iron County Museum and Park—Iron mining complex
**Chelsea**    Gerald E. Eddy Discovery Center—Michigan rocks, minerals, crystals, and mining
**Copper Harbor**    Fort Wilkins Historic State Park—History of copper mining in the area
**Greenland**    Adventure Copper Mine—Tour underground copper mine
**Hancock**    The Quincy Mine Hoist Association—Tour an underground copper mine
**Houghton**    The A. E. Seaman Mineral Museum—Crystal collection, minerals from the Lake Superior copper district

| **Iron Mountain** | Iron Mountain Iron Mine—Iron mine tour |
| **Lake Linden** | Houghton County Historical Museum—Copper mining and refining equipment displays |
| **Mohawk** | Delaware Copper Mine—Mine tour |
| **Mt. Pleasant** | The Museum of Cultural and Natural History, Central Michigan University—Michigan rocks and minerals |
| **Negaunee** | Michigan Iron Industry Museum—Story of Michigan iron industry |
| **Shelby** | Shelby Man-Made Gemstones—Visit a gemstone factory |

**Annual Event**

| **Houghton** | Copper County Mineral Retreat—One week in early August, sponsored by the A. E. Seaman Museum of Michigan Tech. |

## MINNESOTA

**Fee Dig Mines and Guide Services**

None

**Museums and Mine Tours**

| **Calumet** | Hill Annex Mine State Park—Tour an open-pit iron mine |
| **Chisholm** | Ironworld Development Corporation—Iron industry taconite mining tours |
| | The Minnesota Museum of Mining—Indoor and outdoor exhibits |
| | Taconite Mine Tours—Tour of an open-pit iron ore mine |
| **Hibbing** | Mahoning Hull-Rust Mine—Observe an open-pit iron mine |
| **Moose Lake** | Minnesota Agate and Geologic Interpretive Center—Showcases Minnesota's gemstone, the Lake Superior Agate |
| **Pipestone** | Pipestone National Monument—Tour a Native American pipestone quarry |
| **Soudan** | Soudan Underground Mine State Park—Tour an underground iron mine |
| **Virginia** | Mineview in the Sky—View an open-pit iron ore mine |
| | Iron Range Tourism Bureau—Information on mine view sites |

**Annual Event**

| **Moose Lake** | Agate Days—One weekend in July |

## MISSISSIPPI

**Fee Dig Mines and Guide Services**

None

## Museums and Mine Tours
**Starkville**    Dunn-Seiler Museum—Mineral and rock collections

## MISSOURI

### Fee Dig Mines and Guide Services
**Alexandria**    Sheffler Rock Shop—Dig geodes lined with crystals

### Museums and Mine Tours
**Golden**    Golden Pioneer Museum—Large mineral exhibit

**Joplin**    Everett J. Richie Tri-State Mineral Wing—Story of area's lead and zinc mining

**Kansas City**    University of Missouri, Kansas City, Geosciences Museum—Local and regional specimens

**Park Hills**    Missouri Mines State Historic Site—1,100 minerals, ores, and rocks

**Point Lookout**    Ralph Foster Museum, College of the Ozarks—Gemstone spheres and fluorescent minerals

**Rolla**    Mineral Museum, University of Missouri, Rolla—3,500 minerals, ores, and rocks from 92 countries and 47 states

## MONTANA

### Fee Dig Mines and Guide Services
**Alder**    Red Rock Mine and Garnet Gallery—Screen for garnets

**Clinton**    L-Diamond-E Ranch—Sapphire mining pack trips

**Dillon**    Crystal Park Recreational Mineral Collecting Area—Dig for quartz and amethyst crystal

**Hamilton**    Sapphire Studio—Purchase and wash bags of ore for sapphires

**Helena**    Spokane Bar Sapphire Mine and Gold Fever Rock Shop—Dig and screen for sapphires and other gems and minerals

**Libby**    Libby Creek Recreational Gold Panning Area—Pan for gold

**Phillipsburg**    Gem Mountain—Search for sapphires

    Sapphire Country Cabin—Pan or dig for sapphires and gold

    Sapphire Gallery—Wash bags of gravel to look for sapphires

### Museums and Mine Tours
**Butte**    Anselmo Mine Yard—Tour of mining facilities and history of area mining

    The Berkeley Pit—Observation point for closed open-pit copper mine

    Butte-Silver Bow Visitors and Transportation Center—Presents information on area geology and its mining, including local gold and silver mining

| | Mineral Museum, Montana College of Mineral Science and Technology—Gold, fluorescent minerals, and minerals from Butte and MT |
| --- | --- |
| | World Museum of Mining and 1899 Mining Camp—Tour of surface facilities of former silver and zinc mine |
| **Ekalaka** | Carter County Museum—Fluorescent mineral display |
| **Lewistown** | Central Montana Museum—Rocks, minerals, and Yogo sapphires |

## NEBRASKA

### Fee Dig Mines and Guide Services

None

### Museums and Mine Tours

| **Chadron** | Eleanor Barbour Cook Museum of Geoscience—Displays of rocks and minerals |
| --- | --- |
| **Crawford** | Trailside Museum—Displays of western Nebraska geology |
| **Hastings** | Hastings Museum of Natural and Cultural History—Minerals, rocks, fluorescent minerals, and translucent slabs |
| **Lincoln** | University of Nebraska State Museum—Displays of rocks, minerals, and fluorescent rocks |

## NEVADA

### Fee Dig Mines and Guide Services

| **Denio** | Bonanza Opal Mines, Inc.—Dig crystal, white and black fire opal |
| --- | --- |
| | The Opal Queen Mining Company—Dig for crystal, white and black fire opal |
| | Rainbow Ridge Opal Mine—Tailings digging for wood opal |
| | Royal Peacock Opal Mine, Inc.—Dig black and fire opal |
| **Ely** | Garnet Fields Rockhound Area—Hunt for almandine garnets |
| **Reno** | High Desert Gems and Minerals—Gem mine tours |

### Museums and Mine Tours

| **Elko** | Barrick Goldstrike Mines, Inc.—Tour an active gold mine |
| --- | --- |
| **Las Vegas** | Nevada State Museum and Historical Society—Natural history of Nevada |
| **Nelson** | Eldorado Canyon Mine Tours, Inc.—Hard-rock gold mine tour |
| **Reno** | W. M. Keck Earth Science and Mineral Engineering Museum—Collection of minerals and ores |
| **Virginia City** | Chollar Mine—Underground mine tour (gold and silver) |

## NEW HAMPSHIRE

Fee Dig Mines and Guide Services

**Grafton**       Ruggles Mine—Collect up to 150 different minerals
**Laconia**       Deer Hill Mineral Site—Collect amethyst, quartz, and mica
                  Moat Mountain Smokey Quartz Collecting Site—Collect quartz

Museums and Mine Tours

**Contoocook**    The Little Nature Museum—Rocks, minerals, and gems
**Dover**         The Woodman Institute—1,300 specimens including local rocks

## NEW JERSEY

Fee Dig Mines and Guide Services

**Cape May**      Cape May Welcome Center—Hunt for Cape May "diamonds"
**Franklin**      Franklin Mineral Museum and Buckwheat Dump—Tailings diggings
                  for fluorescent minerals and franklinite
**Ogdensburg**    Sterling Hill Mine and Museum—Collect fluorescent minerals

Museum and Mine Tours

**Franklin**      Franklin Mineral Museum—Minerals, rocks, local and worldwide flu-
                  orescent minerals
**Monroe
Township**        Displayworld's Stone Museum—Minerals, hands-on exhibits
**Morristown**    The Morris Museum—Specimens from five continents
**New Brunswick** Rutgers Geology Museum—Specimens from the zinc deposit at
                  Franklin and the zeolite deposits from Paterson, meteorites
**Ogdensburg**    Sterling Hill Mine and Museum—Tour old zinc mine
**Paterson**      The Paterson Museum—Specimens from local basalt flows and basalt
                  flow in the Poona region of India, minerals from NJ and around the
                  world
**Rutherford**    Meadowland Museum—Fluorescent minerals, quartz, minerals from NJ
**Trenton**       New Jersey State Museum—Minerals and rocks, including fluores-
                  cents and magnetite ore

## NEW MEXICO

Fee Dig Mines and Guide Services

**Bingham**       Blanchard Rock Shop—Collect over 84 different kinds of minerals
                  in a former lead mine
**Deming**        Rockhound State Park—Collect a variety of semiprecious stones
**Dixon**         Harding Mine—Harding pegmatite has yielded over 50 minerals

| Gila | Casitas de Gila Guesthouses—Rockhound on 60 acres. Some of the minerals found are white and pink chalcedony, chalcedony roses, red, brown, and yellow jasper, jasper breccia, picture jasper, banded agate, zeolites, geodes, massive hematite, banded rhyolite, andesite, volcanic bombs, scoria, limonite and hematite-banded welded tuff. Pan for gold in the creek. |
| **Magdalena** | Bill's Gems & Minerals—Collect copper and iron minerals at mine dumps |

## Museums and Mine Tours

| **Albuquerque** | Geology Museum, University of New Mexico—Displays of N.M. minerals and geology |
| | Institute of Meteoritics, University of New Mexico—Meteorites |
| | New Mexico Museum of Natural History and Science—3,000 specimens with a focus on N.M. and the southwestern U.S. |
| | The Turquoise Museum—Displays of turquoise |
| **Grants** | New Mexico Mining Museum—Uranium mining |
| **Portales** | Miles Mineral Museum—Displays of minerals, gems, and meteorites |
| **Socorro** | Mineralogical Museum, New Mexico Tech.—10,000 specimens of minerals from N.M., the U.S., and the world |

## Annual Events

| **Socorro** | New Mexico Mineral Symposium—Two days in November |

## NEW YORK

### Fee Dig Mines and Guide Services

| **Herkimer** | Herkimer Diamond Mine and KOA Kampground—Dig for Herkimer "diamonds" |
| **Middleville** | Ace of Diamonds Mine and Campground—Prospect for Herkimer "diamonds," calcite crystals, and dolomite crystals |
| **North River** | The Barton Mine—Hunt for garnets |
| **St. Johnsville** | Crystal Grove Diamond Mine and Campground—Dig for Herkimer "diamonds" |

### Museums and Mine Tours

| **Albany** | New York State Museum—Minerals from New York |
| **Hicksville** | The Hicksville Gregory Museum—9,000 specimens from the major mineral groups, also NJ zeolites, Herkimer "diamonds," fluorescents |
| **New York City** | American Museum of Natural History—Gems, meteorites, emphasis on exceptional specimens from the U.S. |
| **Pawling** | The Gunnison Natural History Museum—Minerals |

# NORTH CAROLINA

## Fee Dig Mines and Guide Services

**Almond**   Almond  Nantahala Gorge Ruby Mine—Sluice for rubies, sapphires, amethyst, topaz, garnet, citrine, smoky quartz

**Boone**   Foggy Mountain Gem Mine—Screen for topaz, garnet, aquamarine, peridot, ruby, star sapphire, amethyst, citrine, smoky quartz, tourmaline, emerald

**Canton**   Old Pressley Sapphire Mine—Sluice for sapphires, zircon, garnet, mica

**Cherokee**   Smoky Mountain Gold & Ruby Mine—Sluice for gold and gems

**Chimney Rock**   Chimney Rock Gemstone Mine—Screen for aquamarine, emerald, ruby, peridot, garnet, quartz, agate, hematite, amethyst, sodalite

**Franklin**   Cowee Mountain Ruby Mine—Sluice for rubies, sapphires, garnets, tourmaline, smoky quartz, amethyst, citrine, moonstone, topaz

Gold City Gem Mine—Sluice for rubies, sapphires, garnets, emeralds, tourmaline, smoky quartz, amethyst, citrine, moonstone, topaz

Mason Mountain Mine and Cowee Gift Shop—Sluice for rhodolite, rubies, sapphires, garnets, kyanite, crystal quartz, smoky quartz, moonstones

Mason's Ruby and Sapphire Mine—Dig and sluice for sapphires (all colors), pink and red rubies

Moon Stone Gem Mine—Sluice for rhodolite garnets, rubies, sapphires, other precious stones

Rocky Face Gem Mine—Sluice for rubies, rhodolite garnets

Rose Creek Mine and Rock Shop—Sluice for rubies, sapphires, garnets, moonstones, amethysts, smoky quartz, citrine, rose quartz, topaz

Sheffield Mine—Sluice for rubies, sapphires, enriched material from around the world

**Hiddenite**   Emerald Hollow Mine-Hiddenite Gems, Inc.—Sluice for rutile, sapphires, garnets, monazite, hiddenite, smoky quartz, tourmaline, clear quartz, aquamarine, sillimanite

**Highlands**   Jackson Hole Gem Mine—Sluice for rubies, sapphires, garnets, tourmaline, smoky quartz, amethyst, citrine, moonstone, topaz

**Little Switzerland**   Blue Ridge Gemstone Mine—Sluice for sapphires, emeralds, rubies, aquamarine, tourmaline, topaz, garnets, amethyst, lepidolite, citrine, moonstone, kyanite, rose, clear, rutilated, and smoky quartz

Emerald Village—Sluice for sapphire, emerald, ruby, aquamarine, tourmaline, topaz, garnet, amethyst, lepidolite, citrine, beryl, moonstone, kyanite, rose, clear, rutilated, and smoky quartz

| | |
|---|---|
| **Marion** | Carolina Emerald Mine and Vein Mountain Gold Camp—Mine for gold, emerald, aquamarine, moonstone, feldspar crystals, garnets, smoky, rose, blue, and clear quartz, tourmaline |
| | Heather Grove Gold and Gem Panning—Pan for gold or a variety of gems and minerals |
| | The Lucky Strike—Sluice for gems and gold panning |
| **Marshall** | Little Pine Garnet Mine—Dig for garnets; can take a horseback ride to the mine |
| **Micaville** | Rock Mine Tours—Dig for emeralds, aquamarine, golden beryl, feldspar, pink feldspar, star garnets, biotite, olivine, moonstone, thulite, black tourmaline |
| **Midland** | Reed Gold Mine State Historic Site—Gold panning |
| **New London** | Cotton Patch Gold Mine—Gold panning |
| | Mountain Creek Gold Mine—Gold panning |
| **Spruce Pine** | Gem Mountain Gemstone Mine—Sluice for sapphires, crabtree emeralds, rubies, Brushy Creek and Wiseman aquamarine |
| | Rio Doce Gem Mine—Sluice for sapphires, emeralds, rubies, aquamarine, tourmaline, topaz, garnets, amethysts, lepidolite, citrine, beryl, moonstone, kyanite, rose, clear, rutilated, and smoky quartz |
| | Spruce Pine Gem and Gold Mine—Sluice for sapphires, emeralds, rubies, aquamarine, tourmaline, topaz, garnets, amethyst, lipidolite, citrine, beryl, moonstone, kyanite, rose, clear, rutilated, and smoky quartz |
| **Union Mills** | Thermal City Gold Mine—Gold and gemstone panning |

## Museums and Mine Tours

| | |
|---|---|
| **Asheville** | Colburn Earth Science Museum—Collection of mineral specimens from NC and the world |
| **Aurora** | Aurora Fossil Museum—Geology of phosphate mine |
| **Franklin** | Franklin Gem and Mineral Museum—Specimens from NC and around the world |
| | Ruby City Gems and Minerals—Specimens from NC and around the world |
| **Gastonia** | Schiele Museum—North Carolina gems and minerals |
| **Greensboro** | Natural Science Center of Greensboro—Specimens from NC and around the world |
| **Hendersonville** | Mineral and Lapidary Museum of Henderson County, Inc.—Minerals and lapidary arts |
| **Linville** | Grandfather Mountain Nature Museum—Specimens from NC |
| **Little Switzerland** | North Carolina Mining Museum and Mine Tour—Tour a closed feldspar mine |

| **Midland** | Reed Gold Mine Historic Site—Gold mine tour |
| **Spruce Pine** | Museum of North Carolina Minerals—Specimens primarily from local mines |

Annual Events

| **Franklin** | Macon County Gemboree—Third weekend in July |
| | "Leaf Looker" Gemboree—Second weekend in October |
| **Spruce Pine** | Original NC Mineral and Gem Festival—Four days at the end of July/beginning of August |

## NORTH DAKOTA

Fee Dig Mines and Guide Services
    None

Museums and Mine Tours

| **Beulah** | Tours at several area lignite strip mines |
| **Dickinson** | Dakota Dinosaur Museum—Displays of rocks and minerals including borax from CA, turquoise from AZ, fluorescent minerals, aurora crystals from AR |
| **Parshall** | Paul Broste Rock Museum—Displays of rocks from the area and around the world |

## OHIO

Fee Dig Mines and Guide Services

| **Hopewell** | Hidden Springs Ranch—Dig for flint (groups only) |
| | Nethers Flint—Dig for flint |

Museums and Mine Tours

| **Cleveland** | The Cleveland Museum of Natural History—The Wade Gallery of Gems and Minerals has over 1,500 gems and minerals |
| **Columbus** | Orton Geological Museum—Rocks and minerals from OH and the world |
| **Dayton** | Boonshoft Museum of Discovery—Minerals and crystals |
| **Glenford** | Flint Ridge State Memorial—Ancient flint quarrying |
| **Lima** | Allen County Museum—Rock and mineral exhibit |

## OKLAHOMA

Fee Dig Mines and Guide Services

| **Kenton** | Black Mesa Bed & Breakfast—Rockhounding on a working cattle ranch |

Howard Layton Ranch—Rockhounding on a working cattle ranch

**Museums and Mine Tours**

**Coalgate**    Coal Country Mining and Historical Museum—Mining museum

**Enid**    The Mr. and Mrs. Dan Midgley Museum—Rock and mineral collection predominantly from OK and the TX shoreline

**Noble**    Timberlake Rose Rock Museum—Displays of barite roses

**Picher**    Picher Mining Museum—Lead and zinc mining

**Tulsa**    Elsing Museum—Gems and minerals

## OREGON

**Fee Dig Mines and Guide Services**

**Federal lands**    Baker City, Jacksonville, Medford, Salem, Unity—Pan for gold

**Klamath Falls**    Juniper Ridge Opal Mine—Hunt for fire opal

**Madras**    Richard's Recreational Ranch—Dig for thundereggs, agate

**Mitchell**    Lucky Strike Geodes—Dig for thundereggs (picture jasper)

**Plush**    Dust Devil Mining Co.—Dig for sunstones

    Ridge Top Mines—Dig for sunstones

    Spectrum Sunstone Mines—Dig for sunstones

**Roseburg**    Cow Creek Recreational Area—Pan for gold

**Yachats**    City of Yachats—Beachcombing for agates and jaspers

**Museums and Mine Tours**

**Central Point**    Crater Rock Museum—Displays of minerals, thundereggs, fossils, geodes, cut and polished gemstones

**Corvallis**    Oregon State University Dept. of Geosciences—Mineral displays

**Hillsboro**    Rice Northwest Museum of Rocks and Minerals—Displays of minerals and crystals

**Redmond**    Peterson's Rock Garden—Unusual rock specimens, fluorescent display

**Sumpter**    Sumpter Valley Dredge State Heritage Area—View a gold dredge, tour historic gold mine towns

**Annual Events**

**Cottage Grove**    Bohemia Mining Days—Four days in July, gold panning and exposition

**Prineville**    Rockhounds Pow-Wow—Mid-June

## PENNSYLVANIA

**Fee Dig Mines and Guide Services**

**Spring Grove**    Jones Geological Services—Guide services for mineral collecting

## Museums and Mine Tours

| | |
|---|---|
| **Ashland** | Museum of Anthracite Mining—Story of anthracite coal |
| | Pioneer Tunnel Coal Mine—Tour an anthracite coal mine |
| **Bryn Mawr** | Museum, Department of Geology, Bryn Mawr College—Rotating display of 1,500 minerals from a collection of 23,500 specimens |
| **Carlisle** | Rennie Geology Museum, Dickinson College—Gem and mineral display |
| **Harrisburg** | State Museum of Pennsylvania—Geology of everyday products |
| **Lancaster** | North Museum of Natural History and Science—Worldwide specimens with a focus on Lancaster County |
| **Lansford** | No. 9 Mine and Museum—Coal mine tour |
| **Media** | Delaware County Institute of Science—Minerals from around the world |
| **Patton** | Seldom Seen Mine—Tour a bituminous coal mine |
| **Philadelphia** | Academy of Natural Science—Exhibit of gems and minerals |
| | Wagner Free Institute of Science—Rocks and minerals |
| **Pittsburgh** | Carnegie Museum of Natural History—One of the premier gem and mineral exhibits in the country |
| **Scranton** | Anthracite Museum Complex—Several anthracite coal-related attractions, including mine tours and museums |
| **Tarentum** | Tour-Ed Mine—Bituminous coal mine tour |
| **Uniontown** | Coal & Coke Heritage Center—Connellsville Coke Region |
| **Waynesburg** | Paul R. Stewart Museum, Waynesburg University—Outstanding mineral collection |
| **West Chester** | Geology Museum, West Chester University—Specimens from Chester County, fluorescent specimens |
| **Wilkes-Barre** | Luzerne County Historical Society—Displays on anthracite coal mining |
| **Windber** | Windber Coal Heritage Center—Exhibits present the heritage of coal mining |

## RHODE ISLAND

### Fee Dig Mines and Guide Services
None

### Museums and Mine Tours

| | |
|---|---|
| **Providence** | Museum of Natural History and Planetarium—Rocks and minerals |

## SOUTH CAROLINA

### Fee Dig Mines and Guide Services

| | |
|---|---|
| **Antreville** | Diamond Hill—Dig your own quartz |

Museums and Mine Tours

| | |
|---|---|
| **Charleston** | The Charleston Museum—Small display of gems and minerals |
| **Clemson** | Bob Campbell Geology Museum—Minerals, meteorites, faceted stones |
| **Columbia** | McKissick Museum, University of South Carolina Campus—Exhibits on geology and gemstones |
| | South Carolina State Museum—Small display of rocks and minerals |

## SOUTH DAKOTA

Fee Dig Mines and Guide Services

| | |
|---|---|
| **Deadwood** | Broken Boot Gold Mine—Pan for gold |
| **Hill City** | Wade's Gold Mill—Pan for gold |
| **Keystone** | Big Thunder Gold Mine—Pan for gold |
| **Lead** | Black Hills Mining Museum—Pan for gold |
| **Wall** | Buffalo Gap National Grassland—Hunt for agates |

Museums and Mine Tours

| | |
|---|---|
| **Deadwood** | Broken Boot Gold Mine—Gold mine tour |
| **Hill City** | Wade's Gold Mill—Guided tour and displays of mining equipment |
| **Keystone** | Big Thunder Gold Mine—Underground mine tour |
| **Lead** | Black Hills Mining Museum—Simulated underground mine tour |
| | Homestead Visitors Center—Gold mining displays |
| **Murdo** | National Rockhound and Lapidary Hall of Fame—Gems and minerals |
| **Rapid City** | Journey Museum—Geology of the Black Hill |
| | South Dakota School of Mines and Technology—Local minerals |

## TENNESSEE

Fee Dig Mines and Guide Services

| | |
|---|---|
| **Ducktown** | Burra Burra Mine—Collect minerals in tailings; garnets, pyite, chalcopyrite, pyrrhotite, actinolite |

Museums and Mine Tours

| | |
|---|---|
| **Ducktown** | Ducktown Basin Museum—Copper mining heritage |
| **Johnson City** | Hands On! Regional Museum—Simulated coal mine |
| **Knoxville** | The Frank H. McClung Museum—Geology of Tennessee |
| **Memphis** | Memphis Pink Palace Museum—Geology and minerals from famous mid-South localities |
| **Murfreesboro** | Middle Tennessee Mineral, Gem, and Fossil Museum—Minerals from Tennessee zinc mines, birthstones, and fluorescent minerals. |

## TEXAS

### Fee Dig Mines and Guide Services

| | |
|---|---|
| **Alpine** | Stillwell Ranch—Hunt for agate and jasper |
| | Woodward Ranch—Hunt for agate, precious opal, and others |
| **Mason** | Lindsay Ranch—Hunt for topaz and other minerals |
| | Seaquist Ranch—Hunt for topaz |
| **Three Rivers** | House Ranch—Hunt for agate |

### Museums and Mine Tours

| | |
|---|---|
| **Alpine** | Last Frontier Museum and Antelope Lodge—Display of rocks from West Texas |
| **Austin** | Texas Memorial Museum of Science and History—Gems and minerals |
| **Canyon** | Panhandle Plains Historical Museum—Gems and minerals from the Texas panhandle |
| **Fort Davis** | Chihuahuan Desert Research Institute—Displays on area mining and minerals |
| **Fort Stockton** | Annie Riggs Memorial Museum—Rocks and minerals of Pecos County and the Big Bend area |
| **Fritch** | Alibates Flint Quarries—View ancient flint quarries |
| **Houston** | Houston Museum of Natural Science—Displays of gem and mineral specimens |
| **Marble Falls** | Granite Mountain—View marble mining operations |
| **Mckenney** | The Heard Natural Science Museum and Wildlife Sanctuary—Rocks and minerals |
| **Odessa** | Odessa Meteor Crater—Meteorite crater |

## UTAH

### Fee Dig Mines and Guide Services

| | |
|---|---|
| **Dugway Mountains** | Dugway Geode Beds—Dig for geodes |
| **Kanab** | Joe's Rock Shop—Dig for septarian nodules |

### Museums and Mine Tours

| | |
|---|---|
| **Bingham Canyon** | Bingham Canyon Mine Visitors Center—Overlook for open-pit copper mine |
| **Eureka** | Tintec Mining Museum—Mineral display and mining artifacts |
| **Helper** | Western Mining and Railroad Museum—Mining exhibits, simulated 1900 coal mine |
| **Hyrum** | Hyrum City Museum—Display of fluorescent minerals |

| Lehi | John Hutchings Museum of Natural History—Minerals linked to mining districts, display of uncut gems |
|---|---|
| Salt Lake City | Museum of Natural History—Mineral classification, Utah ores and minerals, fluorescent minerals |

Place of Interest

| Moab | Moab Rock Shop—Information on rockhounding |
|---|---|

## VERMONT

Fee Dig Mines and Guide Services

| Ludlow | Camp Plymouth State Park—Gold panning |
|---|---|

Museums and Mine Tours

| Barre | Rock of Ages Corporation—Watch granite being quarried |
|---|---|
| Norwich | Montshire Museum of Science—Fluorescent minerals |
| Proctor | Vermont Marble Museum—Story of marble |

## VIRGINIA

Fee Dig Mines and Guide Services

| Amelia | Morefield Gem Mine, Inc.—Dig and sluice for garnet, quartz topaz, and many others |
|---|---|
| Mckenney | Lucky Lake Gem and Mineral Mine of Virginia—Sluice for natural pegmatite minerals and salted material |
| Stuart | Fairy Stone State Park—Hunt for staurolite crystals (fairy stones) |
| Virginia City | Virginia City Gem Mine and Museum—Pan for quartz, ruby, sapphire, garnet, gold |

Museums and Mine Tours

| Big Stone Gap | Harry W. Meador, Jr. Coal Museum—Exhibits and mining equipment |
|---|---|
| Blacksburg | Virginia Tech Geosciences Museum—Large display of Virginia minerals |
| Goldvein | Monroe Park—Tour a mine camp, gold panning demonstrations |
| Harrisonburg | The James Madison University Mineral Museum—Crystals, gems, fluorescent display, specimens from Amelia |
| Martinsville | Stone Cross Mountain Museum—A museum of "Fairy Crosses," specimens of staurolite |
|  | Virginia Museum of Natural History—Minerals and mining exhibits |
| Pocahontas | Pocahontas Exhibition Coal Mine and Museum—Coal mine tour |
| Richmond | University of Richmond Museums—Displays Virginia minerals and a 2,400-carat blue topaz |

## WASHINGTON

### Fee Dig Mines and Guide Services
**Olympia**    Baker-Snoqualmie National Forest—Pan for gold
**Ravensdale**    Geology Adventures, Inc.—Field trips; collect quartz, garnets, topaz, and others

### Museums and Mine Tours
**Castle Rock**    Mount St. Helens National Volcanic Monument—Focus on geology
**Ellensburg**    Kittitas County Historical Museum and Society—Polished rocks
**Pullman**    Washington State University—Silicified wood, minerals
**Seattle**    Burke Museum of Natural History and Culture—Rocks, minerals, the geology of Washington, and a walk-through volcano

## WEST VIRGINIA

### Fee Dig Mines and Guide Services
None

### Museums and Mine Tours
**Beckley**    The Beckley Exhibition Coal Mine—Tour a bituminous coal mine
**Charleston**    The Avampato Discovery Museum at the Clay Center—Exhibits show the story behind West Virginia's geology
**Morgantown**    Museum of Geology and Natural History; W. V. Geological and Economic Survey—Geology of West Virginia

## WISCONSIN

### Fee Dig Mines and Guide Services
None

### Museums and Mine Tours
**Dodgeville**    The Museum of Minerals and Crystals—Local mineral specimens, specimens from around the world
**Hurley**    Iron County Historical Museum—History of area mining, last remaining mine head frame in Wisconsin
**Madison**    Geology Museum, University of Wisconsin at Madison—Minerals, fluorescent minerals, model of Wisconsin cave
**Menasha**    Weis Earth Science Museum, University of Wisconsin, Fox Valley—Official state mineralogical museum of Wisconsin
**Milwaukee**    Milwaukee Public Museum—Displays of geological specimens
University of Wisconsin at Milwaukee—Minerals

| Plateville | The Mining Museum—Lead and zinc mining in the upper Mississippi Valley |
| Potosi | St. John Mine (Wisconsin's 1825 Lead Rush)—Lead mine guided tour |
| Stevens Point | Museum of Natural History, University of Wisconsin—Stevens Point rock and mineral display |

### Annual Events

| Neenah | Quarry Quest—Kid-oriented collecting activities, held in September and sponsored by the Weis Museum, the University of Wisconsin, Fox Valley |
| Menasha | Wonderful World of Agates Symposium—International symposium on Agates, held in July, sponsored by the Weis Musuem, the University of Wisconsin, Fox Valley |

## WYOMING

### Fee Dig Mines and Guide Services

| Shell | Trapper Galloway Ranch—Dig for moss agate |

### Museums and Mine Tours

| Casper | Tate Geological Museum—Rocks and minerals, including Wyoming jade, and fluorescent minerals |
| Cheyenne | Wyoming State Museum—Minerals of Wyoming, coal "swamp" |
| Laramie | Geological Museum, University of Wyoming—Rocks and minerals, fluorescent minerals from Wyoming |
| Saratoga | Saratoga Museum—Minerals from around the world, local geology |
| Worland | Washaki Museum—Geology of Big Horn Basin |

### Annual Events

| Casper | Tate Geological Museum Symposium on Wyoming Geology—June |

# Index by Gems and Minerals

This index lists all the gems and minerals that can be found at fee dig mines in the U.S., and shows the city and state where the mine is located. To use the index, look up the gem or mineral you are interested in, and note the states and cities where they are located. Then go to the state and city to find the name of the mine, and information about the mine.

The following notes provide additional information:

(#)     A number in parentheses is the number of mines in that town that have that gem or mineral.

(*)     Gem or mineral is found in the state, but the mine may also add material to the ore. Check with the individual mine for confirmation.

(FT)    Field trip.

(GS)    Guide service (location listed is the location of the guide service, not necessarily the location of the gems or minerals being collected).

(I)     Mineral has been identified at the mine site but may be difficult to find.

(M)     Museum that allows collection of one specimen as a souvenir.

(MM)    Micromount (a very small crystal which, when viewed under a microscope or magnifying glass, is found to be a high-quality crystal).

(O)     Available at mine but comes from other mines.

(R)     Can be found, but is rare.

(S)     Not the main gem or mineral for which the site is known.

(SA)    "Salted" or enriched gem or mineral.

(U)     Unique to the site.

(Y)     Yearly collecting event.

**Actinolite**  Tennessee: Ducktown

**Agate**  Arkansas: Murfreesboro (S); Michigan: Grand Marais; Montana: Helena (S); New Mexico: Deming; North Carolina: Chimney Rock; Oklahoma: Kenton (2); Oregon: Madras, Yachats; South Dakota: Wall; Texas: Three Rivers
**Banded agate**  Texas: Alpine; New Mexico: Gila

**Fire agate**  Arizona: Safford (2)

**Iris agate**  Texas: Alpine

**Ledge agate**  Oregon: Madras

**Moss agate**  Oregon: Madras, Mitchell; Texas: Alpine (2); Wyoming: Shell

**Polka-dot Jasp-agate**  Oregon: Madras

**Plume agate**  Nevada: Reno (GS)

**Pompom agate**  Texas: Alpine

**Rainbow agate**  Oregon: Madras

**Red plume agate**  Texas: Alpine

**Albite**  Maine: Bethel, Poland (GS), West Paris; New Hampshire: Grafton (I); New Mexico: Dixon

**Albite (Cleavelandite Var.)** Maine: Poland (GS)

**Amazonite**  Virginia: Amelia

**Amber**  Texas: Mason (R); Washington: Ravensdale (GS)

**Amethyst**  Arizona: Glendale; Arkansas: Mt. Ida (SA), Murfreesboro (S); Georgia: Cleveland; Maine: Bethel (R), West Paris; Montana: Dillon; Nevada: Reno (GS); New Hampshire: Grafton (I), Laconia; North Carolina (*): Almond, Boone, Cherokee, Chimney Rock, Franklin (3), Highlands, Little Switzerland, Spruce Pine (3); South Carolina: Antreville

**Amethyst scepters**  Arizona: Tempe

**Amblygonite**  Maine: West Paris

**Amphibolite**  New Hampshire: Grafton (I)

**Andesite**  New Mexico: Gila

**Apatite**  Maine: Auburn, Bethel, Poland (GS), West Paris; New Hampshire: Grafton; New Mexico: Dixon

   **Fluorapatite**  Maine: Poland (GS)

   **Hydroxylapatite**  Maine: Poland (GS)

   **Purple apatite**  Maine: West Paris

**Aplite**  New Hampshire: Grafton (I)

**Aquamarine**  California: Pala; Georgia: LaGrange; Maine: Bethel, Poland (GS); New Hampshire: Grafton (I); North Carolina (*): Boone, Chimney Rock, Franklin, Hiddenite, Little Switzerland (2), Marion, Micaville, Spruce Pine (2) (FT)

   **Brushy Creek Aquamarine**  North Carolina: Spruce Pine (I) (FT)

   **Weisman aquamarine**  North Carolina: Spruce Pine (I) (FT)

**Aragonite**  Arizona: Glendale (GS)

**Arsenopyrite**  Maine: Poland (GS)

**Augelite**  Maine: Poland (GS)

**Aurichalcite**  New Mexico: Magdalena

**Autenite**  Maine: Auburn, Bethel, Poland (GS); New Hampshire: Grafton (I)

**Azurite**  New Mexico: Magdalena

**Barite**  Arizona: Glendale (GS); Arkansas: Murfreesboro (S); Georgia: Lincolnton; New Mexico: Bingham; Washington: Ravensdale (GS)

**Benitoite**  California: Coalinga

**Beraumite**  Maine: Poland (GS)

**Bermanite**  Maine: Poland (GS)

**Bertrandite**  Maine: Poland (GS), West Paris

**Bertranite**  New Hampshire: Grafton (I)

**Beryl**  Delaware: Wilmngton; Georgia: LaGrange; Maine: Auburn, Bethel, Poland (GS), West Paris;  New Hampshire: Grafton (I); New Mexico: Dixon; North Carolina (*): Little Switzerland (2), Spruce Pine (2);  Virginia: Amelia
  **Aqua beryl**  New Hampshire: Grafton (I)
  **Blue beryl**  (see also aquamarine)  New Hampshire: Grafton (I)
  **Golden beryl**  North Carolina: Spruce Pine (FT); New Hampshire: Grafton (I)

**Beryllonite**  Maine: Poland (GS), West Paris

**Beta-Uranophane**  New Hampshire: Grafton

**Biotite**  Maine: Bethel; New Hampshire: Grafton (I); North Carolina: Micaville

**Borate**  California: Boron (Y)

**Bornite**  New Hampshire: Grafton (I)

**Brazillianite**  Maine: Poland (GS)

**Brochantite**  New Mexico: Bingham

**Cacoxenite**  Georgia: Lincolnton

**Calcite**  Arizona: Glendale (GS); Arkansas: Murfreesboro (S); Florida: Ft. Drum; Michigan: Ontonagon; New Hampshire: Grafton; New Mexico: Bingham; New York: Middleville; Texas: Mason; Virginia: Amelia

**Cape May "diamonds"**  See Quartz

**Casserite**  Maine: Poland (GS)

**Cassiterite**  Maine: West Paris; Texas: Mason

**Chalcedony**  Arizona: Safford; Nevada: Reno (GS); New Mexico: Deming
  **White**  New Mexico: Gila
  **Pink**  New Mexico: Gila
  **Chalcedony roses**  New Mexico: Gila

**Chalcopyrite**  Tennessee: Ducktown

**Childrenite**  Maine: Poland (GS)

**Chrysoberyl**  New Hampshire: Grafton (I)

**Chrysocolla**  Arizona: Glendale (GS)

**Citrine**  North Carolina (*): Almond, Boone, Cherokee, Franklin (3), Highlands, Little Switzerland, Spruce Pine (3); Virginia: McKenney

**Clarkite**  New Hampshire: Grafton (I)

**Clevelandite**  California: Pala; Maine: Auburn, Poland (GS), West Paris; New Hampshire: Grafton (I); New Mexico: Dixon

**Columbite**  New Hampshire: Grafton (I); Maine: Bethel, Poland (GS), West Paris

**Compotite**  New Hampshire: Grafton (I)

**Cookeite**  Maine: West Paris

**Copper, pure**  Michigan: Ontonagon, Mohawk

**Copper minerals**  Michigan: Mohawk (M); New Mexico: Magdalena

**Crandalite**  Georgia: Lincolnton

**Cryolite**  New Hampshire: Grafton (I)

**Cymatolite**  New Hampshire: Grafton (I)

**Datolite**  Michigan: Ontonagon

**Dendrites**  New Hampshire: Grafton (I)

**Diadochite**  Maine: Poland (GS)

**Diamond**  Arkansas: Murfreesboro

**Dickinsonite**  Maine: Poland (GS)

**Djurleite**  California: Coalinga

**Dolomite crystals**  New York: Middleville

**Earlshannonite**  Maine: Poland (GS)

**Elabite**  See listing under Tourmaline

**Emerald**  Arkansas: Mt. Ida (SA); Georgia: Cleveland (SA), Dahlonega (SA); North Carolina (*): Almond, Boone, Cherokee, Chimney Rock, Franklin (2), Highlands, Little Switzerland (2), Marion, Micaville, Spruce Pine (2)

    **Crabtree emerald**  North Carolina: Spruce Pine

**Eosphorite**  Maine: Poland (GS)

**Epidote**  Michigan: Ontonagon; Texas: Mason

**Fairfieldite**  Maine: Poland (GS)

**Fairy stones**  (See Staurolite crystals)

**Feldspar**  Delaware: Wilmington; New Hampshire: Grafton (I); North Carolina: Marion, Micaville; Virginia: Amelia

    **Albite feldspar**  Maine: Bethel

**Flint**  Ohio: Hopewell (2)

**Fluoroapatite**  New Hampshire: Grafton (I)

**Fluorescent minerals**  Arizona: Glendale (GS); Kentucky: Marian; New Jersey: Franklin, Ogdensburg; North Carolina: Little Switzerland; Washington: Ravensdale (GS)

**Fluorite**  Arizona: Glendale (GS); Illinois: Rosiclare; Kentucky: Marion; New Mexico: Bingham; Virginia: Amelia; Washington: Ravensdale (GS)

**Franklinite**  New Jersey: Franklin

**Fuchsite**  Georgia: Lincolnton

**Gahnite (spinel)**  Maine: Poland (GS), West Paris

**Gainsite**  Maine: Poland (GS)

**Galena**  Arizona: Glendale (GS); New Mexico: Bingham; Texas: Mason

**Garnets**  Alaska: Juneau; Arizona: Tempe; California: Pala; Connecticut: Roxbury; Delaware: Wilmington; Georgia: Dahlonega (SA); Idaho: St. Maries; Maine: Auburn, Bethel, Poland (GS), West Paris; Montana: Alder, Helena (S); Nevada: Ely; New Hampshire: Grafton (I); New Mexico: Dixon; New York: North River; North Carolina (*): Almond, Boone, Canton, Cherokee, Chimney Rock, Franklin (4), Marshal, Hiddenite, Highlands, Little Switzerland (2), Marion, Spruce Pine (3) (FT); Tennessee: Ducktown; Texas: Mason; Virginia: McKenney, Virginia City (SA); Washington: Ravensdale (GS)
**Almandine garnets**  Maine: Bethel, Poland (GS); Nevada: Ely
**Pyrope garnets**  North Carolina: Franklin
**Rhodolite garnets**  North Carolina: Franklin

**Garnets, Star**  Idaho: Moscow (GS), St. Maries

**Geodes**  Arizona: Safford; Illinois: Hamilton; Missouri: Alexandria; New Mexico: Deming, Gila; Utah: Dugway Mountains
*Lined with:*
**Agate, blue**  New Mexico: Deming
**Aragonite**  Illinois: Hamilton; Missouri: Alexandria
**Barite**  Illinois:Hamilton; Missouri: Alexandria
**Calcite**  Missouri: Alexandria
**Chalcedony**  New Mexico: Deming
**Dolomite**  Missouri: Alexandria
**Goethite**  Missouri: Alexandria
**Hematite**  Missouri: Alexandria
**Kaoline**  Missouri: Alexandria
**Kaolinite**  Illinois: Hamilton
**Opal, common**  New Mexico: Deming
**Pyrite**  Missouri: Alexandria
**Quartz**  Illinois: Hamilton; New Mexico: Deming
**Selenite needles**  Missouri: Alexandria
**Sphalerite**  Missouri: Alexandria

**Gold**  (*) Alabama: Cragford; Alaska: Anchorage, Chugach, Chicken, Copper Center, Fairbanks (3), Girdwood, Juneau, McGrath, Nome, Skagway (2), Talkeetna; Arizona: Apache Junction, Goldfield, Prescott, Wickenburg; California: Coloma, Columbia, Jackson, Jamestown, Mariposa, Nevada City, Pine Grove, Placerville; Colorado: Breckenridge, Granite, Idaho Springs (2), Ouray, Silverton; Georgia: Cleveland, Dahlonega (2), Gainesville; Indiana: Knightstown; Montana: Libby,

Philipsburg; New Mexico: Gila; North Carolina: Cherokee, Marion (3), Midland, New London (2), Union Mills; Oregon: Baker City, Halfway, Jacksonville, Medford, Roseburg, Salem, Unity; South Dakota: Deadwood, Hill City, Keystone, Lead; Virginia: Virginia City (SA); Vermont: Plymouth

**Gold ore**  Colorado: Lakewood (M)

**Gossanite (clear beryl)**  California: Pala

**Goyazite**  Maine: Poland (GS)

**Graftonite**  Maine: Poland (GS); New Hampshire: Grafton (I)

**Granite, graphic**  Maine: Auburn

**Gummite**  New Hampshire: Grafton (I)

**Hedenburgite**  New Mexico: Magdalena

**Hematite**  Georgia: Lincolnton; Montana: Helena; New Mexico: Magdalena; North Carolina: Chimney Rock (SA)
  **Massive**  New Mexico: Gila
  **Hematite**  (banded welded tuft) New Mexico: Gila

**Herderite, hydroxyl**  Maine: Bethel, Poland (GS), West Paris

**Herkimer "diamonds"**  See Quartz

**Heterosite**  Maine: Poland (GS)

**Hiddenite (spodumene)**  California: Pala; North Carolina: Hiddenite

**Hureaylite**  Maine: Poland (GS)

**Ilmenite**  Georgia: Lincolnton

**Iron minerals**  New Mexico: Magdalena

**Iron ore**  Michigan: Iron Mountain (M)

**Jade**  California: Pine Grove

**Jadite**  Montana: Helana (S)

**Jahnsite**  Maine: Poland (GS)

**Jasper**  Arkansas: Murfreesboro (S); California: Pine Grove; Montana: Helena (S); Oklahoma: Kenton; Oregon: Madras, Yachats; Texas: Alpine
  **Brown Jasper**  New Mexico: Deming, Gila
  **Chocolate jasper**  New Mexico: Deming
  **Jasper breccia**  New Mexico: Gila
  **Orange jasper**  New Mexico: Deming
  **Picture jasper**  Oregon: Mitchell
  **Pink jasper**  New Mexico: Deming
  **Red jasper**  New Mexico: Gila
  **Variegated jasper**  New Mexico: Deming
  **Yellow jasper**  New Mexico: Deming, Gila

**Joaquinite**  California: Coalinga

**Kasolite**  New Hampshire: Grafton (I)

**Kosnarite**  Maine: Poland (GS)

**Kunzite**  California: Pala

**Kyanite**  Georgia: Lincolnton; North Carolina (*): Franklin, Little Switzerland

**Laboradorite**  Texas: Alpine

**Lake County "diamonds"**  See Quartz

**Landsite**  Maine: Poland (GS)

**Laueite**  Maine: Poland (GS)

**Lazulite**  Georgia: Lincolnton

**Lepidolite**  Maine: Poland (GS), West Paris; New Mexico: Dixon; North Carolina (*): Little Switzerland
    **Lemon yellow lepidolite**  New Hampshire: Grafton (I)
    **Purple lepidolite**  California: Pala

**Lepidomelane**  New Hampshire: Grafton (I)

**Limonite**  Arizona: Tempe; New Mexico: Gila

**Linarite**  New Mexico: Bingham

**Lithiophyllite**  Maine: Poland (GS); New Hampshire: Grafton (I)

**Lollingite**  Maine: Poland (GS)

**Ludlamite**  Maine: Poland (GS)

**Magnesium oxide**  See Psilomellane

**Malachite**  New Mexico: Magdalena

**Manganapatite**  New Hampshire: Grafton (I)

**Manganese minerals**  New Mexico: Deming

**Manganese oxide minerals**  New Mexico: Deming

**Marcasite**  New Hampshire: Grafton (I)

**McCrillsite**  Maine: Poland (GS)

**Mica**  Delaware: Wilmington; California: Pala; Maine: Auburn, Bethel, Poland (GS); New Hampshire: Grafton (I), Laconia; North Carolina: Canton; Virginia: Amelia
    **Biotite mica**  Maine: Bethel, Poland (GS)
    **Book mica**  California: Pala
    **Muscovite mica**  California: Pala; Maine: Poland (GS)

**Microcline**  Maine: Poland (GS)

**Microlite**  New Mexico: Dixon

**Mitridatite**  Maine: Poland (GS)

**Molybdenite**  New Hampshire: Grafton (I)

**Montebrasite**  Maine: Poland (GS)

**Montmorillonite**  Maine: Poland (GS), West Paris; New Hampshire: Grafton (I)

**Monzaite**  Maine: Poland (GS)

**Moonstone**  North Carolina (*): Franklin (4), Highlands, Little Switzerland, Marion, Micaville, Spruce Pine

**Moraesite**  Maine: Poland (GS)

**Morganite**  California: Pala; Maine: Poland (GS)

**Muscovite**  California: Pala; Georgia: Lincolnton; New Hampshire: Grafton (I); New Mexico: Dixon

**Natrolite**  California: Coalinga

**Neptunite**  California: Coalinga

**Olivine**  North Carolina: Micaville

**Opal**
    **Black fire opal**  Nevada: Denio
    **Common opal**  New Mexico: Deming
    **Crystal opal**  Nevada: Denio
    **Fire opal**  Nevada: Denio (4), Reno (GS); Oregon: Klamath Falls
    **Hyalite opal**  Maine: Bethel
    **Precious opal**  Idaho: Spencer; Texas: Alpine
    **Virgin Valley opal**  Nevada: Reno (GS)
    **White opal**  Nevada: Denio
    **Wood opal**  Nevada: Denio

**Perhamite**  Maine: Poland (GS)

**Parsonite**  New Hampshire: Grafton (I)

**Perlite (black to gray)**  New Mexico: Deming

**Peridot**  Arkansas: Murfreesboro (S); North Carolina (*): Boone, Chimney Rock, Franklin

**Petalite**  Maine: Poland (GS), West Paris

**Phenakite**  Virginia: Amelia

**Phosphosiderite**  Georgia: Lincolnton; Maine: Poland (GS)

**Phosphouranylite**  Maine: Poland (GS)

**Phosphyanylite**  New Hampshire: Grafton (I)

**Pitch Stone** (with seams of red and brown) New Mexico: Deming

**Pollucite**  Maine: Poland (GS), West Paris

**Psilomelane**  New Hampshire: Grafton (I)

**Purpurite**  Maine: Poland (GS); New Hampshire: Grafton (I)

**Pyrite**  Georgia: Lincolnton; Maine: Bethel, Poland (GS); New Hampshire: Grafton (I); New Mexico: Magdalena; Tennessee: Ducktown; Virginia: Amelia; Washington: Ravensdale (GS)

**Pyrophyllite**  Georgia: Lincolnton

**Pyrrhotite**  New Hampshire: Grafton (I); Tennessee: Ducktown

**Quartz**  Arizona: Glendale (GS), Tempe; Arkansas: Jessieville (3), Mt. Ida (6) (Y), Murfreesboro (S), Pencil Bluff, Story (2); California: Pine Grove; Delaware: Wilmington; Georgia: Lincolnton; Maine: Auburn, Poland (GS), West Paris; Michigan: Ontonagon; Montana: Dillon, Helena (S); New Hampshire: Laconia; New Mexico: Bingham, Deming, Dixon; North Carolina: Franklin; Texas: Alpine, Mason; Virginia: Amelia, Virginia City (SA); Washington: Ravensdale (GS)

  **Blue**  Georgia: Lincolnton; North Carolina: Marion

  **Clear**  Georgia: LaGrange; North Carolina (*): Hiddenite, Little Switzerland, Marion, Spruce Pine

  **Milky**  Maine: Bethel

  **Parallel growth**  Maine: West Paris

  **Pseudocubic crystals**  Maine: West Paris

  **Rose**  Maine: Bethel; New Hampshire: Grafton (I); North Carolina (*): Franklin

  **Rutilated**  North Carolina (*): Little Switzerland, Spruce Pine

  **Skeletal quartz**  South Carolina: Antreville

  **Smoky**  Maine: Bethel; Nevada: Reno (GS); New Hampshire: Grafton, Laconia; North Carolina (*): Almond, Boone, Cherokee, Chimney Rock, Franklin (4), Hiddenite, Highlands, Little Switzerland (2), Marion, Spruce Pine (2); Virginia: McKenney

  **Smoky (gem quality)**  New Hampshire: Grafton (I); South Carolina: Antreville

**Quartz "diamonds"**

  **Lake Co. "diamonds" (moon tears)**  California: Lake County

  **Cape May "diamonds"**  New Jersey: Cape May

  **Herkimer "diamonds"**  New York: Herkimer, Middleville, St. Johnsville

**Reddingite**  Maine: Poland (GS)

**Rhodochrosite**  Maine: Poland (GS)

**Rhodolite (garnet)**  North Carolina: Franklin

**Rhyolite, banded**  New Mexico: Gila

**Rochbridgeite**  Maine: Poland (GS)

**Rose rocks**  See Barite

**Rubies**  Arkansas: Mt. Ida (SA); California: Pine Grove; Georgia: Cleveland, Dahlonega (SA); Montana: Helena; North Carolina (*): Almond, Boone, Cherokee, Chimney Rock, Franklin (8), Highlands, Little Switzerland (2), Spruce Pine (3); Virginia: Virginia City (SA)

**Rutile**  Georgia: Lincolnton; Maine: Bethel, Poland (GS); North Carolina: Hiddenite

**Safflorite**  New Hampshire: Grafton (I)

**Sapphires**  Georgia: Cleveland (SA), Dahlonega (SA); Montana: Clinton (GS), Hamilton, Helena, Philipsburg (3); North Carolina (*): Almond, Cherokee, Franklin (8), Hiddenite, Highlands, Little Switzerland (2), Spruce Pine (2); Virginia: Virginia City (SA)

  **Sapphire, blue**  North Carolina: Canton

**Sapphire, grey**  North Carolina: Canton
**Sapphire, white**  North Carolina: Canton
**Sapphire, bronze**  North Carolina: Canton
**Sapphire, pink**  North Carolina: Canton
**Star sapphire**  North Carolina: Boone (SA)

**Scheelite**  Maine: West Paris

**Scoria**  New Mexico: Gila

**Selenite crystals**  New Mexico: Bingham

**Septarian nodules**  Utah: Kanab

**Serpentine**  Montana: Helena (S)

**Siderite**  Maine: Bethel

**Silica minerals**  New Mexico: Deming

**Sillimanite**  New Hampshire: Grafton (I); North Carolina (*): Hiddenite

**Silver**  Michigan: Ontonagon

**Smithsonite**  Arizona: Glendale (GS)

**Sodalite**  North Carolina: Chimney Rock (SA)

**Soddylite**  New Hampshire: Grafton (I)

**Spangolite**  New Mexico: Bingham

**Spessartine**  New Mexico: Dixon

**Spinel**  Montana: Alder

**Spodumene**  Maine: Poland (GS), West Paris; New Mexico: Dixon
  **Altered spodumene**  Maine: West Paris
  **Hiddenite**  California: Pala; North Carolina: Hiddenite

**Staurolite**  New Hampshire: Grafton (I); Virginia: Stuart

**Stewartite**  Maine: Poland (GS)

**Strengite**  Georgia: Lincolnton

**Strunzite**  Maine: Poland (GS)

**Sulfur**  Georgia: Lincolnton

**Sunstone**  Nevada: Reno (GS); Oregon: Plush (3)

**Switzerite**  Maine: Poland (GS)

**Tantalite-Columbite**  Virginia: Amelia

**Thulite**  North Carolina: Micaville

**Thundereggs**  New Mexico: Deming; Oregon: Madras, Mitchell

**Tobemite**  New Hampshire: Grafton (I)

**Topaz**  Georgia: Cleveland (SA); Maine: Poland (GS); Montana: Helena; New Hampshire: Grafton (I); North Carolina (*): Almond, Boone, Cherokee, Franklin (2), Little

Switzerland, Marion, Spruce Pine (3); Texas: Mason (2); Virginia: Amelia, McKenney
**Pink topaz** Washington: Ravensdale (GS)

**Torberite** Maine: Poland (GS)

**Tourmaline** Arizona: Tempe; California: Mesa Grande; Maine: Auburn (2), Poland (GS), West Paris; New Hampshire: Grafton (I); North Carolina (*): Boone, Franklin (2), Little Switzerland, Marion, Spruce Pine (3); Texas: Mason; Virginia: Amelia, McKenney
**Bi-colored** California: Pala
**Black tourmaline** California: Pala; Georgia: LaGrange; Maine: Auburn, Bethel, Poland (GS), West Paris; New Hampshire: Grafton (I); North Carolina: Spruce Pine (FT)
**Gem tourmaline** Maine: West Paris
**Green tourmaline** California: Pala; Maine: West Paris
**Pink tourmaline** California: Pala

**Triphyllite** Maine: Poland (GS), West Paris; New Hampshire: Grafton (I)

**Triplite** Maine: Poland (GS)

**Turquoise** Nevada: Reno (GS)

**Uralolite** Maine: Poland (GS)

**Uranite** Maine: Bethel, Poland (GS); New Hampshire: Grafton (I) (species with gummite-world-famous)

**Uranium minerals** New Hampshire: Grafton (I); North Carolina: Little Switzerland

**Uranophane** New Hampshire: Grafton (I)

**Vandendriesscheite** New Hampshire: Grafton (I)

**Variscite** Georgia: Lincolnton; Nevada: Reno (GS)

**Vesuvianite** Maine: West Paris (I)

**Vivianite** New Hampshire: Grafton (I); Maine: Poland (GS)

**Voelerkenite** New Hampshire: Grafton (I)

**Volcanic Bombs** New Mexico: Gila

**Wardilite** Maine: Poland (GS)

**Whitlockite** Maine: Poland (GS)

**Whitmoreite** Maine: Poland (GS)

**Willemite** Arizona: Glendale (GS)

**Woodhouseite** Georgia: Lincolnton

**Wodginite** Maine: Poland (GS)

**Wulfenite** Arizona: Glendale (GS)

**Zeolites** New Mexico: Gila

**Zircon** Maine: Bethel, Poland (GS), West Paris; New Hampshire: Grafton (I); North Carolina: Canton; Texas: Mason

# Annual Events

## JANUARY

Quartzite, AZ, Gem and Mineral Shows—January–February

Tucson, AZ, Gem and Mineral Shows—End of January–mid-February

## FEBRUARY

Quartzsite, AZ, Gem and Mineral Shows—January–February

Tucson, AZ, Gem and Mineral Shows—End of January–mid-February

## MARCH

Boron, CA, Rock Bonanza—Weekend before Easter

Scottsdale, AZ, Minerals of Arizona—Symposium 1 day in March or April

## APRIL

Boron, CA, Rock Bonanza—Weekend before Easter

Dahlonega, GA, World Open Gold Panning Championship—Third Saturday of April

Scottsdale, AZ, Minerals of Arizona—Symposium 1 day in March or April

## MAY

Augusta, ME, Maine Mineral Symposium—Second full weekend in May

Poland, ME, Maine Pegmatite Workshop—One week at the end of May or beginning of June

## JUNE

Casper, WY, Tate Geological Museum Symposium on Wyoming Geology

Poland, ME, Maine Pegmatite Workshop—One week at the end of May or beginning of June

Prineville, OR, Rockhounds Pow-Wow—Mid-June

## JULY

Cottage Grove, OR, Bohemia Mining Days—Four days in July

Franklin, NC, Macon County Gemboree—Third weekend in July

Menasha, WI, Wonderful World of Agate Symposium—July

Moose Lake, MN, Agate Days—One weekend in July

## AUGUST

Houghton, MI, Copper County Mineral Retreat—One week in early August

Spruce Pine, NC, Original North Carolina Mineral and Gem Festival—Four days at the beginning of August

## SEPTEMBER

Coloma, CA, Marshall Gold Discovery State Historic Park: Gold Rush Live—End of September–beginning of October

Neenah, WI, Quarry Quest—September

## OCTOBER

Coloma, CA, Marshall Gold Discovery State Historic Park: Gold Rush Live—End of September–beginning of October

Dahlonega, GA, Gold Rush Days—Third weekend in October

Franklin, NC, "Leaf Looker" Gemboree—Second weekend in October

Jasper, GA, Pickens County Marble Festival—First weekend in October

Keokuk, IA, Rocktober Geode Fest—One weekend in early October

Mt. Ida, AR, Quartz Crystal Festival and World Championship Dig—Second weekend in October

## NOVEMBER

Socorro, NM, New Mexico Mineral Symposium—Two days in November

## DECEMBER

No information available.

# State Gem and Mineral Symbols

| STATE | GEMSTONE | MINERAL | STONE/ROCK |
|---|---|---|---|
| Alabama | Star Blue Quartz (1990) | Hematite (1967) | Marble (1969) |
| Alaska | Jade (1968) | Gold (1968) | |
| Arizona | Turquoise (1974) | Fire agate | Petrified Wood |
| Arkansas | Diamond | Quartz crystal | Bauxite |
| California | Benitoite | Gold | Serpentine (1965) |
| Colorado | Aquamarine (1971) | Rhodochrosite | Yule Marble |
| Connecticut | Garnet (1977) | | |
| Delaware | | | Sillimanite |
| Florida | Moonstone | | Agatized coral |
| Georgia | Amethyst | Staurolite | Quartz |
| Hawaii | Black Coral | | Lava |
| Idaho | Star Garnet (1967) | | |
| Illinois | | Fluorite (1965) | |
| Indiana | | | Limestone |
| Iowa | | | Geode |
| Kansas | | | |
| Kentucky | Freshwater Pearl | Coal | Kentucky Agate |
| Louisiana | Agate | | Petrified Palm |
| Maine | Tourmaline (1971) | | |
| Maryland | | Patuxent River Stone | |
| Massachusetts | Rhodonite | Babingtonite | Plymouth Rock, Dighton Rock, Roxbury Conglomerate |
| Michigan | Isle Royal Greenstone (Chlorostrolite) (1972) | | Petosky Stone (1965) |
| Minnesota | Lake Superior Agate | Iron | |
| Mississippi | | | Petrified Wood (1976) |
| Missouri | | Galena (1967) | Mozarkite (1967) |

| STATE | GEMSTONE | MINERAL | STONE/ROCK |
|---|---|---|---|
| Montana | Yogo Sapphire & Agate (1969) | | |
| Nebraska | Blue Agate (1967) | | Prairie Agate (1967) |
| Nevada | Virgin Valley Blackfire Opal (1987) (Precious) Turquoise (1987) (Semiprecious) | Silver (Official Metal) | Sandstone (1987) |
| New Hampshire | Smoky Quartz | Beryl | Granite |
| New Jersey | | | Stockton Sandstone |
| New Mexico | Turquoise (1967) | | |
| New York | Garnet (1969) | | |
| North Carolina | Emerald (1973) | | Granite/Unakite |
| North Dakota | | | Teredo Wood |
| Ohio | Flint (1965) | | |
| Oklahoma | | | Barite Rose |
| Oregon | Sunstone (1987) | | Thundereggs (1965) |
| Pennsylvania | | | |
| Rhode Island | | Bowenite | Cumberlandite |
| South Carolina | Amethyst | | Blue Granite |
| South Dakota | Fairburn Agate (1966) | Rose Quartz (1966) (Mineral/Stone) | |
| Tennessee | Tennessee River Pearls | | Tennessee Limestone and Agate |
| Texas | Texas Blue Topaz (1969) Lone Star Cut (1977) (Gemstone Cut) | | Petrified Palmwood (1960) |
| Utah | Topaz | Copper | Coal |
| Vermont | Grossular Garnet | Talc | Granite, Marble, Slate |
| Virginia | | | |
| Washington | Petrified Wood (1975) | | |
| West Virginia | Mississippian Coral, Lithostrotionella | | |
| Wisconsin | | Galena (1971) | Wausau Red Granite (1971) |
| Wyoming | Nephrite Jade (1967) | | |

# Finding Your Own Birthstone

Following is a listing of fee dig sites presented in this four-volume guide where you can find your birthstone! Refer to the individual mine listings for more information on individual mines.

**Garnet (January Birthstone)** Alaska: Juneau; Arizona: Tempe; California: Pala; Connecticut: Roxbury; Delaware: Wilmington; Georgia: Dahlonega (SA); Idaho: St. Maries; Maine: Auburn, Bethel, Poland (GS), West Paris; Montana: Alder, Helena (S); Nevada: Ely; New Hampshire: Grafton (I); New Mexico: Dixon; New York: North River; North Carolina (*): Almond, Boone, Canton, Cherokee, Chimney Rock, Franklin (4), Marshal, Hiddenite, Highlands, Little Switzerland (2), Marion, Spruce Pine (3) (FT); Tennessee: Ducktown; Texas: Mason; Virginia: McKenney, Virginia City (SA); Washington: Ravensdale (GS)
**Almandine garnets** Maine: Bethel, Poland (GS); Nevada: Ely
**Pyrope garnets** North Carolina: Franklin
**Rhodolite garnets** North Carolina: Franklin
**Garnets, star** Idaho: Moscow (GS), St. Maries

**Amethyst (February Birthstone)** Arizona: Glendale; Arkansas: Mt. Ida (SA), Murfreesboro (S); Georgia: Cleveland; Maine: Bethel (R), West Paris; Montana: Dillon; Nevada: Reno (GS); New Hampshire: Grafton (I), Laconia; North Carolina (*): Almond, Boone, Cherokee, Chimney Rock, Franklin (3), Highlands, Little Switzerland, Spruce Pine (3); South Carolina: Antreville

**Amethyst scepters** Arizona: Tempe

**Aquamarine or Bloodstone (March Birthstone)**

**Aquamarine** California: Pala; Georgia: LaGrange; Maine: Bethel, Poland (GS); New Hampshire: Grafton (I); North Carolina (*):Boone, Chimney Rock, Franklin, Hiddenite, Little Switzerland (2), Marion, Micaville, Spruce Pine (2) (FT)
**Brushy Creek aquamarine** North Carolina: Spruce Pine (I) (FT)
**Weisman aquamarine** North Carolina: Spruce Pine (I) (FT)

**Bloodstone** No listing

**Diamond (April Birthstone)** Arkansas: Murfreesboro

**Emerald (May Birthstone)** Arkansas: Mt. Ida (SA); Georgia: Cleveland (SA), Dahlonega (SA); North Carolina (*): Almond, Boone, Cherokee, Chimney Rock, Franklin (2), Highlands, Little Switzerland (2), Marion, Micaville, Spruce Pine (2)
**Crabtree emerald** North Carolina: Spruce Pine

**Moonstone or Pearl (June Birthstone)**

**Moonstone** North Carolina (*): Franklin (4), Highlands, Little Switzerland, Marion, Micaville, Spruce Pine

**Pearl** No listing

**Ruby (July Birthstone)** Arkansas: Mt. Ida (SA); California: Pine Grove; Georgia: Cleveland, Dahlonega (SA); Montana: Helena; North Carolina (*): Almond, Boone, Cherokee, Chimney Rock, Franklin (8), Highlands, Little Switzerland (2), Spruce Pine (3);Virginia: Virginia City (SA)

**Peridot or Sardonyx (August Birthstone)**

**Peridot** Arkansas: Murfreesboro (S); North Carolina (*): Boone, Chimney Rock, Franklin

**Sardonyx** No listing

**Sapphire (September Birthstone)** Georgia: Cleveland (SA), Dahlonega (SA); Montana: Clinton (GS), Hamilton, Helena, Philipsburg (3); North Carolina (*): Almond, Cherokee, Franklin (8), Hiddenite, Highlands, Little Switzerland (2), Spruce Pine (2); Virginia: Virginia City (SA)
    **Sapphire, blue** North Carolina: Canton
    **Sapphire, grey** North Carolina: Canton
    **Sapphire, white** North Carolina: Canton
    **Sapphire, bronze** North Carolina: Canton
    **Sapphire, pink** North Carolina: Canton
    **Star sapphire** North Carolina: Boone (SA)

**Opal or Tourmaline (October Birthstone)**
**Opal**
    **Black fire opal** Nevada: Denio
    **Common opal** New Mexico: Deming
    **Crystal opal** Nevada: Denio
    **Fire opal** Nevada: Denio (4), Reno (GS); Oregon: Klamath Falls
    **Hyalite opal** Maine: Bethel
    **Precious opal** Idaho: Spencer; Texas: Alpine
    **Virgin Valley opal** Nevada: Reno (GS)
    **White opal** Nevada: Denio
    **Wood opal** Nevada: Denio
**Tourmaline** Arizona: Tempe; California: Mesa Grande; Maine: Auburn (2), Poland (GS), West Paris; New Hampshire: Grafton (I); North Carolina (*): Boone, Franklin (2), Little Switzerland, Marion, Spruce Pine (3); Texas: Mason; Virginia: Amelia
    **Bi-colored** California: Pala
    **Black tourmaline** California: Pala; Georgia: LaGrange; Maine: Auburn, Bethel, Poland (GS), West Paris; New Hampshire: Grafton (I); North Carolina: Spruce Pine (FT)
    **Gem tourmaline** Maine: West Paris

**Green tourmaline**  California: Pala; Maine: West Paris
**Pink tourmaline**  California: Pala

**Topaz (November Birthstone)** Georgia: Cleveland (SA); Maine: Poland (GS); Montana: Helena; New Hampshire: Grafton (I); North Carolina (*): Almond, Boone, Cherokee, Franklin (2), Little Switzerland, Marion, Spruce Pine (3); Texas: Mason (2); Virginia: Amelia, McKenney
**Pink topaz**  Washington: Ravensdale (GS)

**Turquiose or Lapis Lazuli (December Birthstone)**

**Turquoise**  Nevada: Reno (GS)

**Lapis Lazuli** No listing

The preceding list of birthstones is taken from a list adopted in 1912 by the American National Association of Jewelers ("The Evolution of Birthstones" from *Jewelry & Gems—The Buying Guide* by Antoinette Matlins and A. C. Bonanno; GemStone Press, 2005).

# Finding Your Anniversary Stone

The following is a listing of fee dig sites contained in this four-volume guide where you can find the stone that is associated with a particular anniversary.

**First: Gold (Jewelry)** Alabama: Cragford; Alaska: Anchorage, Chugach, Chicken, Copper Center, Fairbanks (3), Girdwood, Juneau, McGrath, Nome, Skagway (2), Talkeetna; Arizona: Apache Junction, Goldfield, Prescott, Wickenburg; California: Coloma, Columbia, Jackson, Jamestown, Mariposa, Nevada City, Pine Grove, Placerville; Colorado: Breckenridge, Granite, Idaho Springs (2), Ouray, Silverton; Georgia: Cleveland, Dahlonega (2), Gainesville; Indiana: Knightstown; Montana: Libby, Philipsburg; New Mexico: Gila; North Carolina: Cherokee, Marion (3), Midland, New London (2), Union Mills; Oregon: Baker City, Halfway, Jacksonville, Medford, Roseburg, Salem, Unity; South Dakota: Deadwood, Hill City, Keystone, Lead; Vermont: Plymouth; Virginia: Virginia City (SA)
**Gold ore** Colorado: Lakewood (M)

**Second: Garnet** Alaska: Juneau; Arizona: Tempe; California: Pala; Connecticut: Roxbury; Delaware: Wilmington; Georgia: Dahlonega (SA); Idaho: St. Maries; Maine: Auburn, Bethel, Poland (GS), West Paris; Montana: Alder, Helena (S); Nevada: Ely; New Hampshire: Grafton (I); New Mexico: Dixon; New York: North River; North Carolina (*): Almond, Boone, Canton, Cherokee, Chimney Rock, Franklin (4), Marshal, Hiddenite, Highlands, Little Switzerland (2), Marion, Spruce Pine (3) (FT); Tennessee: Ducktown; Texas: Mason; Virginia: McKenney, Virginia City (SA); Washington: Ravensdale (GS)
**Almandine garnets** Maine: Bethel, Poland (GS); Nevada: Ely
**Pyrope garnets** North Carolina: Franklin
**Rhodolite garnets** North Carolina: Franklin

**Garnets, star** Idaho: Moscow (GS), St. Maries

**Third: Pearl** No Listing

**Fourth: Blue topaz** No listing

**Fifth: Sapphire** Georgia: Cleveland (SA), Dahlonega (SA); Montana: Clinton (GS), Hamilton, Helena, Philipsburg (3); North Carolina (*): Almond, Cherokee, Franklin (8), Hiddenite, Highlands, Little Switzerland (2), Spruce Pine (2); Virginia: Virginia City (SA)
**Sapphire, blue** North Carolina: Canton
**Sapphire, grey** North Carolina: Canton
**Sapphire, white** North Carolina: Canton

**Sapphire, bronze** North Carolina: Canton
**Sapphire, pink** North Carolina: Canton
**Star sapphire** North Carolina: Boone (SA)

**Sixth: Amethyst** Arizona: Glendale; Arkansas: Mt. Ida (SA), Murfreesboro (S); Georgia: Cleveland; Maine: Bethel (R), West Paris; Montana: Dillon; Nevada: Reno (GS); New Hampshire: Grafton (I), Laconia; North Carolina (*): Almond, Boone, Cherokee, Chimney Rock, Franklin (3), Highlands, Little Switzerland, Spruce Pine (3); South Carolina: Antreville

**Amethyst scepters** Arizona: Tempe

**Seventh: Onyx** No listing

**Eighth: Tourmaline** Arizona: Tempe; California: Mesa Grande; Maine: Auburn (2), Poland (GS), West Paris; New Hampshire: Grafton (I); North Carolina (*): Boone, Franklin (2), Little Switzerland, Marion, Spruce Pine (3); Texas: Mason; Virginia: Amelia, McKenney
  **Bi-colored** California: Pala
  **Black tourmaline** California: Pala; Georgia: LaGrange; Maine: Auburn, Bethel, Poland (GS), West Paris; New Hampshire: Grafton (I); North Carolina: Spruce Pine (FT)
  **Gem tourmaline** Maine: West Paris
  **Green tourmaline** California: Pala; Maine: West Paris
  **Pink tourmaline** California: Pala

**Ninth: Lapis Lazuli** No listing

**Tenth: Diamond (Jewelry) Diamond** Arkansas: Murfreesboro

**Eleventh: Turquoise** Nevada: Reno (GS)

**Twelve: Jade** No listing

**Thirteenth: Citrine** North Carolina (*): Almond, Boone, Cherokee, Franklin (3), Highlands, Little Switzerland, Spruce Pine (3)

**Fourteenth: Opal**
  **Black fire opal** Nevada: Denio
  **Common opal** New Mexico: Deming
  **Crystal opal** Nevada: Denio
  **Fire opal** Nevada: Denio (4), Reno (GS); Oregon: Klamath Falls
  **Hyalite opal** Maine: Bethel
  **Precious opal** Idaho: Spencer; Texas: Alpine
  **Virgin Valley opal** Nevada: Reno (GS)
  **White opal** Nevada: Denio
  **Wood opal** Nevada: Denio

**Fifteenth: Ruby** Arkansas: Mt. Ida (SA); California: Pine Grove; Georgia: Cleveland, Dahlonega (SA); Montana: Helena; North Carolina (*): Almond, Boone, Cherokee, Chimney Rock, Franklin (8), Highlands, Little Switzerland (2), Spruce Pine (3); Virginia: Virginia City (SA)

**Twentieth: Emerald**  Arkansas: Mt. Ida (SA); Georgia: Cleveland (SA), Dahlonega (SA); North Carolina (*): Almond, Boone, Cherokee, Chimney Rock, Franklin (2), Highlands, Little Switzerland (2), Marion, Micaville, Spruce Pine (2)
**Crabtree emerald**  North Carolina: Spruce Pine

**Twenty-fifth: Silver**  Michigan: Ontonagon

**Thirtieth: Pearl**  No Listing

**Thirty-fifth: Emerald**  Arkansas: Mt. Ida (SA); Georgia: Cleveland (SA), Dahlonega (SA); North Carolina (*): Almond, Boone, Cherokee, Chimney Rock, Franklin (2), Highlands, Little Switzerland (2), Marion, Micaville, Spruce Pine (2)
**Crabtree emerald**  North Carolina: Spruce Pine

**Fortieth: Ruby**  Arkansas: Mt. Ida (SA); California: Pine Grove; Georgia: Cleveland, Dahlonega (SA); Montana: Helena; North Carolina (*): Almond, Boone, Cherokee, Chimney Rock, Franklin (8), Highlands, Little Switzerland (2), Spruce Pine (3);Virginia: Virginia City (SA)

**Forty-fifth: Sapphire**  Georgia: Cleveland (SA), Dahlonega (SA); Montana: Clinton (GS), Hamilton, Helena, Philipsburg (3); North Carolina (*): Almond, Cherokee, Franklin (8), Hiddenite, Highlands, Little Switzerland (2), Spruce Pine (2); Virginia: Virginia City (SA)
**Sapphire, blue**  North Carolina: Canton
**Sapphire, grey**  North Carolina: Canton
**Sapphire, white**  North Carolina: Canton
**Sapphire, bronze**  North Carolina: Canton
**Sapphire, pink**  North Carolina: Canton
**Star sapphire**  North Carolina: Boone (SA)

**Fiftieth: Gold** (*) Alabama: Cragford; Alaska: Anchorage, Chugach, Chicken, Copper Center, Fairbanks (3), Girdwood, Juneau, McGrath, Nome, Skagway (2), Talkeetna;  Arizona: Apache Junction, Goldfield, Prescott, Wickenburg; California: Coloma, Columbia, Jackson, Jamestown, Mariposa, Nevada City, Pine Grove, Placerville; Colorado: Breckenridge, Granite, Idaho Springs (2), Ouray, Silverton; Georgia: Cleveland, Dahlonega (2), Gainesville; Indiana: Knightstown; Montana: Libby, Philipsburg; New Mexico: Gila; North Carolina: Cherokee, Marion (3), Midland, New London (2), Union Mills; Oregon: Baker City, Halfway, Jacksonville, Medford, Roseburg, Salem, Unity; South Dakota: Deadwood, Hill City, Keystone, Lead; Vermont: Plymouth; Virginia: Virginia City (SA)
**Gold ore**  Colorado: Lakewood (M)

**Fifty-fifth: Alexanderite**  No Listing

**Sixtieth: Diamond**  Arkansas: Murfreesboro

# Finding Your Zodiac Stone

The following is a listing of fee dig sites contained in this four-volume guide where you can find the stone that is associated with a particular zodiac sign. Refer to the individual mine listings for more information.

**Aquarius (January 21–February 21) Garnet** Alaska: Juneau; Arizona: Tempe; California: Pala; Connecticut: Roxbury; Delaware: Wilmington; Georgia: Dahlonega (SA); Idaho: St. Maries; Maine: Auburn, Bethel, Poland (GS), West Paris; Montana: Alder, Helena (S); Nevada: Ely; New Hampshire: Grafton (I); New Mexico: Dixon; New York: North River; North Carolina (*): Almond, Boone, Canton, Cherokee, Chimney Rock, Franklin (4), Marshal, Hiddenite, Highlands, Little Switzerland (2), Marion, Spruce Pine (3) (FT); Tennessee: Ducktown; Texas: Mason; Virginia: McKenney, Virginia City (SA); Washington: Ravensdale (GS)
**Almandine garnets** Maine: Bethel, Poland (GS); Nevada: Ely
**Pyrope garnets** North Carolina: Franklin
**Rhodolite garnets** North Carolina: Franklin
**Garnets, star** Idaho: Moscow (GS), St. Maries

**Pisces (February 22–March 21) Amethyst** Arizona: Glendale; Arkansas: Mt. Ida (SA), Murfreesboro (S); Georgia: Cleveland; Maine: Bethel (R), West Paris; Montana: Dillon; Nevada: Reno (GS); New Hampshire: Grafton (I), Laconia; North Carolina (*): Almond, Boone, Cherokee, Chimney Rock, Franklin (3), Highlands, Little Switzerland, Spruce Pine (3); South Carolina: Antreville
**Amethyst scepters** Arizona: Tempe

**Aries (March 22–April 20) Bloodstone** (green chalcedony with red spots) No listing

**Taurus (April 21–May 21) Sapphire** Georgia: Cleveland (SA), Dahlonega (SA); Montana: Clinton (GS), Hamilton, Helena, Philipsburg (3); North Carolina (*): Almond, Cherokee, Franklin (8), Hiddenite, Highlands, Little Switzerland (2), Spruce Pine (2); Virginia: Virginia City (SA)
**Sapphire, blue** North Carolina: Canton
**Sapphire, grey** North Carolina: Canton
**Sapphire, white** North Carolina: Canton
**Sapphire, bronze** North Carolina: Canton
**Sapphire, pink** North Carolina: Canton
**Star sapphire** North Carolina: Boone (SA)

**Gemini (May 22–June 21) Agate**  Arkansas: Murfreesboro (S); Michigan: Grand Marais; Montana: Helena (S); New Mexico: Deming; North Carolina: Chimney Rock; Oklahoma: Kenton (2); Oregon: Madras, Yachats; South Dakota: Wall; Texas: Three Rivers
**Banded agate**  Texas: Alpine; New Mexico: Gila
**Fire agate**  Arizona: Safford (2)
**Iris agate** Texas: Alpine
**Ledge agate**  Oregon: Madras
**Moss agate**  Oregon: Madras, Mitchell; Texas: Alpine (2); Wyoming: Shell
**Polka-dot Jasp-agate**  Oregon: Madras
**Plume agate**  Nevada: Reno (GS)
**Pompom agate**  Texas: Alpine
**Rainbow agate** Oregon: Madras
**Red plume agate**  Texas: Alpine

**Cancer (June 22–July 22) Emerald**  Arkansas: Mt. Ida (SA); Georgia: Cleveland (SA), Dahlonega (SA); North Carolina (*): Almond, Boone, Cherokee, Chimney Rock, Franklin (2), Highlands, Little Switzerland (2), Marion, Micaville, Spruce Pine (2)
**Crabtree emerald**  North Carolina: Spruce Pine

**Leo (July 23–August 22) Onyx** No listing

**Virgo (August 23–September 22) Carnelian** No Listing

**Libra (September 23–October 23) Chrysolite or Peridot Chrysolite** No listing
**Peridot**  Arkansas: Murfreesboro (S); North Carolina (*): Boone, Chimney Rock, Franklin

**Scorpio (October 24–November 21) Beryl**  Delaware: Wilmington; Georgia: LaGrange; Maine: Auburn, Bethel, Poland (GS), West Paris; New Hampshire: Grafton (I); New Mexico: Dixon; North Carolina (*): Little Switzerland (2), Spruce Pine (2); Virginia: Amelia
**Aqua beryl**  New Hampshire: Grafton (I)
**Blue beryl** (see also aquamarine)  New Hampshire: Grafton (I)
**Golden beryl**  North Carolina: Spruce Pine (FT); New Hampshire: Grafton (I)

**Sagittarius (November 22–December 21) Topaz**  Georgia: Cleveland (SA); Maine: Poland (GS); Montana: Helena; New Hampshire: Grafton (I); North Carolina (*): Almond, Boone, Cherokee, Franklin (2), Little Switzerland, Marion, Spruce Pine (3); Texas: Mason (2); Virginia: Amelia
**Pink topaz**  Washington: Ravensdale (GS)

**Capricorn (December 22–January 21) Ruby**  Arkansas: Mt. Ida (SA); California: Pine Grove; Georgia: Cleveland, Dahlonega (SA); Montana: Helena; North Carolina (*): Almond, Boone, Cherokee, Chimney Rock, Franklin (8), Highlands, Little Switzerland (2), Spruce Pine (3); Virginia: Virginia City (SA)

The preceding list of zodiacal stones has been passed on from an early Hindu legend (taken from *Jewelry & Gems—The Buying Guide* by Antoinette Matlins and A. C. Bonanno; GemStone Press, 2005).

The following is an old Spanish list, probably representing Arab traditions, which ascribes the following stones to various signs of the zodiac (taken from *Jewelry & Gems—The Buying Guide* by Antoinette Matlins and A. C. Bonanno; GemStone Press, 2005).

**Aquarius (January 21–February 21) Amethyst**  Arizona: Glendale; Arkansas: Mt. Ida (SA), Murfreesboro (S); Georgia: Cleveland; Maine: Bethel (R), West Paris; Montana: Dillon; Nevada: Reno (GS); New Hampshire: Grafton (I), Laconia; North Carolina (*): Almond, Boone, Cherokee, Chimney Rock, Franklin (3), Highlands, Little Switzerland, Spruce Pine (3); South Carolina: Antreville
**Amethyst scepters**  Arizona: Tempe

**Pisces (February 22–March 21)** Undistinguishable

**Aries (March 22–April 20) Quartz**  Arizona: Glendale (GS), Tempe; Arkansas: Jessieville (3), Mt. Ida (6) (Y), Murfreesboro (S), Pencil Bluff, Story (2); California: Pine Grove; Delaware: Wilmington; Georgia: Lincolnton; Illinois: Hamilton; Maine: Auburn, Poland (GS), West Paris; Michigan: Ontonagon; Montana: Dillon, Helena (S); New Hampshire: Laconia; New Mexico: Bingham, Deming, Dixon; North Carolina: Franklin; Texas: Alpine, Mason; Virginia: Amelia, Virginia City (SA); Washington: Ravensdale (GS)
**Blue**  Georgia: Lincolnton; North Carolina: Marion
**Clear**  Georgia: LaGrange; North Carolina (*): Hiddenite, Little Switzerland, Marion, Spruce Pine
**Milky**  Maine: Bethel
**Parallel growth**  Maine: West Paris
**Pseudocubic crystals**  Maine: West Paris
**Rose**  Maine: Bethel; New Hampshire: Grafton (I); North Carolina (*): Franklin
**Rutilated**  North Carolina (*): Little Switzerland, Spruce Pine
**Skeletal quartz**  South Carolina: Antreville
**Smoky**  Maine: Bethel; Nevada: Reno (GS); New Hampshire: Grafton, Laconia; North Carolina (*): Almond, Boone, Cherokee, Chimney Rock, Franklin (4), Hiddenite, Highlands, Little Switzerland (2), Marion, Spruce Pine (2); Virginia: McKenney
**Smoky (gem quality)** New Hampshire: Grafton (I); South Carolina: Antreville
**Quartz "diamonds"**
**Lake Co. "diamonds" (moon tears)**  California; Lake County
**Cape May "diamonds"**  New Jersey: Cape May
**Herkimer "diamonds"** New York: Herkimer, Middleville, St. Johnsville

**Taurus (April 21–May 21) Rubies, Diamonds**

**Rubies** Arkansas: Mt. Ida (SA); California: Pine Grove; Georgia: Cleveland, Dahlonega (SA); Montana: Helena; North Carolina (*): Almond, Boone, Cherokee, Chimney Rock, Franklin (8), Highlands, Little Switzerland (2), Spruce Pine (3);Virginia: Virginia City (SA)

**Diamond** Arkansas: Murfreesboro;

**Gemini (May 22–June 21) Sapphire** Georgia: Cleveland (SA), Dahlonega (SA); Montana: Clinton (GS), Hamilton, Helena, Philipsburg (3); North Carolina (*): Almond, Cherokee, Franklin (8), Hiddenite, Highlands, Little Switzerland (2), Spruce Pine (2); Virginia: Virginia City (SA)

**Sapphire, blue** North Carolina: Canton

**Sapphire, grey** North Carolina: Canton

**Sapphire, white** North Carolina: Canton

**Sapphire, bronze** North Carolina: Canton

**Sapphire, pink** North Carolina: Canton

**Star sapphire** North Carolina: Boone (SA)

**Cancer (June 22–July 22) Agate and Beryl**

**Agate** Arkansas: Murfreesboro (S); Michigan: Grand Marais; Montana: Helena (S); New Mexico: Deming; North Carolina: Chimney Rock; Oklahoma: Kenton (2); Oregon: Madras, Yachats; South Dakota: Wall; Texas: Three Rivers

**Banded agate** Texas: Alpine; New Mexico: Gila

**Fire agate** Arizona: Safford (2)

**Iris agate** Texas: Alpine

**Ledge agate** Oregon: Madras

**Moss agate** Oregon: Madras, Mitchell; Texas: Alpine (2); Wyoming: Shell

**Polka-dot Jasp-agate** Oregon: Madras

**Plume agate** Nevada: Reno (GS)

**Pompom agate** Texas: Alpine

**Rainbow agate** Oregon: Madras

**Red plume agate** Texas: Alpine

**Beryl** Delaware: Wilmington; Georgia: LaGrange; Maine: Auburn, Bethel, Poland (GS), West Paris; New Hampshire: Grafton (I); New Mexico: Dixon; North Carolina (*): Little Switzerland (2), Spruce Pine (2); Virginia: Amelia

**Aqua beryl** New Hampshire: Grafton (I)

**Blue beryl** (see also aquamarine) New Hampshire: Grafton (I)

**Golden beryl** North Carolina: Spruce Pine (FT); New Hampshire: Grafton (I)

**Leo (July 23–August 22) Topaz** Georgia: Cleveland (SA); Maine: Poland (GS); Montana: Helena; New Hampshire: Grafton (I); North Carolina (*): Almond, Boone, Cherokee, Franklin (2), Little Switzerland, Marion, Spruce Pine (3); Texas: Mason (2); Virginia: Amelia

**Pink topaz** Washington: Ravensdale (GS)

**Virgo (August 23–September 22) Bloodstone** (green chalcedony with red spots) No listing

**Libra (September 23–October 23) Jasper** Arkansas: Murfreesboro (S); California: Pine Grove; Montana: Helena (S); Oklahoma: Kenton; Oregon: Madras, Yachats; Texas: Alpine
**Jasper braccia** New Mexico: Gila
**Brown Jasper** New Mexico: Deming
**Chocolate jasper** New Mexico: Deming
**Orange jasper** New Mexico: Deming
**Picture jasper** New Mexico: Gila; Oregon: Mitchell
**Pink jasper** New Mexico: Deming
**Variegated jasper** New Mexico: Deming
**Yellow jasper** New Mexico: Deming, Gila

**Scorpio (October 24–November21) Garnet** Alaska: Juneau; Arizona: Tempe; California: Pala; Connecticut: Roxbury; Deleware: Wilmington; Georgia: Dahlonega (SA); Idaho: St. Maries; Maine: Auburn, Bethel, Poland (GS), West Paris; Montana: Alder, Helena (S); Nevada: Ely; New Hampshire: Grafton (I); New Mexico: Dixon; New York: North River; North Carolina (*): Almond, Boone, Canton, Cherokee, Chimney Rock, Franklin (4), Marshal, Hiddenite, Highlands, Little Switzerland (2), Marion, Spruce Pine (3) (FT); Tennessee: Ducktown; Texas: Mason; Virginia: McKenney, Virginia City (SA); Washington: Ravensdale (GS)
**Almandine garnets** Maine: Bethel, Poland (GS); Nevada: Ely
**Pyrope garnets** North Carolina: Franklin
**Rhodolite garnets** North Carolina: Franklin

**Sagittarius (November 22–December 21) Emerald** Arkansas: Mt. Ida (SA); Georgia: Cleveland (SA), Dahlonega (SA); North Carolina (*): Almond, Boone, Cherokee, Chimney Rock, Franklin (2), Highlands, Little Switzerland (2), Marion, Micaville, Spruce Pine (2)
**Crabtree emerald** North Carolina: Spruce Pine

**Capricorn (December 22–January 21) Chalcedony** Arizona: Safford; Nevada: Reno (GS); New Mexico: Demin

# Some Publications on Gems and Minerals

## Jewelry Artist (Lapidary Journal)
300 Chesterfield Parkway, Suite 100
Malvern, PA 19355
Phone: (610) 232-5700
Subscriptions: (800) 676-4336
www.lapidaryjournal.com

## Rocks & Minerals
c/o Heldref Publications
1319 18th Street, NW
Washington, DC 20036-1802
Subscriptions: (866) 802-7059

## Rock & Gem
c/o Miller Magazines, Inc.
Maple Court, Suite 232
Ventura, CA 93003-3517
www.rockngem.com

## Gold Prospector
Gold Prospectors Association of
America, Inc.
43445 Business Park Drive
Temecula, CA 92590
Phone: (800) 551-9707
www.goldprospectors.org

## Colored Stone
300 Chesterfield Parkway, Suite 100
Malvern, PA 19355
Phone: (610) 232-5700
www.colored-stone.com

## The Mineralogical Record
P.O. Box 35565
Tucson, AZ 85740
Phone: (520) 297-6709
Fax: (520) 544-0815
www.mineralogicalrecord.com

Other sources of information are local and regional rock, gem, and mineral clubs and federations, and rock, gem, and mineral shows. Many times clubs offer field trips and some shows have collecting trips associated with their annual event. Among these are The American Federation of Mineralogical Societies (www.amfed.org), which lists member clubs, and Bob's Rock Shop (www.rockhounds.com), which has a U.S. club directory (supplied information).

# Send Us Your Feedback

## Disclaimer

The authors have made every reasonable effort to obtain accurate information for this guide. However, much of the information in the book is based on material provided by the sites and has not been verified independently. The information given here does not represent recommendations, but merely a listing of information. The authors and publisher accept no liability for any accident or loss incurred when readers are patronizing the establishments listed herein. The authors and publisher accept no liability for errors or omissions. Since sites may shut down or change their hours of operations or fees without advance notice, please call the site before your visit for confirmation before planning your trip.

The authors would appreciate being informed of changes, additions, or deletions that should be made to this guide. To that end, a form is attached, which can be filled out and mailed to the authors for use in future editions of the guide.

## Have We Missed Your Mine or Museum?

This is a project with a national scope, based on extensive literature search, phone and mail inquiry, and personal investigation. However, we are dealing with a business in which many owners are retiring or closing and selling their sites. In addition, many of the mines, guide services, and smaller museums have limited publicity, known more by word of mouth than by publication. Thus, it is possible that your operation or one you have visited was not included in this guide. Please let us know if you own or operate a mine, guide service, or museum, or have visited a mine, guide service, or museum that is not in the guide. It will be considered for inclusion in the next edition of the guide. Send updates to:

Treasure Hunter's Guides
GemStone Press
Route 4, Sunset Farm Offices
P.O. Box 237
Woodstock, VT 05091

## Do You Have a Rockhounding Story to Share?

If you have a special story about a favorite dig site, send it in for consideration for use in the next edition of the guide.

## A Request to Mines and Museums:

For sites already included in this guide, we request that you put us on your annual mailing list so that we may have an updated copy of your information.

## Notes on Museums

In this guide we have included listings of museums with noteworthy gem, mineral, or rock collections. We particularly tried to find local museums displaying gems or minerals native to the area where they are located. This list is by no means complete, and if you feel we missed an important listing, let us know by completing the following form. Since these guides focus specifically on gems and minerals, only those exhibits have been recognized in the museum listings, and we do not mention any collection or exhibits of fossils. See our sequel on fossils for information on fossil collections.

## READER'S CONTRIBUTION

I would like to supply the following information for possible inclusion in the next edition of *The Treasure Hunter's Guide*:

**Type of entry:**  ☐ fee dig  ☐ guide service  ☐ museum  ☐ mine tour
☐ annual event

**This is a:**  ☐ new entry  ☐ entry currently in the guide

**Nature of info:**  ☐ addition  ☐ change  ☐ deletion

*Please describe (brochure and additional info may be attached):*

_____

_____

_____

_____

Please supply the following in case we need to contact you regarding your information:

Name: _____

Address: _____

_____

_____

Phone: ( ) _____

E-mail: _____

Date: _____

# FIELD NOTES

# FIELD NOTES

# FIELD NOTES

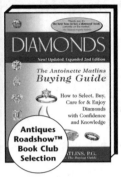

# Now You Can Have the "Professional's Advantage"!
## With Your OWN Jeweler's Loupe—
# The Essential "TOOL OF THE TRADE"!

Personally selected by the authors, this valuable jeweler's aid is *now available to the consumer* from GemStone Press. And GemStone Press includes, FREE, a copy of "The Professional's Advantage: How to Use the Loupe and What to Look For," a $5.00 value, written with the jewelry buyer in mind. You can now *have more fun while shopping and make your choice with greater confidence*. This is not just a magnifying glass. It is specially made to be used to examine jewelry. It will help you to—

- *Enjoy* the inner beauty of the gem as well as the outer beauty.
- *Protect yourself*—see scratches, chips, or cracks that reduce the value of a stone or make it vulnerable to greater damage.
- *Prevent loss*—spot weak prongs that may break and cause the stone to fall from the setting.
- *Avoid bad cutting*, poor proportioning and poor symmetry.
- *Identify the telltale signs* of glass or imitation.
  . . . *And much more, as revealed in "The Professional's Advantage"!*

You'll love it. You'll enjoy looking at gems and jewelry up close—it makes this special experience even more exciting. And sometimes, as one of our readers recently wrote:

*"Just having the loupe and looking like I knew how to use it changed the way I was treated."*

### CALL NOW AND WE'LL RUSH THE LOUPE TO YOU.
### FOR TOLL-FREE CREDIT CARD ORDERS:
# 800-962-4544

| Item | Quantity | Price Each | TOTAL |
|---|---|---|---|
| Standard 10X Triplet Loupe | _____ | $29.00 | = $_____ |
| Bausch & Lomb 10X Triplet Loupe | _____ | $44.00 | = $_____ |
| "The Professional's Advantage" Booklet | 1 per Loupe | $ 5.00 | = ˙ Free |
| Insurance/Packing/Shipping in the U.S.* | 1st Loupe | $ 7.95 | = $   7.95 |
| *Outside U.S.: Specify shipping method (insured) and provide a credit card number for payment. | Each add'l | $ 3.00 | = $_____ |

TOTAL: $_____

Check enclosed for $_____ (Payable to: GEMSTONE PRESS)
Charge my credit card: ❏ Visa ❏ MasterCard
Name on Card _____
Cardholder Address: Street _____
City/State/Zip _____ E-mail _____
Credit Card # _____ Exp. Date _____
Signature _____ CID# _____
*Please send to:* ❏ Same as Above ❏ Address Below    Phone (____)_____
Name _____
Street _____
City/State/Zip _____ Phone (____)_____

*Phone, mail, fax, or e-mail orders to:*
GEMSTONE PRESS, Sunset Farm Offices, Rte. 4, P.O. Box 237, Woodstock, VT 05091
*Tel: (802) 457-4000 • Fax: (802) 457-4004 • Credit Card Orders: (800) 962-4544*
**sales@gemstonepress.com • www.gemstonepress.com**
Generous Discounts on Quantity Orders

Prices subject to change

ASK ABOUT OTHER GEM ID INSTRUMENTS — REFRACTOMETERS • DICHROSCOPES • MICROSCOPES • AND MORE
**FOR CREDIT CARD ORDERS CALL 800-962-4544** (8:30AM–5:30PM ET Monday–Friday)

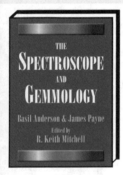

# Buy Your *"Tools of the Trade"*...

## Gem Identification Instruments directly from *GemStone Press*

Whatever instrument you need, GemStone Press can help.
Use our convenient order form, or contact us directly for assistance.

### Complete Pocket Instrument Set
# SPECIAL SAVINGS!
#### BUY THIS ESSENTIAL TRIO AND SAVE 12%
Used together, you can identify 85% of all gems with these three
portable, pocket-sized instruments—the essential trio.
10X Triplet Loupe • Calcite Dichroscope • Chelsea Filter

**Pocket Instrument Set:**
**Premium:** With Bausch & Lomb 10X Loupe • RosGem Dichroscope • Chelsea Filter  **only $197.95**
**Deluxe:** With Bausch & Lomb 10X Loupe • EZview Dichroscope • Chelsea Filter  **only $179.95**

| ITEM / QUANTITY | PRICE EA.* | TOTAL $ |
|---|---|---|
| **Pocket Instrument Sets** | | |
| _____ **Premium:** With Bausch & Lomb 10X Loupe • RosGem Dichroscope • Chelsea Filter | $197.95 | $ _____ |
| _____ **Deluxe:** With Bausch & Lomb 10X Loupe • EZview Dichroscope • Chelsea Filter | $179.95 | _____ |
| **Loupes—Professional Jeweler's 10X Triplet Loupes** | | |
| _____ Bausch & Lomb 10X Triplet Loupe | $44.00 | _____ |
| _____ Standard 10X Triplet Loupe | $29.00 | _____ |
| _____ Darkfield Loupe | $58.95 | _____ |
| • Spot filled diamonds, identify inclusions in colored gemstones. Operates with mini maglite (optional). | | |
| **Analyzer** | | |
| _____ Gem Analyzer (RosGem) | $299.00 | _____ |
| • Combines Darkfield Loupe, Polariscope, and Immersion Cell. Operates with mini maglite (optional). | | |
| **Calcite Dichroscopes** | | |
| _____ Dichroscope (RosGem) | $135.00 | _____ |
| _____ Dichroscope (EZview) | $115.00 | _____ |
| **Color Filters** | | |
| _____ Chelsea Filter | $44.95 | _____ |
| _____ Synthetic Emerald Filter Set (Hanneman) | $32.00 | _____ |
| _____ Tanzanite Filter (Hanneman) | $28.00 | _____ |
| _____ Bead Buyer's & Parcel Picker's Filter Set (Hanneman) | $24.00 | _____ |
| **Diamond Testers and Tweezers** | | |
| _____ SSEF Diamond-Type Spotter | $150.00 | _____ |
| _____ Diamondnite Dual Tester | $269.00 | _____ |
| _____ Diamond Tweezers/Locking | $10.65 | _____ |
| _____ Diamond Tweezers/Non-Locking | $7.80 | _____ |
| **Jewelry Cleaners** | | |
| _____ Ionic Cleaner—Home size model | $85.00 | _____ |
| _____ Ionic Solution—16 oz. bottle | $20.00 | _____ |

# Buy Your *"Tools of the Trade..."*
## Gem Identification Instruments directly from *GemStone Press*
Whatever instrument you need, GemStone Press can help.
Use our convenient order form, or contact us directly for assistance.

| ITEM / QUANTITY | PRICE EA.* | TOTAL $ |
|---|---|---|
| **Lamps—Ultraviolet & High Intensity** | | |
| _____ Small Longwave/Shortwave (UVP) | $72.00 | _____ |
| _____ Large Longwave/Shortwave (UVP) | $199.95 | _____ |
| _____ Viewing Cabinet for Large Lamp (UVP) | $175.00 | _____ |
| _____ **Purchase Large Lamp & Cabinet together** | $339.95 | _____ |
| **and save $35.00** | | |
| **Other Light Sources** | | |
| _____ Solitaire Maglite | $11.00 | _____ |
| _____ Mini Maglite | $15.00 | _____ |
| _____ Flex Light | $29.95 | _____ |
| **Refractometers** | | |
| _____ Precision Pocket Refractometer (RosGem RFA 322) | $625.00 | _____ |
| • operates with solitaire maglite (additional—see above) | | |
| _____ Refractive Index Liquid 1.81—10 gram | $69.95 | _____ |
| **Spectroscopes** | | |
| _____ Spectroscope—Pocket-sized model (OPL) | $98.00 | _____ |
| _____ Spectroscope—Desk model w/stand (OPL) | $235.00 | _____ |
| **Scale** | | |
| _____ GemPro50 Carat Scale | $174.95 | _____ |

**Shipping/Insurance per order in the U.S.: $7.95 first item,** SHIPPING/INS. $_____
**$3.00 each add'l item; $10.95 total for pocket instrument set.**

Outside the U.S.: Please specify *insured* shipping method you prefer
and provide a credit card number for payment. **TOTAL $ _____** **

---

Check enclosed for $ _____ (Payable to: GEMSTONE PRESS)
Charge my credit card: ❑ Visa ❑ MasterCard
Name on Card _____ Phone (_____)_____
Cardholder Address: Street _____
City/State/Zip _____ E-mail _____
Credit Card # _____ Exp. Date _____
Signature _____ CID # _____
*Please send to:* ❑ Same as Above ❑ Address Below
Name _____
Street _____
City/State/Zip _____ Phone (_____)_____

*Phone, mail, fax, or e-mail orders to:*
**GEMSTONE PRESS, P.O. Box 237, Woodstock, VT 05091**
*Tel:* **(802) 457-4000** • *Fax:* **(802) 457-4004**
*Credit Card Orders:* **(800) 962-4544 (8:30AM–5:30PM ET Monday–Friday)**
**sales@gemstonepress.com • www.gemstonepress.com**
## Generous Discounts on Quantity Orders

**TOTAL SATISFACTION GUARANTEE**
If for any reason you're not completely delighted
with your purchase, return it in resellable condition
within 30 days for a full refund.

*Prices, manufacturing specifications, and terms subject to change
without notice. Orders accepted subject to availability.

**All orders must be prepaid by credit card, money order or check
in U.S. funds drawn on a U.S. bank.

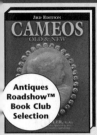

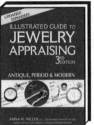
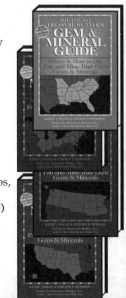

*Please send me:*

**CAMEOS OLD & NEW, 3RD EDITION**
_____ copies at $19.95 (Quality Paperback) *plus s/h\**

**COLORED GEMSTONES, 2ND EDITION: THE ANTOINETTE MATLINS BUYING GUIDE**
_____ copies at $18.99 (Quality Paperback) *plus s/h\**

**DIAMONDS, 2ND EDITION: THE ANTOINETTE MATLINS BUYING GUIDE**
_____ copies at $18.99 (Quality Paperback) *plus s/h\**

**ENGAGEMENT & WEDDING RINGS, 3RD EDITION: THE DEFINITIVE BUYING GUIDE**
_____ copies at $18.95 (Quality Paperback) *plus s/h\**

**GEM IDENTIFICATION MADE EASY, 3RD EDITION:**
**A HANDS-ON GUIDE TO MORE CONFIDENT BUYING & SELLING**
_____ copies at $36.95 (Hardcover) *plus s/h\**

**GEMS & JEWELRY APPRAISING, 2ND EDITION**
_____ copies at $39.95 (Hardcover) *plus s/h\**

**ILLUSTRATED GUIDE TO JEWELRY APPRAISING, 3RD EDITION**
_____ copies at $39.99 (Hardcover) *plus s/h\**

**JEWELRY & GEMS AT AUCTION: THE DEFINITIVE GUIDE TO BUYING & SELLING**
**AT THE AUCTION HOUSE & ON INTERNET AUCTION SITES**
_____ copies at $19.95 (Quality Paperback) *plus s/h\**

**JEWELRY & GEMS, 6TH EDITION: THE BUYING GUIDE**
_____ copies at $19.99 (Quality Paperback) *plus s/h\**
_____ copies at $24.99 (Hardcover) *plus s/h\**

**THE PEARL BOOK, 3RD EDITION: THE DEFINITIVE BUYING GUIDE**
_____ copies at $19.99 (Quality Paperback) *plus s/h\**

**THE SPECTROSCOPE AND GEMMOLOGY**
_____ copies at $49.95 (Quality Paperback) *plus s/h\**

**TREASURE HUNTER'S GEM & MINERAL GUIDES TO THE U.S.A., 4TH EDITIONS:**
**WHERE & HOW TO DIG, PAN AND MINE YOUR OWN GEMS & MINERALS—**
**IN 4 REGIONAL VOLUMES** $14.99 per copy (Quality Paperback) *plus s/h\**
_____ copies of NE States _____ copies of SE States _____ copies of NW States _____ copies of SW States

\* In U.S.: Shipping/Handling: $3.95 for 1st book, $2.00 each additional book.
Outside U.S.: Specify shipping method (insured) and provide a credit card number for payment.

---

Check enclosed for $_____ (Payable to: GEMSTONE Press)

Charge my credit card: ❏ Visa ❏ MasterCard

Name on Card (PRINT) _____ Phone (_____)_____

Cardholder Address: Street _____

City/State/Zip _____ E-mail _____

Credit Card # _____ Exp. Date _____

Signature _____ CID # _____

*Please send to:* ❏ Same as Above ❏ Address Below

Name (PRINT) _____

Street _____

City/State/Zip _____ Phone (_____)_____

*Phone, mail, fax, or e-mail orders to:*
**GEMSTONE PRESS,** Sunset Farm Offices,
Rte. 4, P.O. Box 237, Woodstock, VT 05091
*Tel:* (802) 457-4000 • *Fax:* (802) 457-4004
*Credit Card Orders:* (800) 962-4544
(8:30AM–5:30PM ET Monday–Friday)
sales@gemstonepress.com • www.gemstonepress.com
**Generous Discounts on Quantity Orders**

Prices subject to change

# Try Your Bookstore First

MAY        2008